HEI
SUFFICIENT

Christina Stapley

Author of Herbwise Naturally
Herbcraft Naturally

Best Wishes,
Christina Stapley

HEARTSEASE BOOKS

DEDICATION

For Anna, Deborah and Iemke, with love and thanks.

Photography
Christina Stapley

ISBN: 0-9522336-3-0

Printed in England by St Richard's Press Ltd
Chichester. West Sussex. PO19 2TU.

With thanks to David for his support and help in preparing the graphics and colour pages.

Herbs can be powerful substances whether applied as oils or in other forms. The author cannot take responsibility for reader's use of recipes or possible allergic reactions. Please note cautionary guidelines with recipes, particularly with dyes.

CONTENTS

January - February..7 - 31

March - April ....32 - 54

May - June ....55 - 75

July - August...76 - 96

September - October..97 - 119

November - December.......................................120 - 137

Herb Cultivation...138 - 150

Bibliography.. - 151

List of Suppliers .... - 152

Index ....153 - 160

ILLUSTRATIONS

Chamomile seat, winter honeysuckle, black hellebore i

Herb swags, seed collage ii

Astrology beds, Solomon's seal, greater knapweed, bugle iii

Knot garden, view through knot, miniature knot iv

Spring knot garden, blessed thistle, Easter garland v

Spring flowers, balsam poplar buds, bramble dyed blouse vi

Astrology bed, self heal, willow herbar vii

Wines and preserves, violet sugar, candied lovage viii

Spring harvest, violets in strawberry basket viii

Making rose petal jelly, posy, honeysuckle and jasmine arch ix

Entrance to covered way ix

Ringlet on ragwort, mullein moth caterpillar x

Painted lady on Greek valerian, hedgehog, bee on elecampane x

Astrology beds, Aries and Virgo, Cancer, Leo xi

Harvesting flowers, making hypericum and verbascum oils xii

Moist pot-pourri, stem basket before trimming xii

Clove pinks, clove pink conserve, agrimony xiii

Lavender fringe, starting star mobile, add 'rays' to mobile xiv

Completed leaf mat xiv

Alpha in the serenity, view from serenity xv

Knot in summer xvi

Virgo bed, yarrow in Libra, milk thistle brightens Sagittarius xvii

Tarragon in Scorpio xvii

Pokeweed, ripe pokeberries, dyer's bistort xviii

Snowberries and guelder berries xviii

Dyed wool samples, dyed silks and leaf prints xix

Rosehips over chamomile, basket in progress xx

Christmas conserves, wines, liqueurs, chocolates, ... xxi

Pomander beads, autumn harvest ball xxi

Christmas swags, sprayed seedheads, spicy sack mixture xxii

Weaving on the peg loom, back of waistcoat xxiii

Frosted teazle, motherwort, St John's wort xxiv

DIAGRAMS

Plan of Astrology Garden 12

Plan of Miniature Knot Garden 17

Tree of Life seed design 30

Willow Herbar ....40 - 41

Stem Basket 75

Lavender Fringe 92

Lavender Star Mobile 94

Leaf Mats 96

Basket 118

January - February

Silvered mornings with icy fingers
drawing jewelled webs upon the glass,
reaching deep within each crack.
Bone chilling, finger numbing cold,
relentless before all but sunbeams -
swordshafts of power
releasing winter's grip.
Naked branches reach across the hillside,
leafless and stark in their emptiness.
Clothed as if for decency
by shrouds of traveller's joy.
A wren darts from twig to twig,
half-hidden.
An orange sun hangs in a grey sky
laden with snow.
It falls in whirls and eddies
leaving a soft, sacred silence.
A smooth surface, violated
by paw prints of warm life -
in stillness is the birth of movement.

In the Garden

ALREADY the sweet, heady perfume of winter honeysuckle, *(Lonicera fragrantissima)* fills the air immediately outside my front door and around seats in sheltered corners of the garden. Grown against a south-facing wall, the honeysuckle often opens its beautiful flowers just before Christmas; to fragrance those precious hours of sunlight between then and March. As the honeysuckle fades, the rosemary at the other side of my door becomes a mass of flowers, welcoming all who pass. Perfume and bright flowers at the windows, outside and in, are especially important at this season.

The yellow winter jasmine brightens my outlook, catching the sunlight as the flowers peer in at the edges of the windows. When severe weather is forecast you may like to save their beauty by pressing them. (see page 27)

Beyond the windows, the true beauty of the design of a herb knot garden is appreciated as perfectly after a light fall of snow, or a heavy frost, as it is in full summer with green hedges and flower filled beds. The essence of peace which touches our perception of a very personal paradise, is drawn by nature at her most powerful to pierce our shield of everyday cares. Designing a knot or series of beds is simplified by making a miniature 3-D plan with dried flowers and foliage in oasis. (see page 15)

Good management of the garden, hand in hand with nature is also needed to encourage wildlife to work with you. Together you can create a pleasure garden which supplies food, physic and raw materials for all. Whether you are led to knowledge by books or experience, herbs are perfect companions along the way. Over the years they have tempted me to study botany, geology, geography, history, astrology and medicine - all in the course of coming to know and respect the plants as individual characters. Even exploring the needs of local wildlife, and ways in which birds, animals and insects can aid you as a gardener, opens an encyclopedia of knowledge.

The wonder of cobwebs strung from seedhead to seedhead, bejewelled by frost and sparkling in the first shafts of sunlight on a bright winter's morning, can only be revealed in a garden where the stage has already been set. Once the framework has been created, the temptation to cut down all 'untidy' dried stems in autumn should be resisted. Seedheads and berries are stores of winter food for birds. On cold mornings it will be a delight to watch noisy mobs of finches and tits plunder this storehouse.

Seeds

YOU will already have gathered those seeds you need for the following year and if your stores are like mine, you will generally find there are some to spare. These may be put out for wildlife on very cold days, shared with friends and a small amount used for sheer pleasure in a decorative collage, see the Tree of Life design.

Sorting seeds will inevitably bring their great variety of size, shape, colouring and texture to your notice. A good place to begin in coming to know and appreciate any plant.

When sown in trays in a mix of compost and garden soil and watered with warmed rainwater, you will also find how differently each seedling responds. Some, such as parsley and tobacco seem to need the very best conditions and may take weeks to germinate. Everything from boiling water to being sown by a woman at full moon, preferably at midnight, has been tried with parsley. I found my best results were spontaneous germination of the whole crop after burglars tipped the seed tray on end.

Over a number of years I have experimented with sowing seeds in trays indoors at different phases of the moon. I find there may be some truth in ancient instructions to sow seeds just before or just after a new moon. Traditionally, plants which give a harvest of roots should be sown with the moon waning, and those giving flowers and seeds, when it is waxing. I always set the trays where they will receive moonlight as well as sunlight.

When sowing several types of seed in one tray, I try to select those likely to germinate around the same time. Basil, French marigolds, biennial clary sage, sweet mignonette, milk thistle, blessed thistle, weld, flax, marjoram, hyssop, dill, Greek oregano, lobelia, coreopsis, borage, helichrysum, salad rocket, safflower, calendula and dyer's chamomile have all germinated within 7 days in some years - but there is no guarantee. Most other herb seeds will take only a little longer before they germinate and appear above ground. Patience can be rewarded 3 weeks or more later however. A tray which has not produced seedlings after this time may still be set outside in shade in early summer, and give you a wonderful surprise long afterwards. The most common disappointment, especially if you mix your garden soil with seed compost, is that the first precious green shoots which you so carefully nurture prove to be weeds. Unless these are taking over the tray do not be in a hurry to remove them until the true crop appears, as you may take out your seeds as well.

As they develop they may cluster together in tiny, intertwined perfection, (dill and hyssop) or need their own space, (alkanet, milk thistle, sunflower). Always ensure they have light from both sides, or the tray is turned more than once a day if possible. Beware of sowing seeds too early if you do not have a greenhouse where they can be grown on until frosts have ended. The medicinal thistles, sunflowers and nasturtiums will all quickly need potting on and can be sown late outdoors. Those herbs which will take longest to germinate and grow, need an earlier start, tobacco, henna, anise, costmary, chervil, hollyhock, indigo, chamomile, marshmallows, arnica and savory can all be in this category.

Some, such as sweet cicely, angelica and cowslips, need frost to germinate and will be better in seedtrays set outside rather than refrigerated. Pots of seeds in compost in the fridge have, in my experience, only annoyed other members of the family and are risking culinary disaster. Wherever your seedtrays are, do label them carefully and make sure the labels will not be washed away when watering. Some seedlings such as dyer's chamomile quickly have pretty, frilled leaves showing an easily recognized 'adult' form. Alkanet too will be soft and furry from the beginning, but many herb seedlings are very similar and can easily be mistaken for each other for some time. The most spectacular of the real 'characters' is the castor oil plant. The bean like pod emerges from it's shell white and earthshaking in the seedtray, raising the compost in the air. This is followed by the red 'swan-like necks' of the stem looping upwards, their leaves yet hidden beneath the jumbled earth. As the closed leaves finally break surface and rise slowly to open, first as a duck's beak and then fully, opposite each other, you almost feel obliged to applaud. The whole process has taken up to three days.

Flowers

WITH our seeds sown, or sorted ready, we may find sunny days drawing us out into the garden to begin any new constructions of pergolas, or to mend trellis and fencing. Towards the end of this period we may be greeted by clumps of fragrant violets, many half hidden by leaves as if tucked in to keep warm. The recipe for violet liqueur is one to try in abundant years. Early primroses and the odd bright celandine, too often greeted as unwelcome weeds, can be added to our pressed flower collection, together with the beauty of small ivy and cyclamen leaves. Another herb which spreads at a prodigious rate and is more likely to be gathered wild, is the coltsfoot. The sunny yellow flowers are looked upon as a tonic to the spirits in northern countries, where they appear through the snow and are the first flowers of spring. Here we can gather them in February and March to make a warming wine with ginger and lemons - good for colds and chilled joints, as well as reviving the spirits, and ready by autumn of the same year.

Before the coltsfoot flowers, snowdrops and hellebores with white, green or dusky pink flowers have already graced the herb garden amongst the evergreens. All have provided remedies in the past.

Indoors

LEMON and rose-scented geraniums, lemon verbena, pineapple and tangerine sages, and the less hardy lavenders such as *Lavandula dentata,* add their fragrances to the tranquilizing effect of that idyllic perfume in the leaves of *Pelargonium graveolens.* I bring them in along with young bays, silver rosemary and the tender patchouli for protection against frost, and in return they offer clouds of fragrance at the lightest touch and a steady harvest.

All of these overwintered plants may suffer a similar 'depression' to our own at the darkest point of the year, and will benefit from a dose or two of nettle or comfrey tea. Rainwater collected and brought to room temperature is also better than tap water to induce stronger growth. If they have become starved of light and nutrients, producing pale, spindly growth, cut them back and water with 4 drops Bach Rescue Remedy and 2 drops Bach Olive Remedy in a large jug of water. Repeat as necessary at intervals of a few days. Leaves from lemon and rose-scented geraniums and pineapple or tangerine sage can be used in preserves - see recipes. Also the brown, dried leaves of geraniums are a good addition to pot-pourri. Fresh geranium leaves are wonderful templates for craft projects such as the Tree of Life design for the seed collage and can be used for leaf printing. (see page 52)

Planning

AT this time of year it is natural to review the state of your garden and any new ideas you may have for plantings. A few years ago I was doing just that when reading Culpeper's herbal. As I looked at individual herbs, reading his introductory sentence of which planet rules that particular plant, the idea of making an astrology garden to explore these relationships came into my mind. The subject of his belief in planets causing diseases would be too complex to pass on, but I felt confident that this different approach to looking at the natures of the herbs would be fascinating. As I hoped, many people coming round my garden have also found it so.

The Astrology Garden

MEDICAL astrology is a very ancient science, developed before the horoscope astrology which is now the only form most people are aware of. The signs of the zodiac each govern certain parts of the body, following the doctrine that the macrocosm of the universe is repeated in the microcosm of man. This link is continued as particular planets are associated both with the signs and organs in the human body.

Culpeper enlightens us on the classification of herbs in several passages in his herbal. While Martial herbs are those with hot, prickly natures such as blessed thistle, nettle, basil and horseradish; he also includes those which like to grow close to the sites of enduring fires such as forges. Mars is coupled with Aries and Scorpio in the zodiac, and since Aries rules the head and stomach and Scorpio the sexual organs; Martial herbs prove their nature by treating diseases or injuries in these areas of the body. Sometimes the placing of a herb is not because it belongs to the planet ruling the sign, but because it belongs to the planet in opposition to it. So we find both herbs of Mars and Venus in Aries, to cure diseases by a sympathetic reaction, or the opposite, working by antipathy.

When I began the garden I measured out a large enough area to take 12 beds. A circular astrology garden appealed to me, but the best site still available required the astrology to take on a more rectangular form. In using an existing bank next to the lawn, I set 6 beds back to back with 6 more - see plan. With the rise in height where the 2 rows of beds met, this had the advantage for much of the year of hiding the bed behind. A friend painted the signs of the zodiac on marker tiles for me while I studied Culpeper day after day, making and revising lists of herbs under the various planets.

My final choices were made firstly by matching their therapeutic values for those parts of the body to be treated under the sign, and secondly on consideration of the long term maintenance and appearance of the beds. I discovered that in some beds, especially those where the influence of Venus is strongest, setting a number of rampant herbs together seemed impossible to avoid. For this reason every spring, I spend more time dividing plants in the astrology than in any other area.

Herbs ruled by the Sun are equally endowed with the gift of spreading a mass of seedlings. The familiar families of plants in modern classification, Compositae, Umbelliferae etc have no consistent correlations with planetary influence.

As we pass from one section to another through the book, the corresponding two signs of the zodiac in the astrology garden will be detailed and discussed.

ARIES	**PISCES**
Mars	*Jupiter*
cowslip	agrimony
holy thistle	alexanders
rosemary	costmary
self heal	rose

TAURUS	**AQUARIUS**
Venus	*Saturn*
lovage	fumitory
mint	hellebore
tansy	knapweed
violet	wintergreen

GEMINI	**CAPRICORN**
Mercury	*Saturn*
elecampane	comfrey
horehound	heartsease
lavender	mullein
valerian	Solomon's seal

CANCER	**SAGITTARIUS**
Moon	*Jupiter*
clary sage	clove pinks
hyssop	houseleek
lemon balm	milk thistle
wormwood	sage

LEO	**SCORPIO**
Sun	*Mars*
angelica	basil
bay	chives
calendula	lady's mantle
motherwort	tarragon

VIRGO	**LIBRA**
Mercury	*Venus*
fennel	pennyroyal
parsley	strawberry
savory	violet
southernwood	yarrow

Before the first two, Capricorn and Aquarius, here are the words of Culpeper which began my research; "physic without astrology is like a lamp without oil".

Of course the astrological considerations I have given in placing the herbs are not the whole story. There are also the implications of gathering these herbs at the right times with reference to the heavens, and more astrological involvement in preparing the medicines. Sowing the seeds according to the right phase of the moon is child's play when compared to the knowledge and application required for medical astrology, Paracelsus (born 1483), was one of it's most famous champions and also the father of modern medicine.

Planting the Garden

FROM December 21st to January 21st **Capricorn** is the ruling sign, dominated by Saturn. Culpeper writes that Saturn "loves his bones" and so we may expect to find herbs which treat sprains, dislocations, broken bones and rheumatic diseases under this planet. The knees in particular may be the joints affected, together with problems in the ears and skin. Saturn can also be linked with depression and melancholia. This does not mean that everyone under this sign is obliged to suffer from all, or any of the above. The astrologer - physician would set out a chart of the positions of the planets for the onset of the disease and from this find the likely heavenly cause. The birth chart of the patient was a secondary consideration, showing possible health trends and weaknesses.

Culpeper classifies Saturnine herbs both as treating these problems and being of a cold and slimy nature - not very complimentary. My choice of herbs, being limited by the space available, I selected **Comfrey** with it's admittedly slimy juice and wonderful healing properties, as the best herb to apply to broken bones and torn ligaments. As effective in this role now as it was seen to be then. (Also providing a source of green mulch and liquid feed for plants in the astrology garden.) **Mullein** was applied for stiffness of the sinews in the period when the herbal was written (17th century). Its modern use in treating ear problems as a healing oil and helping dry eczema gave me further reason to include it as a herb of Capricorn.

Also classified as under Saturn I found **Solomon's Seal** which enjoyed a good reputation used as a poultice of the pounded root on deep bruising, especially black eyes. Perhaps it helped when ears were boxed. It was certainly well regarded for treating broken bones. Distilled water from the roots helped skin problems.

The last herb in my bed of Capricorn I allow to spread between the others for its pretty, cheering nature, a help for depression if ever there was one - and a treatment for skin rashes, eczema etc; **Heartsease.** The tricoloured flower faces have attracted charming country names, such as 'Cuddle me' and 'Three faces in a hood'. Culpeper associates it particularly with the sign of Cancer where I also encourage it to spread.

One herb is still needed to complete Capricorn and this is the **Melancholy thistle,** *Carduus heterophyllus,* a herb which Culpeper regarded as capable of making a melancholy man "merry as a cricket". I have searched for a plant of this herb for some time and now have seeds to sow this year. Hopefully, it's perennial nature will mean it should become a permanent resident in the astrology garden.

In **Aquarius** Saturn continues to rule, with the joints most at risk - now being the ankles. Difficulties caused by poor circulation may also enter the diagnosis. Culpeper sets one herb above the others as he writes "Saturn presents it to the world as a cure for his own disease, and a strengthener of the parts of the body he rules". You may be surprised to know he is referring to a herb often regarded as a weed in modern gardens. **Fumitory** is also known as earth smoke for the ethereal nature of it's silvered blue/green leaves. It was administered in the form of a syrup or decoction for a number of ailments associated with the liver and spleen and the powdered herb given for melancholy.

Black hellebore *Helleborus niger*, also then called the Christmas herb and now the Christmas rose, was regarded with rightful caution by Culpeper. He wrote "It is an herb of Saturn, and therefore no marvel if it has some sullen conditions with it...". He recommends purifying the poisonous root before treating melancholy diseases, gout and jaundice.

Wintergreen which grows at the 'foot' of the hellebore, spreading a mat of thick, almost succulent, leaves, was well known for treating wounds and sores. The subsequent use in ointments and rubs for rheumatic pains appears not to have been tried at the time.

Behind the wintergreen, rising to 1m (3ft) tall in summer and drawing many bees and butterflies to this bed, is **Greater knapweed.** Wounds, sores and inflammations were all treated with this lovely herb, better known nowadays as a wild flower.

Cultivation details for comfrey and heartsease can be found in Herbwise Naturally and those for mullein in Herbcraft Naturally. The black hellebore, fumitory, greater knapweed, Solomon's seal and wintergreen will be found in the Cultivation section.

Chamomile seat

(top right) *Winter honeysuckle*
(above) *Black hellebore*

January - February

Herb swags

Seed collage

Astrology beds

Greater knapweed

Solomon's seal

Bugle

January - February

Knot garden

(Left) *View thro' 'Knot'*

Miniature Knot

Garden Feature

Miniature Gardens for Design

WHEN planning new beds for the coming season, or even re-arranging existing plantings, making sample miniature gardens is the perfect aid to design. A block or two of oasis, a few seeds to mark the paths, a ruler and pencil, templates for complex patterns and some dried flowers and foliage, are all you need for a simple lay-out. It is impossible to use the actual herbs in many cases. Substitute whatever dried herbs you have available within the colour ranges, remembering to represent differences in size between one herb and another.

For gravel paths, celery seed or the larger coriander seed work well, while wooden stepping blocks and fences can be represented by using flakes of cinnamon stick. Arches may be constructed of florists wire, lapping cane or cardboard strips. Rocks around pools, or on mounds, can be made of pieces of dried root ginger and grass is well represented with dill weed glued down. Trees may be shown with thrift or horehound seedheads; wild basil is a little less useful as it can be fragile. Lady's mantle makes a delicate tree to be added only at the last minute.

If you wish to keep your miniature garden as a decoration, it should be made to fit inside a box, casket, basket or display frame. Be sure to leave sufficient headroom beneath the lid for your choice of herbs. The oasis is set into the box first and then the shapes of the beds marked out. Next glue the paths with a craft glue which will dry clear. Sprinkle or pour on the seeds to cover. Pat them well down and turn the garden upside down over newspaper to be sure they are firmly secured. Add more glue and seeds if necessary and repeat. Any grass areas are also glued down at this point. Add rocks, fences, arches etc.

Have ready a selection of different coloured dried herb flowers to give yourself plenty of choice. See the table below. Prepare them by cutting across multiple flower heads such as tansy to give both single flowers and some small 'bushes' of flowers with 1cm (⅜in) stems. Lavender and mints can often produce a number of flower heads from one spike if you can cut between them working down the stem, discarding some flowers for pot-pourri as you go. Germander can be treated in the same way to give foliage with pairs of leaves for representing hedges. Work from the centre of your garden outwards. Each flower is pushed gently into the oasis on its individual stem. The joy of oasis is that you can arrange and re-arrange them until you are happy with the effect. You may even set the finished garden on the side and look at it for a few days, before deciding to take it apart and begin again with a different planting in mind.

The table of herb flowers according to colour, and key to the diagram of the garden illustrated, will give you ideas. Enjoy experimenting. For more actual garden plans, see Herbcraft Naturally - p104-108.

Key to Miniature Garden

ALTHOUGH all of the herbs are shown on the planning diagram, which may be produced before or after the miniature garden is made; I have selected only those which make most visual impact for the actual garden. In choosing other herbs to represent them I have matched flower colours and height and breadth.

In this way tall, yellow flowered elecampane is well represented by clusters of tansy on long stems. While omitting the green foliage of sweet cicely, white thrift heads give a good idea of their likely spread and show white flowers. Germander sprigs make excellent hedging and here show sage, germander and box, reminding us of the uniformity of hedge heights and breadth needed.

Savory with a few flowers, or many, as tiny foliage sprigs or much taller growth; is versatile and has been used in several roles. Lady's mantle also resembles flowering angelica as one tall sprig, while flattened sprays of the herb laid over the arches of the covered way, suggest the golden hop. Some compromises are made for flower colour with the tiny flowers of *Santolina rosmarinafolia* representing both clusters of primroses and cowslips and individual pot marigolds. Choosing dried herbs from the available stock to represent your plans will limber up your imagination ready for the true design work.

SYMBOL	HERB	REPRESENTED BY
E	Elecampane	tansy
O	Oregano	oregano
Sc	Sweet cicely	white thrift
G	Germander, sage, box	germander
W	Winter savory	winter savory
P	Pot Marigold	santolina rosmarinafolia
Pr	Primrose	santolina rosmarinafolia
C	Cowslip	santolina rosmarinafolia
Ma	Golden Marjoram	santolina rosmarinafolia
F	Fennel	tall sprig savory
Ep	Evening primrose	lady's mantle
Gv	Greek valerian	tall savory, few flowers
A	Angelica	lady's mantle
Cp	Clove pinks	oregano florets
H	Honeysuckle	peppermint flowers
L	Lavender	lavender
M	Marshmallow	savory
R	climbing Rose	savory or germander on long stem
Gh	Golden hop	lady's mantle
Mi	Mints	eau-de-cologne mint flowers
Y	Yarrow	yarrow
Sn	Sneezewort	yarrow

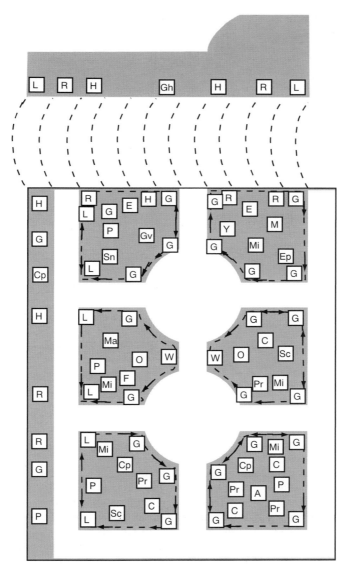

Preserves

JANUARY is traditionally the month when an abundance of cheaper citrus fruits in shops and markets turns our thoughts to making marmalade and preserves. With a growing family at home, I remember buying a whole box of each fruit every year and storing them in a cold porch. These were not only for making marmalade, but also to keep us supplied with our fill of fresh fruit for plentiful vitamin C at a time when colds and 'flu' are at their height.

As ever, the role of herbs is to add exciting flavours and their health-supporting properties to our store cupboard contents. If you feel bored with old marmalade recipes and would like a change, these original flavours cannot be bought and are well worth the experiment. The roots can be dug and candied now, or autumn candies used. Elecampane root adds a spicy, warming zing to a recipe on the tart side and offers the additional bonus of its medicinal properties, which are used for asthma and chesty coughs. You would have to eat prodigious quantities to use it as a cough marmalade - but it may help to ease winter's ills. Sweet cicely root has a softer, liquorice like flavour and adds sweetness to the recipe.

If you feel you haven't the time to follow the whole method for marmalade, you can still add the candied root to tinned ready prepared fruit, along with the sugar.

In this section I have added both a sweet and a savoury jelly recipe. Rosemary orange jelly is quick to make and flavours roast duck, fish and vegetable pies wonderfully. You may find many more uses.

Scented geranium jelly is even simpler. It gives the last touch of perfection to a sponge cake as a fragrant sweet filling, whether the cake has been baked in a tin lined with lemon-scented geranium leaves or not. If you are using this method, remember to wash the leaves in cold water first. Pat dry with paper kitchen towel. Tear each leaf almost in half to release the flavour before laying in the greaseproof lined tin and pouring in the mixture. The jelly is also delicious spread on warm scones.

For a breakfast spread with a spicy zing, using the candied root given below;-
Grapefruit and Elecampane Marmalade
3 grapefruit, approx 900g (2lb) fruit
2 large lemons   40g (1½oz) candied elecampane root
1.8 kg (4lb) sugar   2.25 litres (4 pints) water

Wash and dry fruit. Remove a thin layer of rind using a vegetable peeler, put the rinds (in chunky or fine strips) into the preserving pan. Next lift away the white pith of the fruits and opening them into segments, remove stringy lengths of skin and pips from the soft fruit. Put all the pith, skin and pips into a square of muslin or muslin straining bag and tie securely. Pour the water into the pan over the rinds and soft fruit segments. Add the muslin bag of pips etc.

Set the pan on a moderate heat and simmer until the liquid is reduced by half. This may take 1-1½ hours. Add the sugar and finely chopped candied elecampane root. Keep stirring over a slow heat until the sugar has dissolved. Bring to the boil and continue boiling until the setting point is reached - approximately 20-30 minutes. Test for this by dripping a spoonful onto a cold saucer and putting it aside to cool. As soon as the cold marmalade wrinkles as you touch the surface, it is done. Move the pan off the heat for a few minutes before filling jars which have been sterilised with boiling water and kept warm. Cover and label.
*Makes 2.7-3.2kg (6-7lb) marmalade

For a sweeter, less adventurous recipe;-
Grapefruit and Sweet Cicely Marmalade
Make as above, substituting 50g (2oz) candied sweet cicely root for the
elecampane.
Note: When buying fruit for marmalade it is worth looking out for lemons and
oranges labelled as free of chemical sprays. These may be available.

To candy Sweet Cicely or Elecampane root
100g (4oz) cleaned and chopped root
170g (6oz) sugar
275ml (½ pint) water

When the root is dug, the fine rootlets and any discoloured areas are discarded.
(The root of sweet cicely can be intricately swirled in growth.) The healthy main
root is peeled and chopped into small cubes. Add the root to the water with 50g
(2oz) of sugar. Keep stirring over a low heat until the sugar has dissolved. Bring to
the boil and boil gently for about 20-25 minutes, until soft enough to allow a fork
through the root easily. Set aside to cool.

Strain the root and layer with an equal weight of sugar in a covered dish. After
24 hours turn the root and sugar to be sure the root remains moist. By this time a
syrup will be forming. Leave for a further 24 hours. Pour the syrup and root back
into the pan and bring to the boil briefly. Strain out the root. If it is to be used
straight away in marmalade add the herb at this stage. To keep it for longer,
sprinkle with sugar before setting on a rack to dry in a warm oven. Store in layers
between greaseproof paper in a tin or jars. The strained sweet cicely syrup
remaining may be used to flavour a fruit pudding, or thickened as a glaze over an
apple tart.

There are few fresh harvests of herbs for preserves at this time of year.
However the first flowers may open on the rosemary in February if it is in it's
favourite position against a south facing wall. The lovely, delicate flowers are our
cue to begin harvesting on sunny days when there is no danger of really sharp frost
on the night following. A little flowering rosemary can safely be taken on most
days. Cover the bush for a night or two after a large harvest if the weather turns
really cold. Even when the weather forbids an outdoor harvest, the lemon and rose-
scented pelargoniums set along my windowsills offer their flavours.

Do use leaves from your own plants so that you are sure they have not been
sprayed recently with pesticides. Do not buy a plant and use the leaves
immediately for the recipe.

Scented Geranium Jelly
3 cups sugar
½ cup herb infusion
100 ml (4 fl oz) liquid pectin

Strained juice of 1 large lemon made up
to 1 cup with apple juice

Pour 1 cup of boiling water over about 4 tablespoons of torn fresh leaves of lemon-
scented geraniums. This will be about 7 or 8 large leaves. Simmer gently to reduce

the liquid by half. Strain. While this is simmering pour the sugar and fruit juices into a large pan and prepare 2 jam jars by sterilising with boiling water. Keep these warm.

Add the herb infusion to the sugar and fruit juices and bring slowly to the boil, making sure the sugar has dissolved before turning up the heat. Once boiling, add the liquid pectin and stir well. Boil for 2 minutes and remove the pan from the heat. Skim. Set one torn fresh geranium leaf in each warmed jar and pour in the jelly. Seal.

*Makes 900g (2lb) jelly

Rosemary Orange Jelly

3 cups sugar   100 ml (4 fl oz) liquid pectin
½ cup herb infusion   1 cup freshly squeezed orange juice

Always pound rosemary with a pestle or the rolling pin to bring out the flavour before using in a recipe. Pour one cup of boiling water over 3 tablespoons washed and chopped, flowering herb. Simmer till the liquid is reduced by half. While this is simmering put the sugar and orange juice into a large pan and prepare 2 jars as in the recipe above. Add the strained herb infusion to the sugar and fruit juice and heat gently, stirring to dissolve the sugar. When the sugar is dissolved, turn up the heat, bringing the jelly to the boil. Add the liquid pectin and stir well. Boil for 2 minutes. Remove from the heat. Skim off any scum. Pour the jelly into the warmed jars. Seal and label.

Herb Teas

F RESH rosemary will also make a warming tea which renews your mental energy as well as increasing circulation. Take one top of rosemary (flowering if possible) about 10cm (4ins) long, wash it and pound it on a board using the rolling pin to bring out the full flavour before pouring on the boiling water. Avoid rosemary tea while pregnant.

For a dried tea to warm and revitalise mix the following;
2 parts rosemary   ½ part lavender
1 part thyme   ½ part flaked cinnamon stick
1 part angelica leaf (optional)

Mix and make as below. After a few days change to a different tea for a while.

Herb tea method

I N general use one or two fresh tops of the herb, or one teaspoon of dried herb, per cup. Never make herb tea in a metal teapot. Try to keep a particular pot or jug just for herb teas. Warm the pot first and pour the boiling water over torn fresh herb or dried blend. Cover and leave to stand for about 5 minutes. Strain into a cup, adding honey if liked as a sweetener. All herb teas are potentially medicinal and should be restricted to one cup per day unless you require the medicinal effect.

Wines and Liqueurs

HOME winemaking sprang from a combination of seeking ways of using a welcome surplus of fruit, vegetables and herbs from the garden, and enjoying a tasty tipple with friends. Hospitality on a budget can be achieved with a very small input of time on your part. It is fun to make wines and liqueurs through the year so that as each gallon or more of a wine is ready to drink, there are new wines to follow on. The recipes which appear in each of the 6 sections of this book have not appeared in my previous works. Wines which are detailed in Herbcraft Naturally will be mentioned in the following sections at the appropriate time of year.

The first wine to be made in any year is Coltsfoot and I have talked to winemakers who found the flowers alone gave a poor result. Remembering this, I teamed them with lemon, grapefruit and ginger for added flavour in my own recipe. This has proved a popular wine with my friends and family and I was soon persuaded to double the quantity. The wine should be ready to drink between late autumn and Christmas of the same year.

Since you will almost certainly be gathering coltsfoot flowers from the countryside, be sure to do so away from the traffic fumes. If you are fortunate enough to see the yellow flowers appearing in a friend's garden or allotment, they will be only too happy for you to take both the flowers and plants, for they spread rapidly. Coltsfoot is such an unpopular herb/weed with gardeners, you must also ensure your crop has not been sprayed with weedkiller just before you arrived on the scene. It can be found on dry, chalky soil in the south of England, both high on hillsides and at the edges of low-lying wet fields. It rejoices in old railway embankments and waste ground. Occasionally coltsfoot will appear in gardens and on allotments, and I have also seen it on sandy patches of riverbank along the Tees in the north. The flowers open before the leaves, which gives the herb the old name of son-before-father. Cut the flowers only, removing all green parts from behind them.

Coltsfoot, Lemon & Ginger Wine

Approx 1.2 - 1.5 litres (2-2½ pints) coltsfoot flowers
25g (1oz) fresh ginger root (or 15g pack dried ginger pieces)
1.35 kg (3lb) sugar

25g (1oz) fresh bakers yeast	Optional; 2 Campden tablets
1 slice bread, toasted	4.5 litres (8 pints) water
1 lemon	1 grapefruit

Put the thickly sliced lemon and grapefruit rinds and broken or cut pieces of ginger into a large preserving pan with 3 litres (5½ pints) of water. Stir in the granulated or caster sugar over a low heat until it is dissolved. Bring the liquor to simmering and simmer for 10 minutes. Meanwhile wash the trimmed flowers a few at a time in a sieve under a running cold tap. Put them into a fermenting bucket or earthenware crock with the juices of the fruit and crushed Campden tablets if these are to be used. Pour over the hot syrup. (The purpose of the tablets is to kill any natural yeasts in the flowers and give a controlled fermentation. Since this is a modern refinement in winemaking and I favour older methods - I look upon this step as optional and will merely comment that I do occasionally use them.) Since Campden tablets kill yeasts you must leave your wine for 24 hours before adding the yeast you wish to work, see below.

Add a further 1.5 litres (2½ pints) of boiling water and spread the fresh yeast on toasted bread. When the liquor is at bloodheat, float the yeast on toast on the surface. Cover and leave for 24 hours. Remove the toast, pressing the liquid out of it and back into the wine, which should now be frothing and fermenting. Stir the wine with a wooden spoon and cover again. The wine is stirred night and morning daily for 7 days while being kept in a warm, steady temperature ideally about 21°C, 70°F.

If, during this time the frothing appears to die down and stirring does not produce a fizzing sound, add a handful of chopped raisins to feed the yeast. After 7 days, syphon the wine into a sterilised demi-john or pass the liquor through a fine sieve into a jug and pour in. Fill the demi-john past the height at which it begins to narrow to the neck, but not completely to the top, and fit the bored bung with fermentation lock inserted. Bottle when fermentation has ended.

FOR those with the patience to wait 1, 2 or 3 years for a very special treat, liqueurs are made in minutes and need even less attention than wines. This first liqueur of the year could not be simpler and even before the sugar is added, the wonderful fragrance will delight you.

Violet Liqueur

AS the first violets open each year, I find myself assessing the possible harvest and making the difficult decision whether there may be sufficient flowers for liqueur or syrup, as well as violet sugar and candied flowers for cakes.

To gather over 25g (1oz) of petals requires a large number of flowers when all the green parts have been removed. You will need a very large, or several smaller patches of the deeply scented *Viola odorata* to provide them. However, you do not need them all to be in flower at the same time, so long as you have sensitive scales which can register only 10g or less. With sufficient flowers to register on your scale on the first occasion, you can then count these and keep a record of how many flowers you pick, prepare and add to the spirit on each successive dry day.

You should aim to pick at least 32g (1¼oz) of petals, the more flowers you add, the stronger the flavour will be. 50g (2oz) of petals is even better.

You will need;
At least 32g (1¼oz) violet petals - all green parts removed
35cl (12 fl oz) 1 'half bottle' brandy or eau-de-vie
¾ rounded teaspoon ground orris root powder
1½ teaspoon ground coriander seed
1 teaspoon whole aniseed
¾ cup caster sugar

Fill a screwtop jar to within an inch or two of the brim with the neat spirit, leaving space only for the other ingredients. Keep the spirit bottle ready for later. Only perfect flowers should be picked on a dry day, preferably in the mid or late morning. Remove the green parts of the flowers, allowing the petals to fall into a bowl of cold water. Immerse them briefly in the water to remove any insects or dust and gently pat dry between two layers of paper kitchen towel. Put straight into the spirit. Replace the screwtop and swirl the flowers in the liquor. The freshly ground coriander seed, whole aniseed and ground orris root may be added when you have at least half the flowers in the spirit, or after the last flowers. Do not add the sugar at this stage. Label the jar with details of the amount of violets and date.

Keep the tightly closed and labelled jar in a warm, dark cupboard for 6 weeks, giving the contents a swirl every so often. At the end of this time strain the spirit through a coffee filter paper to remove even the orris powder, and stir in the sugar gradually. You will find it will dissolve as you continue stirring, do not heat the liqueur or you will lose the alcohol. If a little residue remains it does not matter, simply pour this into the original bottle with the spirit.

Having added the sugar you will need a second spirit bottle to take the extra volume. Label your liqueur and date it. Hide the bottles in the back of a cupboard and do not taste for at least one year. The longer you leave it the better the treat will be. If you taste it before it is ready the flavour will be too harsh to enjoy.

For more details of wine and liqueur making see Herbcraft Naturally.

In the Home

HERBS have always held a role of improving the quality of our lives - whether through flavouring food, aiding health and beauty, or adding soothing and refreshing fragrances to homes. When windows and doors may be tightly closed against cold or wet weather, a clean sweep of fragrance through centrally heated rooms can be just as welcome as it was in the dark draughty halls of past centuries. Fresh rushes were once strewn on the floors with sweet-smelling herbs amongst them. The recipe below is a modern alternative to freshen your floor coverings.

Carpet sprinkle
(dried ingredients)
6 tablespoons heavily scented rose petals
1 tablespoon eau-de-cologne mint leaves
1 rounded tablespoon ground orris root
1 dessertspoon cloves
Grind all the ingredients together and store in a sealed jar. Sprinkle generously over the carpet to be freshened. Leave for 10-15 minutes with the door closed. Vacuum the carpet.

ADDED perfume from pot-pourri will enrich a warm atmosphere. If you are already harvesting and drying herb flowers and foliage through the year, you will have a ready supply of ingredients stored in boxes with a little silica gel to keep them dry, or in brown paper sacks or screwtop jars. Pot-pourri requires a curing time of 6 weeks before it is set in bowls or pots to be opened for a short period each day. The following recipes are worth the wait. The sooner you mix the ingredients, the sooner you will be enjoying them. The first recipe is sweet and rich.

Rose Arbour Pot-Pourri
(dried ingredients)
4 cups heavily scented rose petals
2 cups rose geranium leaves (these may be removed brown and crisp from the plants on the windowsill)
1 stick cinnamon (broken into small pieces)
¼ cup eau-de-cologne mint leaves
3 tablespoons marjoram
1 tablespoon ground calamus or orris root
½ tablespoon star anise pods and seeds
¼ teaspoon vanilla perfume or extract
4 drops essential oil of rose geranium

Mix the dried flowers and leaves together in a bowl. Add the spices and fixative root (available from healthfood shops). Stir well together. Pour in the vanilla perfume or extract, or torn vanilla pod. Lastly add the oil of geranium one drop at a time. Spoon the mix into a screwtop jar and seal, placing the jar in a warm, dark cupboard for 6 weeks to 'cure'. At the end of this time the perfumes will have blended together and the pot-pourri will be ready to set in a covered dish which is only opened to the light and air for an hour each day. Set the bowl in a warm place where the airflow will waft the fragrance about the room. Replace the lid.

The second recipe is a lighter blend with subtle undertones;

Summer Garden Pot-Pourri

(dried ingredients)

2 cups jasmine flowers	1 cup lemon verbena
1 cup rosebuds	½ cup lavender
1 tablespoon limeflowers	1 tablespoon flowering catmint
2 tablespoons pot marigold petals	1 tablespoon sandalwood chips
1 stick cinnamon, crushed	½ teaspoon ground cloves
1 tablespoon orris root	4 drops essential oil of sandalwood
5 drops aromatherapy oil of jasmine	1 drop essential oil of geranium

Mix the dried flowers and herbs, adding the spices and fixative root as above. Add the oils carefully, one drop at a time. Essential oil of jasmine would be even better and you would need only 3 drops if you have this. Here I have substituted aromatherapy oil which is the essential oil already diluted in a carrier - this is due to the high cost of the pure oil. If you can afford the pure essential oil - so much the better. With the blend made, store it in a dark screwtop jar in a warm cupboard for 6 weeks to cure as before - the really delicious perfume will be worth waiting for.

Craft

Ivy Berry Dye

DYES from natural materials are always unpredictable as so many factors affect them. The temperature of the dyebath and hardness of the water are easier to control than the pH of the soil in which the plant has grown, rainfall over the previous 2 or 3 weeks, maturity of the herb and so on. For me, much of the fun of dyeing is waiting to see exactly which shade will emerge from the dyebath. Sometimes it is a disappointment which can be over-dyed using another herb. At others it can be a brilliant surprise.

The metal of the dyepan, and mordant used, are the greatest factors. For this reason, unless you are mordanting with alum, a stainless steel dyepan is best. If you mordant with chrome to bring out orange or red shades then this pan should also have a lid, as the light must be excluded during mordanting and dyeing. Wear rubber gloves when dyeing and keep all measuring spoons, stirring rods, pans and so on for dyeing only.

For this first recipe of the year I generally use alum as a mordant and will detail this below. I have also used chrome to obtain a much brighter, lime green. For instructions for the chrome mordant see page 89. The dye liquor is exactly the same in both cases.

Depending on their location, ivy berries can ripen to a glossy black as early as the end of December, or as late as March. Do gather berries for dyeing as soon as you see they are ready. Never think you can return a week later, for the birds may well have been there before you.

Harvest
To dye 50g (2oz) wool or a silk scarf and embroidery thread, gather 225g (8oz) ripe berries.

Preparation of Wool
Thoroughly wash raw fleece and soak clean fleece or a skein of spun wool in cold water for 2 hours before mordanting. With skeins ensure the ties are sufficiently loose to allow the dye to reach the strands within them.

To Mordant with Alum
Put 15g (½ oz) alum powder (available from chemists) into a jam jar. Add ½ teaspoon cream of tartar. Pour on a little hot water and stir until dissolved. Add to 2.8 - 3.4 litres (5-6 pints) of cold water in a large dyepan. Heat slowly and add the wool when the water is hand-hot. Simmer gently for 45 minutes for fine wool, or 1 hour for coarse. It can then be dried to dye another day or squeezed dry and entered into the prepared dye liquor.

The same amounts can be used for silk. In this case the silk fabric or thread is put straight into the cold mordant and a very low heat applied. Once the liquor is approaching simmer, but not actually simmering, remove from the heat.

Leave to one side overnight to give the silk time to take up the mordant. If you wish to treat wool and a little silk at once, add the silk when you have removed the pan from the heat.

To Prepare the Dye
Add the ripe ivy berries to 2.8 - 3.4 litres (5-6 pints) of water in a dyepan. Simmer steadily for about 1 hour. It will not matter if the water boils. A pink colouring will appear first. This does not set in the wool. As the berries soften, encourage them to release their juice by crushing them against the side of the pan, either with a wooden spoon kept just for dyeing, or the pestle from a mortar and pestle.

After 1 hour set the dye liquor aside to cool. Strain off the berries. Enter the gently squeezed, mordanted wool when the liquor is hand-hot. Simmer for 45 minutes. Lift out the wool using a wooden spoon or rod and sprinkle in ¼ - ½ teaspoon of iron. (Ferrous sulphate is available from dye suppliers - see appendix). Stir into the liquor and re-enter the wool. Continue simmering for 15 minutes. Set aside from the heat. When the dyebath has cooled to about hand-hot, pre-mordanted silk may be added. Leave to stand overnight.

For Wool
Remove from the dyebath next morning, rinse 3 times in cold water and drip dry outdoors. A plastic apron will protect you from accidental splashes. Care should also be taken not to drop or splash dye on carpets or sides. **Result** -An attractive shade of grey-green.

For Silk
Leave the silk to soak in the dyebath for 2 or 3 days before rinsing and dripping dry outside. Generally deeper shades are obtained on silk.

Safety
Alum is a safe mordant to use with children. Chrome is very toxic and the room should be well ventilated while this is on the stove. For other safety considerations see page 89.

When gathering ivy berries for dyeing you may also like to pick a selection of foliage and flowers for pressing.

Flowers and Foliage to press

C HOICES are limited at this time of year but you need not stray far into the garden to pick a few lovely flowers. Winter honeysuckle and winter jasmine are perfectly situated along a south-facing wall to frame windows or doorways. Ivy growing on a house or garden wall, or over a tree-stump, is another welcome source of material for pressing. Small leaves often have the best markings. The beauty of cyclamen leaves has made them a favourite of mine and there may be some fresh growth of tansy or fennel to supply that first vivid green of early spring. Celandines may also splash the drab February hedgerows with bright colour.

All of these flowers and leaves may be pressed as well between blotting paper in a heavy book, as in a flower press. The ivy and cyclamen will need extra weight on top. Once they are fully dry, store them in a scrapbook or old telephone book, (they can then be filed alphabetically) in a dry dark place.

They may be used to create original cards, designs for embroidery, or decorate boxes. See Herbcraft Naturally.

Herb Swags

B RIGHT and perfumed flowers and foliage make a swag both attractive and enjoyable over several months.

You will need: secateurs or strong scissors. Florists wire or strong thread. Seagrass or raffia.

HERBS FOR COLOUR		HERBS FOR PERFUME
bergamot	oregano	hyssop
bistort	rosebuds	lavender
clove pinks	santolina flowers	mints
helichrysum	St John's wort	santolina
Jerusalem sage	tansy	thymes
lavender	yarrow	

To make: cut 3 cords of seagrass at least 1½ times the length of the completed swag. Tie together close to one end with more seagrass or strong thread. Lay the seagrass on a flat surface and work a tight plait, taking first the left cord over the one in the centre and then the right. Stop at intervals to free the long ends of seagrass which will have twisted around each other as you work. Tie again at the end of the plait.

Make up several bunches of individual herbs, or two or three together. These can be a little wider than the plait, or up to three times the width. As you bring the bunches together, carefully remove all lower flowering stems to give flatter, bare ends as a base for the next bundle which will be laid over these. Offcuts may be saved in small jars or boxes either for adding to pot-pourri, or using in making miniature gardens.

Once you have prepared 5 or 6 bunches by tying them with crochet thread or florists wire, you can lay them in order. Rearrange them until you have the best contrasts or shades of colour for your finished effect.

If you are making 2 swags to hang at either side of a door or fireplace, remember to check that you have sufficient materials to repeat either the whole swag, or key touches of dominant herbs. With the order of herbs decided, set the first bunch to overlap one end of the plait, completely hiding the seagrass. Either tie or stitch it in place with strong crochet thread, or bind it on with florists wire, which is then taken in a continuous length around further bunches.

Lay each bunch so that the flowers or foliage covers the bound or stitched stems of the previous one. If you wish to leave a free end of seagrass to scroll round against the wall, stop working about 46cm (18ins) away from the end and lay your last bunch of herbs facing the other way. Your last tie may be covered by a ribbon bow, or a large dried flower or two set over it, with the stems tucked into bunches already secured.

For a shorter, heavier swag over a doorway, plait 3 bunches of 3-6 cords of seagrass or raffia, adding wider bunches of flowers. Knock panel pins into the wall to support the swag in the desired, finished shape. Lift the swag into position and press the raffia plait over the pins, to secure.

Tree of Life Seed Design

THE collage seen in the illustration measures 23cm x 28.5cm (9 x 11ins) with a tree trunk 21cm (8¼ins) tall and 5.5cm (2½ins) across at the widest point. It may be repeated with leaf shapes of varying sizes.

For my initial design, I began by cutting out the shape of the tree trunk with short branches in a dark coloured felt, and trimmed this until I was satisfied with the result when laid against a light background. I then drew a faint outline in pencil on the white card mount, adding the mounded hill shape below it. For the large leaf shapes I drew faint outlines around the leaves of lemon-scented geranium, laid flat. Small leaf shapes are easily drawn freehand, or more of the smaller leaves can be used from the plant.

The placing of the seeds in the various leaf areas may be followed from the diagram or varied, according to your taste and availability of materials. A number of seeds, such as coriander, dill, celery, star anise and possibly angelica, can be bought in wholefood shops. Others, such as French marigold, calendula and honesty, each with their own very individual characters, are available from garden seed suppliers. Some, such as alexanders, may be gathered wild in autumn near the sea on the south or west coasts. Borage is a good alternative. Milk thistle, dyer's broom, woad and sweet cicely may be more difficult to find, in which case substitutes can be made.

The joy of seed collage is in searching amongst those seeds you have to hand for the greatest contrasts in size, shape, shade and texture, and exploring many possibilities before finally reaching for the glue. When you do feel ready to make lasting decisions, begin working on the leaves at the top of the picture and work down. In this way you will avoid leaning on work you have already finished. Very little glue is needed. It can be applied with a cocktail stick to a small area of the card at a time and the seeds laid individually in place, or poured on, according to their size.

Calendula seedcases are particularly useful for encasing seeds and giving a smooth, rounded outline. I have also used the empty seedcases from the dyer's broom for narrow branches as these twist as they 'explode' open in sunlight, producing a striking effect.

The cinnamon for the trunk is cut and prised off cinnamon sticks as flakes and these are laid in rows working up the trunk of the tree. Each layer is laid partly over the one below, and many fragments overlap slightly to give the feeling of raised bark patterns.

The ground roots which I have sprinkled on as 'soil' are calamus root and galingale. Orris root and cinnamon or other powders could be substituted. To complete your picture it is best placed in a deep mount or display frame to lift the glass away from the larger seeds.

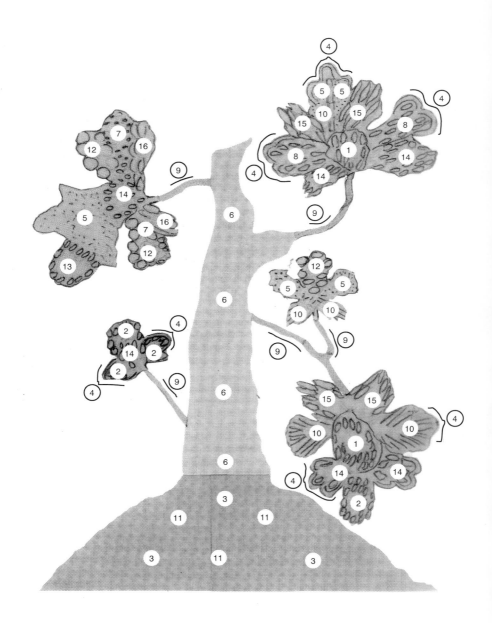

Seeds Key

1	alexanders
2	angelica
3	calamus root
4	calendula seedcases
5	celery
6	cinnamon stick
7	coriander
8	dill
9	dyer's broom seedpods
10	French marigold
11	galingale
12	honesty
13	milk thistle
14	star anise
15	sweet cicely
16	woad

March - April

A time of sweet nurturing -
Ewe with her lambs, gardeners their seeds.
Clear frosty nights of bright, bright stars
cradle days of brilliant sun - warm air.
Contrast is everywhere.
Stark earth and dried seedheads
foster new life in tansy green.
Buds bursting, birds nesting, re-creation.
Winter sleepers waken - tortoiseshell
flies out to bask too soon.
A time of new energy,
birds building nests, gardeners tend soil.
Blackthorn winter with cold, cold wind
threatens blossom's promise of fruit to come.
Contrast is everywhere.
Yellows of dandelion, primrose and daffodil
herald white flowers, and pink partners blue.
The triumph of spring renewed.
Rejoined, precious circle of the year.

In the Garden

IN the garden, March is a month of awakening promise, when the robin follows the gardener's digging to feast on newly exposed worms. As frosty mornings are followed by brilliant, deceptively warm afternoons, we may be tempted to clear beds of the protection of dead stems and divide perennial herbs too early. If the urge to 'spring clean' the garden is too strong to resist, then newly divided or planted herbs must be given a good protection of mulch, and perhaps a cover for a night or two.

Young forget-me-nots and wild strawberries offer good ground cover until annuals can be planted out. The blackthorn flowers seem still to herald a period of bitter winds even as the climate has changed, and the tradition of the 'blackthorn winter' lives on. North and east winds in March and April can threaten the very existence of thymes, rosemary and bay, especially if they are in wet soil. Covering plants with a net curtain is the best protection from frost. Good drainage is also most important for the Mediterranean herbs in winter. Rosemary may thrive better with broken eggshells stirred into the surrounding earth.

Before setting myself to tidy the herb beds I remove all weeds from the bark and gravel paths in my garden. This can be done when the beds are still too wet to be disturbed. I always find herb seedlings here. These need to be carefully removed and planted in the beds or potted on. In recent years the late spring has been very dry and the gravel and bark areas have proved the best situations for seedlings to germinate and grow. I have been especially thankful that I have never fallen to the temptation of using weedkillers, for I would have missed so many wonderful surprises. One herb seedling which must be potted or moved while very small, is fennel. A larger plant is extremely difficult to remove as the taproot goes straight down into the earth.

Plant Division

In any herb garden the enthusiastic growth of many herbs will mean paying special attention to division and control at this point in the year. The vibrant green of new tansy leaves which for me define 'spring green', will often reveal that the roots appear to have been spreading silently underground all winter. The table of plants to divide will give you a guide to those herbs which also need a generous allowance of extra space around them when first planted as innocent young seedlings.

Pests

Snails and woodlice are revealed, as tubs, flower pots and edging stones are moved while putting the garden in order. Essential oil of pine can be dripped beneath them to deter snails in particular and slugs to a lesser extent. A few drops added to a jar of petroleum jelly, which is then kept sealed for 24 hours before smearing it around trays and pots of young seedlings, can also help to keep them safe. I have tried laying rosemary in a thick layer around young plants against slugs, although a good covering of juniper is better. However the most successful protection when planting out seedlings has so far been given by tearing up fresh comfrey leaves, and laying these around the herb you wish to protect. The snail will prefer the comfrey, eating that instead. The only drawback to this method is, of course, that the comfrey has to be replaced as it is eaten. Check there is some left each morning and evening.

Both comfrey and stinging nettles are putting on a spurt of new growth as the stems of the long-lasting coltsfoot flowers are slowly clothed in fresh young leaves; their naked stalks comforted. By mid-March the bees will be about on sunny days and an occasional peacock or tortoiseshell butterfly explores the garden, drawn through the open window from its winter home along the ceiling beams in our bedroom. The ladybirds are busy on nettles, sage leaves, chervil, lovage, lemon balm and motherwort. Already established in the garden, they have enjoyed the protection of dead leaves and stems. They will be ready for the first aphids and quickly lay young on affected plants later in the year.

Birds are also busy about the garden. While thrushes are particularly welcome as they help the gardener by eating snails, some birds can be a real nuisance. They have an annoying habit of pecking off the attractive flower buds of primroses and cowslips, before they have time to bloom.

In my garden pheasants and partridges can be the culprits, and to give them a sharp reminder they are not welcome, I set the seedheads of Scotch thistles around and over the young plants in bud. After a few days these can generally safely be removed. If small birds are the culprits, often sprigs of curry plant set thickly about the plants will discourage them, as they hate the smell. This method can also be used with young peas and beans. Alternatively, garlic will deter them.

In the vegetable garden a number of useful combinations of herbs and other plants may be used for protection. See Herbwise Naturally.

Propagation

Sage bushes offer fragrant cover for cabbages against pests. These can be earthed up in March to encourage their stems to grow roots. The 'layered' plants are ready to transplant in May. Cuttings of sage and the early shoots of mint will grow roots readily, set in a clear jar of water on the kitchen windowsill in late March or April. Rosemary sprigs seem to prefer the privacy of a dark vase when rooting. All will be encouraged by changes of water and an occasional addition of comfrey tea. Give them 4 drops of Rescue Remedy in the initial water.

Sage, rosemary, germander, winter savory, hyssops, box, lavender, snowberry, santolina, thymes, elder, honeysuckle and curry plant will all root successfully as 7.5 -10cm (3-4ins) cuttings taken with a 'heel' if possible, rather than cut straight across. Strip the lower leaves of each cutting, putting the stems into a pot or jar of treated water. To prepare the water add 4 drops of Bach Rescue Remedy and 2 drops of Bach Walnut remedy.

The gardener at the Bach Centre near Oxford told me some years ago that he used this remedy in water when moving plants or taking cuttings, and I have found it helpful ever since. When given to human patients it treats fear of new places. It may seem a quaint idea at first for a plant to be apprehensive, but there is now plentiful scientific evidence to show they are far more aware of their surroundings than had been thought.

Leave the stems in this while preparing deep pots of a mix of half soil and half potting compost. Dip the cuttings into hormone rooting compound before setting them in the pots, about 2.5 - 4cm (1-1½ins) apart. Keep the pots under cover at night and on cold days in a cold frame or greenhouse and ensure the soil remains moist but not wet.

Plant Conditions

The red spears of lovage thrust skywards in a giant clump, warm weather enabling them to shoot up by several inches in a few days. Fresh, and wondrously tempting for salads and soup, the young stems still need protection from sharp frosts which can give severe damage, impairing growth later in the year.

While herbs such as Greek valerian and sweet cicely show their young growth to full advantage in compact beauty, other herbs are less appealing after winter frosts. Winter savory and hyssop may yet be brown and even appear to have died. Do not be hasty in removing them however, as nine times out of ten, April will see them suddenly sprout fresh leaves and recovery is then a joy to see. The most important aids to their survival are good drainage in relatively poor soil. Hyssop may be cut back further, if green shoots which were left in autumn have died. Do not cut back too harshly. To remain healthy, rosemary bushes should be harvested, cutting them back by almost two thirds.

Craft Harvests

While moving about the garden, steadily tidying , craft enthusiasts should watch out for fibres which have been left by rotting stems of nettle, or members of the mallow family. Sometimes as certain stems are cut in autumn, lengths fall and lay on the damp earth through the winter. By spring these may be weathered down to reveal the bare fibres, and can be gathered carefully to prepare for papermaking, or even spinning - see Herbcraft Naturally.

As you dead-head daffodils, remember these can be saved for dyeing wool and the leaves harvested later and dried to make mats. Dandelion flowers gathered from the garden as you weed are also a brilliant dye source. As I work I take joy in the amazing variety of leaf forms and textures, pressing some alongside the spring flowers, for this is when they show the best shades of green or variegation. Many, I note, will be superb specimens for leaf printing.

If you grow thornless or wild bramble and have not cut it back in the autumn, it can be trimmed now, supplying tips of new growth for dyeing, or longer lengths in March for basketry. Make sure it is well supported. Often as I tend the bramble at the far end of the orchard I find the blackbirds nearby, looking harassed and tired, busily working away to feed their young family. The juniper provided a safe nesting place for them one year. The cypressus hedge is another favourite site.

The beauty of the bramble leaves may well be lost on those who struggle with the thorns, but they are truly lovely and serve well for leaf printing. As for basketry, March sees the end of the winter period for gathering and preparing stems to weave or make garlands. It is also a good point in the year to plant a basketry source such as willow and watch it grow into a living arch, seat or herbar. Last year we chose to plant a willow herbar to be used as a skittle alley in the children's area of the garden. This project is detailed in the garden feature for this section.

Feeding

Roses and shrubs such as bay need attention at this time. To help prevent mildew and fungal problems on roses later in the year, see they are watered well and make up the horsetail infusion given in Herbwise Naturally. Water them with this 2 or 3 weeks running, the first time foliage only and then the roots. This has fungicidal properties and doubles as a mineral rich tonic. Bay will benefit from a good dose of strong nettle infusion as an iron tonic after the frosts. Lift any mint in small containers, giving it fresh compost ready for the new growth. Re-plant.

Seedlings

With all this activity in the garden do not forget to maintain care of your young seedlings still under protection. On still, sunny days the greenhouse can be opened, or they may be set outside in a sheltered position. Beware of subjecting them to a strong breeze or sudden chill.

Basil is particularly subject to damage from draughts. I have lost a whole tray simply by leaving a nearby door open on a day which turned colder while I was out. Prick out seedlings with 4 leaves to give them space and sufficient nutrients to develop well. Keep them watered without having them awash. Light from more than one side is important. Damping off in greenhouses can be treated with chamomile. Set a handful of chamomile flowers (dried flowers are available from wholefood stores), in a shallow dish of water and leave this in sunlight for a few hours. Strain off the flowers and water the affected plants with the liquid.

Sow more seeds best suited to outdoor conditions in prepared seedbeds in the garden in April.

Nasturtiums, chervil, marjoram, calendula, borage, sunflower, foxgloves, woad, soapwort, salad rocket, Greek valerian, salad burnet, St John's wort, motherwort, evening primrose, mullein, teazle, agrimony, betony, fennel, dyer's chamomile, greater burdock will all do well in natural conditions. The sowing time before or just after New Moon may again be followed - perhaps with some, and not others, to keep a recorded experiment. It is interesting to do this over a few years and then compare results.

Herbs to divide in Spring

ajuga   alecost
avens - traditional harvest of herb bennet roots for pot-pourri is on March 25th, Lady Day
bergamot - this should be lifted, the dead centre of the root
   discarded and the new outer growth replanted
chives - excess bulbs can be pickled
comfrey - remember you are unlikely to be able to move it
   without leaving a second plant behind
golden marjoram   oregano
golden rod   periwinkle
gypsywort   self-heal
lady's bedstraw   soapwort

lemon balm
lovage – dry as fixative
marshmallow
mints
mugwort
nettle

St. John's wort
sweet cicely
tansy
tarragon
thrift
yarrow

The Astrology Garden

PISCES, the sign of the fishes, is entered by the sun about February 21st, but the sign Aquarius also rules in part until the 27th, so it is March before Pisces comes truly into it's own. As the fishes imply, it is a watery sign, ruled by Jupiter and Neptune. The feet and particularly the toes are the centre of attention for treatment, with causes of problems in this part of the body mainly being infections and poor liver function. Circulation may also be affected. Gout and dropsy both figure here.

For liver function in particular I chose to include **Agrimony** in this bed. Culpeper writes that it removes diseases in any part of the body governed by Jupiter under several signs, including Pisces. Therefore, he tells us, it "must needs be good for the gout, either used outwardly in oil, or ointment, or inwardly in an electuary ….". Since it was also credited with opening and cleansing the liver, being beneficial to the bowels and healing inward wounds; it was, and remains, a worthwhile herb.

My own use includes winemaking with the flowering tops, which are also a good dye and dried for pot-pourri. The tiny yellow flowers on the spires of hairy stems add ethereal beauty to the elegant, lower leaves.

Alexanders, another herb of Jupiter is recommended by Culpeper for opening a stoppage of the liver and spleen and provoking urine. While agrimony remains at ground level at the beginning of March. Alexanders is already tall with many tasty green leaves. It makes an excellent green vegetable from January onwards.

Lungwort, often better known by it's Latin name, pulmonaria, is in the bed in place of the moss, also named lungwort, which grows on oaks and beeches. Modern herbal medicine gives both for similar conditions, and pulmonaria is, I feel, qualified as a 'watery' herb in treatment of the lungs.

Culpeper's first comments on **Sage** are that Jupiter claims it and it is good for the liver. Sage is also an excellent antibacterial herb for the infections mentioned above. I chose to include the medicinal purple sage in this bed, although green could equally well be used.

Culpeper's remarks on **Roses** are wonderful to read. He places red roses under Jupiter and writes that they "strengthen the heart, the stomach and the liver,". The sugar, syrup, water, and honey he mentions, are all worth making. Whenever a patient needs love in their treatment, a rose preparation is given.

Costmary, or alecost as it is also known, has white flowers, resembling chamomile, alongside the agrimony. These rise on tall stems above the long, silvery grey leaves. Another herb of Jupiter, it was known in Culpeper's day for cleansing, putrefaction and opening obstructions. He writes it "is an especial friend and help to evil, weak and cold livers". The leaves can be dried for pot-pourri and sachets against moths, as well as their old use in making ale.

Aries - March 21st - April 21st
The sign of the Ram is a hot, fiery sign, ruled as it is by the planet Mars. Martial herbs are defined by Culpeper as those of a hot, prickly nature and plants which love to grow close to the blacksmiths forge. The sign relates to the head and stomach.

Blessed or holy thistle, *Carduus benedictus,* stands out, not only as an extraordinary herb with a fascinating seedhead for flowercrafts, but also because Culpeper singles it out as a herb of Mars under Aries. Since Mars governs choler he writes the herb is good for yellow jaundice and is also good to treat vertigo. Where some virtues he quotes come from sympathy with Mars, it was used equally to treat diseases caused by Venus; being a herb under the planet in opposition. (Mars and Venus are opposites.)

Garlic, which Culpeper clearly dislikes, although he gives it all credit for a long list of treatments, is also under Mars. He follows this catalogue of ailments with "more peculiar virtues … it hath a special quality to discuss inconveniences coming by corrupt agues and stinking waters" - as also by taking poisons. Against this, he accused it of sending evil vapours to the brain, resulting in strange visions.

As a gardener, I have to admit including it in Aries as much to protect the rose planted immediately behind, in Pisces, as to represent purging the head.

Rosemary I thought would be readily recognised as a Martial herb, having both a hot and prickly nature and for our sign, once again purging the head of phlegm and aiding the stomach in digestion. However, Culpeper writes that the sun claims privilege in it, but places it under Aries. It is as wondrously useful as a herb in physic and in daily household needs, now, as it was in his day - in cookery, wines, fragrant preparations, and cosmetics.

Culpeper places the tiny wild thyme, also called **Mother of thyme** under Aries as a plant ruled by Venus, the planet in opposition to Mars. A thyme vinegar was made to apply to the head to relieve pain. Mother of thyme is a charming addition to the herb bed, making a perfect shelter for the roots of the **Cowslips** alongside, also herbs of Venus. He recommends an ointment of the flowers for wrinkles, spots and sunburn and for all infirmities of the head from heat and wind. They were given for palsy as they strengthen the brain; the conserved flowers being eaten with nutmeg. I have never tried this recipe but love to preserve the flowers for cake decoration and pick them for winemaking. Perhaps the ointment which had a reputation for adding beauty, or at least restoring what was lost, might have an appeal in the modern world too.

Self heal, which flowers alongside, or just after the cowslips, is given by Culpeper as a herb of Venus for inward and outward wounds. It was also applied as juice with oil of roses to the head as a painkiller. Wherever we find the common name of Carpenters Herb as here, we may be assured it has had a considerable reputation for treating wounds. At the end of his entry, Culpeper goes so far as to say neither physician nor surgeon would be needed if self-heal and sanicle were available. The pretty purple flowers attract many bees in summer and have spread happily into the lawn where they are welcome to remain.

Marjoram is the last herb in Aries. Culpeper places sweet marjoram under Aries and Mercury, hailing it as an excellent remedy for the brain, and comfortable to the stomach. I have chosen to include both a 'crinkle leaf' golden marjoram and a dwarf marjoram for their respective beauty in foliage, and in the case of the dwarf - pretty white flowers which attract the bees. The low growing marjoram is, perhaps a variation on *Origanum heracleoticum* or winter marjoram.

So the beds are filled with some herbs in flower from spring through to autumn to give maximum interest and pleasure. The cultivation details for garlic, marjoram, sage, cowslips, thyme and rosemary can all be found in Herbwise Naturally. Those of agrimony and costmary are included in Herbcraft Naturally. Details of the blessed thistle, alexanders and self-heal are in Cultivation.

Garden Feature

Willow Herbar

IN the Medieval period the word 'herber' seems to have referred to a garden area devoted to herbs. Perhaps as a shortened version of 'herbarium'. By the time Thomas Hill wrote "The Gardener's Labyrinth" in the 16th century, however, he is using the term "upright herbar" to mean a covered alley or walkway.

He tells us they may be made with ash or willow and be square, or made "in arch manner winded", with vines, cucumbers, roses and herbs spreading over them. Thomas Hill recommends ash poles for the arched herbar, as willow needs replacing or repairing every three years. From this we can gather the willow had not taken root and grown.

Now as then, our herbar provides welcome shade to be enjoyed on hot summer days. Whether we wish to sit, stand or walk beneath it, the feathery screen will be appreciated. An archway may be left open in the side of the herbar, or the other 'end' can be used to frame a view from a shaded seat. The closed rounded end in the diagram could house a seat. In the case of our herbar we decided to use this enclosed area for skittles, placing a narrow seat opposite the archway further along. This gives us a cool walkway, shaded seat and a skittle alley for visiting children. Unlike the early herbars ours rooted and sprouted new shoots in 2 months, despite a very dry start.

Materials

Once you have decided on the form you wish your herbar to take, some measurements will be required in order to estimate the materials needed. First and second year rods are available from specialist nurseries in wetland areas, such as Somerset.

For the herbar detailed below we needed 90 second year rods of *Salix viminalis* and 5 bundles of 60 first year rods. Note: more first year rods would be needed to work basketweave along both long sides. We only worked one long side due to the proximity of the fence. The only other requirements being strong garden twine or string, a measure, and garden tools.

Dimensions:

Length	5.64m	(18ft 6ins)
Width	1.80m	(6ft)
Width of Side Arch	1.04m	(3ft 5ins)
Height	2.50m	(8ft 4ins)

Distance between side rods approx: 25.5 - 30.5cm (10-12ins)
Base Basketweave approx: 33cm (13ins) deep

The willow had been cut several weeks before and was delivered at the beginning of the second week in March. Within a few days the herbar was 'in situ'. As the weather was very cold, I worked the basketweave at the base of the herbar in several sessions on different days.

To Begin

As soon as the willow is delivered, store it in shady conditions, to keep it damp. Use a dibber to prepare holes approximately 23cm (9ins) deep for the rods at either side of each archway in the herbar sides. For any open side arches miss 3 holes where the opening is to be. Those holes at either side of the opening and those at the open end of the herbar will need to be larger as these will have to take extra rods. You should have an uneven number of arches between all openings for the final basketweave.

Pair second year rods, tying their thin ends together to make arches. While they are still laid on the ground, tie on two or three lengths of the thinner ends of first year rods to give strength where the top of the arch will be. The ties should be made securely **(a)** with non-rotting garden twine.

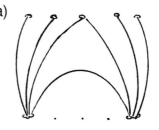

Set 2 together in the holes at the open end/s of your herbar. Work along making a tunnel effect by setting the rods into their prepared holes. Firm these in as you go. Where you reach a side opening, set all 4 rods into the holes on the closed side of the herbar first. Then insert the first and second rods at the left side of the 'doorway'. Take the others and set them beside the rod at the other side of the doorway. This will give a vaulted effect (see diagram a).

To complete the tunnel with a rounded end, use single second year rods set into the ground (as in diagram b,) keeping them the same distance apart as before. Once again, the thin ends of the rods are reinforced with lengths of the first year rods. Weave the first 2 rods at either side of the rounded end diagonally upwards, over and under the rods of the straight sides. Take all central rods alternately under or over the top of the end arch and continue weaving them under and over arches for their full length (see diagram b).

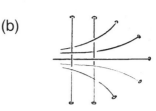

(b)

Sides

Starting at the first arch made, insert a first year rod into the ground alongside the second year rod.

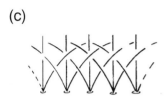

(c)

Take it diagonally upwards weaving it under and over the following rods to begin a lattice effect. Repeat this on the same side of the next arch, and those following, until you reach the end. Work back again in the same way. This time place one first year rod at the other side of each second year rod and weave it under and over second year and first year rods (see diagram c).

Basketweave

This is best worked on a damp, overcast day. If the rods are brittle, soak them for several hours in cold water before weaving. Take a particularly flexible first year rod and kinking it first about one quarter of the way along, fold it around the 'edge' of the end arch (see diagram d). Work it with your fingers first or it may split. As you lay it around the second year rod, give it a slight twist and work the short end in and out of the first arches leaving the end facing into the

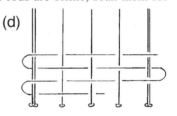

(d)

herbar. Take the long end of the weaver and work this in and out of the arches as far as it will go.

Continue until you reach the other end, weaving new lengths in as they are needed. Bring the weaver around the edge and begin working back along for the second row. Always avoid putting too much strain on the thickest part of the rod by trying to bend it at the edge. Work the joins so that the thicker end of the rod is laid amongst the weaving and thinner ends are used at the edge turns.

Joins

If the end of the rod is too thick to work leave this pointing back into the herbar and lay the next rod over this on the inside with a short length free. Continue weaving until the basketweave is about 33cm (13ins) deep. Trim.

Watering

If the weather is dry you will need to decide whether supplying the amount of water this number of trees could take up is justifiable. With the herbar illustrated we allowed nature to decide it's fate, as once watering was started we would have felt obliged to continue. The speed with which green shoots appeared after the first rain, almost two months later, confirmed we had been right not to water.

Maintenance
Trim as necessary spring and autumn.

Main Harvests - Quick Reference

Angelica -   the first cut of angelica leaves can be taken for rhubarb and angelica wine in April.

Bramble-tips - fresh green shoots about 10cm (4ins) long for dyeing.

Coltsfoot -   Harvest for wine or to dry for medicinal use.

Cowslip -   flowers from your garden for candying, sugar, syrup, or wine. Wild flowers are protected.

Daffodil -   use dead heads for dyeing.

Dandelion -   flowers for dyeing and wine.

Herb bennet - harvest root for pot-pourri. Traditionally dried on Lady Day, March 25th if weather suitable.

Lovage -   use fresh growth in salads and soups. Candy stems and make jelly.

Nettle -   fresh in tea and soup, or as vegetable. See savoury nettle pancakes in Herbwise Naturally. Dry for tea later in the year. Nettle syrup, wine or beer, shampoo. Leaves and roots to dye wool. Make liquid feed for plants.

Balsam Poplar - prune long branches to reduce height and use for basketry or plant supports. Remove buds which are sticky and fragrant for furniture polish or to dry for pot-pourri.

Primrose -   candy flowers or use in sugar, syrup or wine. Press. Dry for pot-pourri.

Rosemary -   harvest flowering rosemary for vinegar, tea, honey, flavouring rhubarb, cakes, jellies, and liqueur. Dry on stems for pot-pourri and sachets - or to grind to powder for culinary use. Also use fresh or dried in cosmetic recipes.

Sweet cicely - use fresh leaves for sweetening recipes. Also with rhubarb in jam.

Violet -   candy sweet violet flowers, make sugar, syrup or liqueur. Dry for pot-pourri.

Spring - Knot garden

Blessed thistle

Easter garland

March - April

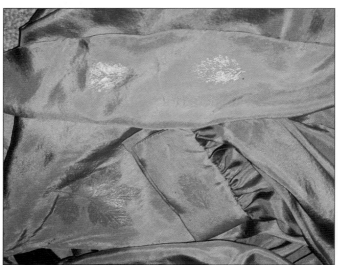

(Top left) *Spring flowers*

(Top right) *Balsam poplar - buds*

Bramble dyed blouse

Astrology bed

(Top right) *Self heal*

Herbar

Wines and preserves

Violet sugar

(Below) *Candied lovage*

Spring harvest, violets in strawberry basket

Preserves

IN March and April new harvests are available in the garden - Lovage is fresh and green, providing tasty stems to candy and strongly flavoured leaves for a tangy jelly. The mass of flowers on the rosemary declares it to be at it's very best. The flowering sprigs are dried for fragrance. Set them in spirit for liqueur or vinegar for seasoning. Rosemary is tasty with young shoots of spearmint in rosemary and mint jelly.

The spring flowers of primroses and violets make perfect cake decorations and sugars for Easter and Mother's day cakes. It is a busy, exciting celebration of new growth to harvest fresh angelica for winemaking with rhubarb and young angelica, or sweet cicely leaves to sweeten the rhubarb jam. Rosemary as fresh sprigs or ground dried herb is also a wonderful spicy flavouring when cooking rhubarb. See Herbwise Naturally for recipe. Nettles are another traditional harvest for their valued health-giving properties. I have partnered them with angelica in a rich syrup to cleanse and revitalise after the winter. Nettle acts as a diuretic as well as supplying important vitamins and minerals. It appears again as dried herb in the tea recipe. Rosemary, mint and nettle make another good spring combination in a shampoo to thoroughly restore your hair after the trauma of winter.

The last main harvest at this time is that of the poplar buds from the balsam poplar. Sticky, resinous and fragrant, I gather them as I harvest young branches for basketry. They may be added to pot-pourri once they have been dried, or give their powerful perfume to the furniture polish recipe.

Lovage and Grapefruit Jelly

3 cups sugar
1 cup grapefruit juice

½ cup herb infusion
100 ml (4 fl oz) liquid pectin

Pour 1 cup of boiling water over 4 tablespoons of washed and chopped lovage leaves in a pan. Bring to the boil and simmer steadily until the liquid is reduced to half the amount. Meanwhile put the sugar and grapefruit juice into a larger pan and strain the ½ cup of herb infusion over them. Bring slowly to the boil, making sure the sugar is fully dissolved by stirring before turning up the heat. Once the jelly is boiling, remove from the heat and add the liquid pectin, stirring well. Return to the heat and boil rapidly for 2 minutes. Stand to cool slightly, before filling 2 or 3 jars which have been prepared by washing and filling with boiling water to sterilise them. Cover. Seal and label.

This jelly is the perfect accompaniment to meat, fish and vegetarian dishes. It can be stirred into shepherd's pie, spread on a roast in the oven, added to pasta dishes or melted over grilling fish.

Rosemary and Mint Jelly

3 cups sugar
1 cup apple juice

½ cup herb infusion
100 ml (4 fl oz) liquid pectin

Pour 1 cup of boiling water over 3 tablespoons chopped mint and 1 tablespoon of rosemary which has been pounded, removed from the stem and chopped. Flowering rosemary gives a better flavour. Simmer the herbs and water gently in an enamel pan until reduced by half - about 10 minutes. Strain through coffee-filter paper. While simmering, put the sugar and apple juice into a larger pan and prepare 2 or 3 jam jars as above.

Add the strained herb infusion to the sugar and fruit juice and heat gently, stirring until the sugar has dissolved. Turn up the heat and bring to the boil, adding the liquid pectin once boiling point has been reached. Stir well and boil rapidly for 2 minutes. Set aside to cool before filling the prepared jars. Seal, cover and label.

This jelly is delicious with lamb, chicken or other fowl. It can add a very unusual and enjoyable flavour to fish and will also partner nut and bean vegetarian casseroles and loaves.

Candying Lovage stems

CUT sufficient lovage stems (the thickness of your little finger), to give 100g (4oz) with the leaves removed. The leaves can be dried and stored ready for seasoning soups later in the year.

Put the lovage stems into a pan, chopping them into 5-8cm (2-3ins) lengths as you do so. Cover them with water and bring to the boil. Boil them until they are tender when tested with a fork. Drain and take a sharp knife to peel away the thin outer skin. Weigh the peeled stems and layer with an equal weight of sugar in a covered dish. Leave for 2 days, (giving them a stir to turn both sugar and lovage after 24 hours). By this time a syrup will be forming.

Set the sugar syrup and lovage into a pan which you have rinsed with cold water. Bring the syrup to the boil, stirring all the time. Simmer on a very low heat for 5 minutes, still stirring. Drain the stems. Sprinkle with sugar and dry on a rack in a just-warm oven. Store wrapped in clingfilm in tins, or in jars between greaseproof paper layers.

Use to decorate desserts and cakes, add to fruit cakes or the Christmas pudding instead of candied peel. Alternatively, chop into small pieces, wrap in marzipan and cover in chocolate.

Candied Flowers

Sweet violets, primroses and the cowslips which follow, are all edible flowers so long as they are of wild, English stock. Elaborately curled and coloured primulas are not suitable. Cowslips in the wild are protected and should not be gathered. Seeds are readily available with wild flower collections and it is soon possible to grow sufficient in your garden to candy. The method takes time but is one of those annual tasks which I look forward to as a real pleasure. Gather perfect flowers on a dry morning. Prepare immediately. While removing the green parts from the flowers, dipping the petals in cold water to remove any insects or dust, and then laying them on paper kitchen towel to be patted dry; you have plenty of opportunities to really appreciate their beauty. With the flowers or petals washed and dried make the gum arabic solution as follows:-

1 tbsp rose water (if bought from a dispensary - tell the pharmacist it is for cooking)
1 tsp gum arabic powder (available from shops supplying cake icing equipment)

Pour the rose water into a small wide-necked jar or bottle. Sprinkle on the gum arabic. Seal and shake vigorously until it dissolves. Alternatively use 3 times the amount and mix in a food blender or liquidiser. Always add the powder to the liquid. Each petal or flower to be candied must be completely immersed in this so that it is sealed. Remove from the solution onto a plate of caster or granulated sugar. A spoon handle can be used to gently dip and retrieve flowers. Remove any soggy sugar lumps from the centres of the flowers. Sprinkle more sugar over and turn the flower, then set it on greaseproof paper on a rack to dry. An oven which is just-warm can be used to speed the process. Store the candied flowers in layers between greaseproof paper either in jars or tubs. They will keep until the following year for decorating cakes, desserts and home-made chocolates.

Herb Sugars

JUST as sweet violets, primroses and cowslips are candied to add their beauty to cakes and desserts, so the petals may also be used to colour and flavour sugar. The origins of this method can be traced back to Elizabethan kitchens of the well-to-do, where standards of decoration in moulded marchpanes and sugar pastes, were high for special occasions. Some herb sugars and flower conserves were also made to relieve melancholy, which they will readily do for us today. For anyone who enjoys making sweets and fancy desserts, herb coloured sugars are a must. They will keep through the year in a cool, dark cupboard and can be brought out in triumph months later, either to enjoy or to impress an unexpected guest with a unique dish. Day after day you can make a little - or more, as you wish. The sugars cannot be bought; a consideration which makes removing the green parts of the flowers, washing and drying the petals, worthwhile.

With that done, drop your perfect flowers and petals into a cup to measure them. To every cup of flowers add the same amount of white sugar. Grind in an electric grinder and the sugar is coloured in seconds. Tip the damp sugar onto foil on a baking tray and dry it in the oven on the lowest temperature. Crumble the dried sugar into a jar. Label and seal. Sprinkle on cakes, include in the recipes for colouring, make fondant or decorate desserts.

Rhubarb and Sweet Cicely Jam

1.35 kg (3lb) rhubarb   12 sprays of 3 leaves of sweet cicely
1.35 kg (3lb) sugar   1 tsp ground rosemary

Wash and cut the rhubarb stems into 8cm (3ins) lengths. Weigh these and put into the pan with the sprays of sweet cicely leaves which have been washed and torn as they are added. Sprinkle over the level teaspoon of ground rosemary. If you wish to use fresh rosemary add 3 pounded, flowering tops on the stem about 10-15cm (4-6ins).

Cook over a very low heat in a preserving pan until the rhubarb has produced sufficient moisture to add an equal weight of sugar. Stir over a low heat until the

sugar has dissolved and then boil rapidly until setting point is reached. Test by pouring a spoonful onto a cold saucer. When cool, the surface of the jam should wrinkle as you touch it. Once a set is obtained, set aside for a few minutes and then fill jam jars prepared as for the jellies and kept warm.
*Makes approx 2.7kg (6lb)

Nettle and Angelica Syrup

400g (14oz) young nettle tops
170g (6oz) angelica leaves and stems
450g (1lb) sugar for each 600ml (pint)

1 cinnamon stick
2.25 litres (4 pints) water

Gather the nettles wearing rubber gloves for protection. Weigh them first, then wash and discard any damaged leaves. Repeat with the angelica. Put the green herbs into a preserving pan, pouring the cold water over and adding a cinnamon stick broken into 4 pieces. With the pan over a low heat, simmer for 4-5 minutes partly covered. Strain and measure the liquor. To every 600ml (1 pint) add 450g (1lb) sugar and set over a low heat again, stirring until the sugar has dissolved. Bring to the boil, then cool and pour into sterilised bottles. Empty spirit bottles which have been kept sealed and not rinsed, need not be sterilised. Seal and label. The syrup can be made up into a healthy spring drink which acts as a tonic and cleanser to your system. You should note that large quantities will have a diuretic effect and the angelica content means it is not suitable for pregnant women. Topped up with lemonade, or water, it is delicious and refreshing.

Herb Teas

FOR a dried tea to cleanse your system of winter's ills and refresh you in readiness for spring, make the following tasty blend and take 1 cup per day.
2 parts dandelion root (ground very fine)
2 parts nettle
2 parts thyme (dried flowering)
1 part parsley

Herb tea method

IN general use one or two fresh tops of the herb, or one teaspoon of dried herb, per cup. Never make herb tea in a metal teapot. Try to keep a particular pot or jug just for herb teas. Warm the pot first and pour the boiling water over torn fresh herb or dried blend. Cover and leave to stand for about 5 minutes. Strain into a cup, adding honey if liked as a sweetener. All herb teas are potentially medicinal and should be restricted to one cup per day unless you require the medicinal effect.

Wine and Liqueur

MARCH and April offer the best treats of all in the form of sweet wines, which, given a little time to mature, become almost liqueurs - primrose and cowslip. Gone are the days when we picked the spring blooms in woods and fields, now we must make the extra effort to grow them in our own garden. Some old recipes require as much as a gallon of flowers, but my experiments have shown that 1.2 - 1.5 litres (2-2½ pints) of flowers picked into the measuring jug and allowed to settle without pushing them down, is plenty. If you do not have enough of either flower then a very satisfying wine can be made of the two together. In this case, use the cowslip wine recipe. Pick only perfect flowers on a sunny day, in late morning if possible. I usually take a little stool into the garden to be more comfortable, as cowslips in particular take a considerable time to pick. In both cases only the yellow part of the flower is used, I prefer to pick just this part rather than sort them again. On a fine day with the sun's warmth on your back, stopping now and again to listen to birdsong, watch a brimstone or orange tip butterfly or talk to a neighbour, it can be a pleasure. If you are short on patience or time however, why not ask a friend or two round to help you - they will be very happy to drink the wine with you later.

Spiced Primrose Wine

Approx 1.2-1.5 litres (2-2 ½ pints) primrose flowers

1.35 kg (3lb) sugar	25g (1oz) fresh bakers yeast
2 oranges	1 slice bread, toasted
1 lemon	2 Campden tablets
10 cloves	4.5 Litres (8 pints) water

Finely pare the peel of 2 oranges and the lemon, rejecting all white pith. Put the peel with the sugar and flowers into a fermenting bucket. Add the cloves which should have been pounded to release their flavour, but not crushed. Pour over 2.8 litres (5 pints) of boiling water and the juices of 1 orange and 1 lemon. Dissolve the Campden tablets in 600ml (1 pint) of boiling water in a jug before adding. Stir to dissolve the sugar. Leave covered in a warm place (approx 21°C, 70°F) for 24 hours. Add a further 1.2 litres (2 pints) of boiling water with 25g (1oz) fresh bakers yeast spread on a slice of toast. Float this on the liquor and cover again. After 24 hours remove the toast and yeast. The wine should now be fermenting. Leave for 6 days, stirring the wine night and morning. Strain out the flowers, fruit rind and spices, and pour into a sterilised demi-john up to the point where the neck narrows. Add the fermentation lock with a little boiled water inside and leave in a warm place until fermentation has ended. Bottle. This can be drunk at the end of the same year or kept to be savoured in 18 months or 2 years time.

Cowslip Wine

Someone once told me that I was the first person he had met who drank cowslip wine, since he had read of it in the little grey rabbit stories. Cowslips are returning to roadsides and conservation areas and these are rightly protected. It is up to us to buy the seeds and sow them in autumn or winter in our gardens. With frost they germinate and will quickly spread in areas of chalky soil in particular. They prefer to grow amongst grass. Beginning with 6 plants from my mother's garden I had sufficient flowers, 4 years later, to give me 900ml (1½ pints) of the yellow petals, calyx removed - sufficient for 1 gallon of wine. 1.2 litres (2 pints) of flowers, is, of course, even better.

You will need;
Approx 900ml - 1.2 litres (1½ - 2 pints) cowslip flowers
1.35 kg (3lb) white sugar
Fine muslin straining bag
Juice of 1 orange   25g (1oz) fresh bakers yeast
225 g (½ lb) chopped sultanas or raisins   1 slice bread, toasted
4.5 litres (8 pints) water   2 Campden tablets (optional)

Put the sugar, crushed Campden tablets (see coltsfoot, lemon and ginger wine for comments on these) and orange juice into the fermenting bucket or crock. Put the cowslip flowers into a clean fine muslin straining bag or wrap them securely in clean muslin, and add. Pour over 2.8 litres (5 pints) of boiling water, if using the Campden tablets, adding the remaining boiling water 24 hours later with the yeast spread on toast. If the tablets are not used, pour over the full amount of water. In either case, before adding the yeast, see the liquor is at bloodheat and pour the chopped sultanas on top of the bag of flowers to weigh it down and keep it below the surface. After the yeast has been on the must for 24 hours, remove the toast carefully. The wine should be working well by this time. Stir night and morning, keeping the wine covered and weighing down the flowers again after stirring if necessary, for 7 days. Strain into a prepared demi-john as above and seal with a fermentation lock containing a little boiled water. The colour of this wine is a wonderful brilliant yellow. Bottle when fermentation has ceased - and enjoy. This wine is best kept for 2 years when it will be rich and beautiful. Also in the March-April period it is time to make the Rhubarb and Angelica wine and Rosemary Spring Liqueur - see Herbcraft Naturally for recipes. Dandelion and Nettle wines are more alternatives.

In the Home

Rosemary, Mint and Nettle Shampoo
25g (1oz) fresh herbs (about 4 sprigs rosemary, 3 of mint and 5 or 6 nettle tops)
1.2 litres (2 pints) water
50g (2oz) soapwort root
2 drops essential oil of rosemary or essential oil of tea-tree

Personal comfort in the home is as dependant on health and beauty recipes as it is on those for the general care of household items. The old stillroom recipe books included both and you will find them side by side here in the same way.

Wear rubber gloves for protection when gathering and preparing the nettles and other herbs. Choose only perfect leaves and pick flowering rosemary. Rinse the herbs in cold water and pound the rosemary on a board with a rolling pin, or in a mortar, before tearing or chopping the sprigs into a non-aluminium pan. Add 600ml (1 pint) of cold water, set over a moderate heat and simmer for 10 minutes, partly covered with a lid. Set aside - covering the pan and leave overnight to steep.

Next morning put 50g (2oz) of fresh soapwort root which has been washed clean and chopped into short lengths, into a second pan with 600ml (1 pint) of cold water. Bring to the boil and simmer for 20 minutes, again partly covered with a lid. Add to the strained herb infusion and boil gently until the liquor is reduced to 600ml (1 pint) - about 15 minutes. Pour into a sterilised bottle and when cool add the essential oil of rosemary or tea-tree if preferred. Seal and shake to disperse the oil. The shampoo can now be decanted into several smaller bottles (pre-sterilised with screwtops). Keep in a cool place.

Balsam Furniture Polish

A polish which is especially good for antique furniture and perfumes the house as you clean, making you feel calm and refreshed. Essential oil of marjoram also helps to deter woodworm.

225g (8oz) beeswax	25g (1oz) balsam poplar buds
40g (1½ oz) soapflakes	Essential oil of marjoram or thyme - 4-5 drops
1½ cups cold water	Essential oil of geranium - 4 drops
3 cups turpentine	

Note: it is advisable to wear rubber gloves and keep the stove area well ventilated when making the polish. Turpentine is highly inflammable and should be added well away from the heat. An ovenproof pyrex bowl can be set directly over a low heat to melt the beeswax but a thick bottomed glass pan, or double boiler with water boiling in the pan below the beeswax, will be safer.

Set the beeswax to melt. Small blocks will do so fairly quickly but are more expensive than larger blocks available from beekeepers. A large block can be cut with a very hot knife. The turpentine should be gently warmed but kept away from direct heat.

Add the balsam poplar buds to 1½ cups of cold water in a pan. Bring slowly to simmering and simmer for 10 minutes. Strain out the buds through a piece of muslin or coffee filter paper which can then be thrown away. Add the soapflakes, stirring well until they have dissolved.

Remove the melted beeswax from the heat and stir in the turpentine, dribbling it carefully down the side of the bowl or pan. Allow both the beeswax, and turpentine and soap solution to cool to bloodheat, then slowly add the soap to the beeswax. Continue stirring and keep assessing the consistency. Add less if you want a harder polish and all the solution, or as much as you think it needs, to make a furniture cream. (If the soap has cooled too much when the beeswax is ready, you can always re-heat it.)

Lastly, add the drops of essential oil, stirring well before pouring the warm polish into tins or shallow, wide-necked screwtop jars. Seal tightly.

Apply sparingly and rub well for a beautiful shine. This need only be used once in 3 weeks on your furniture.

Craft

Bramble-tip Dye

AT the beginning of April the bramble bushes along country lanes, or perhaps thornless bramble in your garden, will have produced several inches of good new growth. A pair of stout scissors or secateurs and protective gloves will enable you to combine a pleasant walk, or time in your garden, with harvesting. You may even have the added delight of watching a bright yellow brimstone butterfly flitting from one dandelion to another in the hedgerow, or an orange-tip darting about the garden.

Around 100g (4oz) of bramble shoots about 10-15cm (4-6ins) long, will be sufficient to dye 50g (2oz) of wool or a silk scarf. I used 325g (12oz) of bramble tips to dye sufficient silk for a blouse plus a few skeins of silk thread for embroidery. Note: always wear rubber gloves and ensure good ventilation when preparing dyes.

See page 26 for preparation of wool and mordanting wool and silk.

To Prepare the Dye

Add the bramble-tips to 2.8 litres (5 pints) of cold water in the dyepan. Bring to the boil, lower the heat and retain a fast simmer or gentle boil for almost one hour. Stand the pan aside to cool. Strain out the herb and enter the mordanted wool having gently squeezed it almost dry immediately before. Put the pan back on the heat, and again keep the temperature well below boiling.

Stir the wool, making sure all parts receive the dye evenly. After 45 minutes, a soft lemon colour may be achieved. To retain that colour set the pan aside after 10 minutes. Steep overnight before rinsing. For green lift the wool above the surface of the dye and add ¼ -½ teaspoon of iron (ferrous sulphate), stirring the liquor before returning the wool to the pan.

Simmer for a further 15 minutes. The shade of green achieved will depend upon the amount of iron added. A delicate green can be very attractive. Leave the wool to steep overnight. Wash, rinse 3 times in cold water and drip dry outside.

To Dye Silk Fabric

Prepare the mordant and treat as on page 26.

Prepare the bramble-tip dye as above, strain and cool to hand-hot or less. Enter the silk and leave over a very low heat for 15 minutes. Do not bring to simmer. Stand aside and leave covered in a cool place for 2-4 days. Turn the silk, allowing the dye liquor to flow over every inch of the fabric at regular intervals.

When dyeing silk for a garment it is easiest to cut out the pattern pieces first. Machine oversew the edges with great care to prevent fraying. If you do not have a dyepan large enough to allow the silk to be opened out to take up the dye evenly this does not matter. Make up separate dye batches, mix these together and when the dye has cooled to almost hand-hot, enter the alum mordanted silk in a larger bucket or tin bath. Note: although the alum is the only mordant recommended for use with silk, the addition of a little iron to obtain green as the dye is prepared, works well.

When your silk has achieved the colour you would like, remove it from the dye and rinse each piece of fabric well in cold water, drip dry outside. When handling dyed wool or silk the safest way to avoid spots of dye staining carpets, walls or other surfaces, is to take a bowl of water outside and rinse them there if possible. Do not forget your rubber gloves. The silk can now be washed to establish fastness. In my own experiments no colour has subsequently leaked from the fabric when washed by hand in warm water and rinsed in cold. Some items have withstood many such washes.

If you wish to decorate your scarf or garment further, then leaf-printing with cold water dyes provides the perfect opportunity to explore your harvest of fresh leaves from the garden. As you will see in the illustration I used agrimony and meadowsweet leaves on the cuffs and scarf/collar of my blouse. There are many foliage forms in the herb garden and it is a good idea to try a few different samples first.

Note: applying decorative leaf prints can also cover any darker spots of concentrated dye which may appear on the silk as you learn the dye techniques.

Daffodils

Also during this time the daffodils come to an end and need to be dead-headed. Here is another potential harvest for keen dyers. Gather together the dead heads and simmer twice the weight of flower heads to wool for about 50 minutes. Strain and enter alum mordanted wool as above for a bright spring yellow dye.

Nettle

If you are reducing the size of your ever extending nettle patch you will have the opportunity to harvest roots as well as the fresh young leaves for dyeing. An alum mordant, with or without iron, can give good results. Use at least twice the weight of herb to wool. With the root, soak it for several days chopped in the water first. The root and leaf could be mixed after soaking.

Dandelion

Another successful dye source. My lawn is more of a medieval mead and I always race to gather the dandelion flowers before the first cut. Chrome will give you a brilliant egg yolk yellow. See page 89 for details of chrome mordanting. Alum produces a softer colour. With both mordants use twice the weight of flowers to wool.

Flowers and Foliage to press

AS spring advances, more and more flowers are available for pressing. If you have a regular use for them in making up pictures or decorating lampshades for instance, it is a good idea to make notes, dating particular selections. In this way you will know the earliest time your stocks can be replenished in the following year. As with all seasonal harvests, nature leads the way and remains in charge. Never allow dry days to pass while the harvest is at it's best, for a period of rain may always be around the corner.

Gather the flowers and foliage when the weather is dry and settled. Trying to keep delicate flowers from blowing away on a windy day can damage them before you start. Perfect flowers and foliage are a must.

Pick just a few and then return indoors to lay them carefully in the press, rather than taking the press into the garden, unless the day is totally still.

Deep flowers such as water avens with their attractive nodding bonnets should be sliced in half with a kitchen knife to make them thin enough to press well. The extra effort is well worth it for the beautiful results.

Flowers	**Foliage**
alehoof	fennel
alkanet	golden hop
avens	lady's mantle
celandine	meadowsweet
cowslip - yellow and red	salad burnet
forget-me-nots	silverweed
goldlace	sweet cicely
honesty	sweet woodruff
lungwort	tansy (green and variegated)
primrose	wild strawberry
rosemary	
violet	
wild strawberry	

Leaf Printing

THIS can be the most fascinating and absorbing of simple art forms. While a flair for design is a bonus in producing outstanding results, the technique is readily mastered. Whatever your chosen fabric for the completed garment or article, begin by practising on a light or medium weight calico which takes the dye evenly.

All you need to begin is a length, or even scraps of fabric, your chosen cold water dye colour, a fine paintbrush, roller of some sort and a selection of leaves with well-defined veining.

You will soon discover which herbs are your personal favourites. Searching them out amongst the herb beds will encourage you to look more carefully at each plant and see new beauty as you go.

Those which I have come to treasure for leaf printing are: -

agrimony	lemon geranium	sweet woodruff
betony	meadowsweet	wild strawberry
bramble	motherwort	
jasmine	mugwort	

Ivy can also be effective but you need to select the leaves with particular care as they vary in texture. It is a good idea to equip yourself with a set of samples, trying each leaf one side up and then the other, and marking the results alongside, or recording them in a notebook. Some leaves, such as agrimony and lady's mantle can give good results on both sides, while others will only yield an attractive print from the underside.

The next greatest factor in achieving good results is the amount of dye which is applied. Too much will result in a nasty blotch, too little and you may only print parts of the leaf. A thin but smooth covering is to be aimed for, and practice will soon bring you to a knowledge of how much each leaf takes up. Having carefully painted the dye onto the leaf, lay it dye side down in place on the fabric. Using a glass or marble rolling pin which will not absorb the dye, or a craft roller or jam-jar, roll the leaf firmly in place. Lift the leaf carefully away to reveal the print. If part of the leaf has not come out you may paint the leaf again and apply it exactly over the first attempt, rolling a second time. You are more likely to produce a perfect match however, by cutting away the part of the leaf which has not printed, re-painting that and applying it again where you can see the lines will join together. Such small additional prints can be most successful.

If you are not satisfied with your placing of the finished design, or the colour, it can readily be washed out at this stage, enabling you to begin again. Buying jars of yellow, red, blue and green cold water dyes will enable you to mix new colours and a variety of subtle shades. Gold is also worth buying to use alone.

To fix your completed design leave it in a warm, dry atmosphere for 24 hours and then iron on both sides for 1-2 minutes. The fabric can now safely be washed.

As with the blouse illustrated, the paints can add a very original charm to home-dyed silk garments. Silk is a more difficult fabric to use as too much dye will soon run and blotch, but it is well worth the extra care for such beautiful results. An all-over pattern painted on lawn, muslin or cotton can also be exceptionally attractive. The lemon geranium design on the scented sachet perfectly compliments the geranium filling to make a charming present. Samples will help you to decide on new projects.

Leaf printing can also be done on paper. Smooth papers are even more difficult than silk but home-made, slightly more absorbent papers can be perfect for making unique greeting cards. See Herbcraft Naturally for papermaking instructions, both for re-cycled paper and original papers. These are made from nettle, fennel, hollyhock and sunflower fibres, which you will find yourself cleaning away in early spring as you set the garden in order.

Crown of Thorns Easter Garland

THE idea for this project came originally from examining the stark beauty of the milk thistle seedheads, which can give an impression of miniature crowns of thorns in themselves. The milk thistle, otherwise known as the Mary thistle, has a special aptness as the white markings on it's leaves were once seen as drops of the Virgin's milk. Another herb, both flowering and fragrant at this time with a special link to Jesus, is rosemary. In legend this herb is credited with hiding the Virgin Mary and baby Jesus from Herod's soldiers. Rosemary is really, Mary's rose.

To these I added thorn-like spikes of red dogwood to remind us of blood from the wounds inflicted by the thorns, and white blossom for innocence. With a late Easter, sloe blossom could be used, adding yet more thorns to the crown, but for an earlier Easter the white blossom of wild plum can be gathered from hedgerows. Occasional sprays of winter honeysuckle would also add fragrance, and if no other thorny material is available, berberis could be substituted.

The crown can be starkly effective on a wreath made of twisted honeysuckle or vine with the milk thistle seedheads and berberis. Or, a softer effect which needs wet oasis to survive for more than 24 hours, can be set into a garland base or wet oasis strapped to a wooden or metal hoop.

The garland illustrated was made using a wide wooden ring, (originally a basketry rim) and strapping sections of damp oasis to this. Some areas are left without oasis for the dried seedheads (see illustration). The blossom, dogwood and any honeysuckle are pushed into the wet oasis first with some rosemary. Then the milk thistle seedheads are secured in place, before finally adding sufficient short lengths of rosemary to cover the oasis and give an appearance of fresh abundance.

May - June

Sun and earth together,
work a universal alchemy
distilling pharmacy for all life.
The true paradise revealed, the garden
is blessed; heavenly perfumes, open blooms.
Serenity and grace stand tall
as the herbs grow;
soaking the very atmosphere
to heal in welcome warmth.
Summer stretches ahead as if eternal.
In the dusk, herbs unveil
their inner selves.
Shy valerian leaps into life,
it's flowers as white candles
set to burn in darkness.
Velvet marshmallow overpowers the senses,
with simple touch.
Roses, jasmine, honeysuckle,
fill the night.
Moonlight, sunlight, life triumphant.

In the Garden

AFTER the intensive preparation in the garden of March and April, summer tasks are far more relaxed. This allows time to sit and enjoy the sunshine, as well as to harvest the first fruits of your labours. The perennial herbs will now be well established and growing taller in the beds. They offer shade for those seedlings sown out of doors and young seedlings which have been carefully nurtured before planting out.

All young plants should be carefully hardened off. Firstly during the warmest part of the day give them a sheltered position outdoors and then set the pot or tray close to their final site overnight. The same applies to plants which have wintered indoors.

Late frosts have been particularly severe in my garden in the last few years, even at the end of May. For this reason I leave the lemon verbena, pineapple and tangerine sages, frost-shy lavenders and scented geraniums, in their pots in the beds until June. If a sudden turn in the weather threatens them I can then easily take the pots in for a night.

When I finally set these herbs into the warm earth I trim back excess growth for fresh cuttings, or harvest, and with very large geraniums, trim the roots as well. I add a good measure of compost to line the hole, well moistened with a liquid feed of comfrey and nettle to give them a good start to the growing season (recipe in Herbwise Naturally). The plants are also treated with Rescue Remedy and the Bach Walnut remedy to counteract the shock of transplanting - see page number 34.

All young seedlings and newly set plants must also be kept well watered until they are established. Shade them from powerful sunshine in the heat of June days. Supports for tender plants and protection against slugs and snails can be combined to some extent. It is useful with sunflowers for instance, to stake them with branches of rosemary or juniper and set more juniper around the base. An additional plastic collar cut from a squash bottle can also give protection from cold wind if necessary. Dried mint can be sprinkled around seeds when sowing outdoors to deter mice.

It is a pleasurable task setting out carefully tended seedlings and removing ground cover of wild strawberries and forget-me-nots as you go. A time to wander in the garden, taking note of all manner of life.

Wildlife

Often as I am planting out and watering, I keep my camera by my side to catch those special shots which won't wait. I may lift a large comfrey leaf aside to reveal one of many toads in my garden staring up at me, or come upon the blackbirds raiding the first wild strawberries to ripen. A gatekeeper butterfly may join an orange tip on the flowering Spanish sage, making a perfect picture as I approach to cut the aromatic sprigs. To encourage butterflies to lay their eggs on nettles in your garden, cut one third of stems almost to the ground at the beginning of June. This will ensure new growth for their young to feed on. The cut nettles can be soaked in a tub of rainwater to make liquid feed for the plants.

My greatest pleasure in the garden at this time is watching the young blackbirds and thrushes, which I have noted since they were still in the nests. One June day I was joined by a mother, and then baby weasel, emerging from the knot as I sat motionless on the lawn. Even at my side the camera was not near enough then however.

Pests and Predators

The beauty of allowing nature to take on tasks which we might otherwise feel obliged to do ourselves, cannot be over-emphasised. Surely our tampering and need to feel 'in control' often does more harm than good, making new problems to solve. As the aphids arrive to feed on the roses and other herbs, I have seen 'crowds' of sparrows swaying madly on the tall stems to enjoy eating them. In other years aphids on those same herbs have been ignored by the birds, but in their place are many ladybird larvae chewing voraciously through the pests. Blue tits take their share of aphids from the roses on the trellis, and lacewings have emerged from their winter home in the summerhouse to help.

Gardening without pesticides or herbicides, I have created conditions in which nature can shoulder the burden; while I gather my harvests with thought for the well-being of plants and wildlife helpers. The elderflower harvest is always restricted to one third of the flowers on the trees. This leaves a future harvest of berries to be shared again, half for me and half for the birds. It may seem a strange idiosyncrasy, but I always talk to my herbs as I harvest, giving thanks and telling them the use.

Of course, it is not always idyllic in the garden. In some years rain lashes the roses and weighs down tall stems which need support. This may be given using a range of harvests from the garden including branches which have been pruned, as well as bamboo canes.

A careful watch needs to be kept on the foliage of both St John's wort and mullein if their later harvests are to be safeguarded. The mullein moth caterpillar, lovely as it is to look at, munches through the leaves at an alarming rate. I plant mulleins in several areas of the garden and usually some are free of this pest, but they always seem to appear on at least two plants. If you can remove the small black eggs from around the stem at the leaf joints this avoids the problem before the caterpillars begin eating. A good dose of garlic tea at regular intervals may act as a deterrent if applied early enough.

With St John's wort another insect lays it's eggs on the upper side of the topmost leaves, often close to early flowerbuds. The leaves will be seen curled round, holding them tightly cradled. Simply pick these leaves off the plants and destroy them.

When aphids are troublesome on other plants use a strong garlic and pepper spray if the predators in your garden are not sufficient to cope. However, taking this step yourself may stop them from helping out - they won't like garlic either. Elderflowers may be sprinkled amongst delicate leaves and food plants as a deterrent.

Herb Hedges

Late May should see the worst frosts over and the herb hedges of box, germander, sage, winter savory, hyssop and santolina are cut back and clipped neatly into shape before summer growth. Dry by hanging in bunches of 8-10 stems for craft use. If the hedge is your only source of winter savory, clip only the sides, leaving the top to flower before harvesting. With lavender trim the sides in the same way, harvesting the flowers later as they first open. Thyme hedges are trimmed when in flower. In May check for any bushes of lavender or thyme which have succumbed to frost and replace these.

If the thyme has been lost through poor winter drainage, stir in gravel to remedy the situation before replanting. Lavender will prefer a deep hole with compost in the bottom and a good watering of liquid feed below the roots.

The Astrology Garden

IN the astrology garden we have reached **Taurus** - April 21st to May 21st. This section is one of the most difficult for the gardener to manage. The ruling planet is Venus. The link of Venusian plants with treating problems of the reproductive system in another role in Scorpio, seems evident in their rampant growth and spread here. Under Taurus they treat disorders of the throat and neck and those brought about by excesses of all kinds. Being Venusian they are cooling, soothing and cleansing.

Culpeper writes, *Tansy* belongs to "Dame Venus". It was eaten in spring for centuries to cleanse the body of the "cold and moist constitution of winter". In his time it had a reputation for treating threatened miscarriages when applied externally. Internal use should be avoided during pregnancy.

In the garden the over enthusiastic root system quickly explores Aries and Gemini, and the plant will need to be divided in spring or autumn, after the flowering stems have been harvested. I use the dried leaves in moth sachets, the dried flowering tops for flowercrafts and miniature gardens, and fresh flowering tansy for dyeing.

The herb of choice for Culpeper is *Lovage* with as strong a root system, this time taking nourishment from deeper soil. Once again it will need dividing every second or third year. Definitely it is a herb of the Sun, under the sign Taurus, Culpeper writes: "If Saturn offend the throat ...., this is your cure". He recommends it for treating all agues, the throat in quinsy, inward gripings and infection.

A deeply cleansing herb, lovage makes a perfect seasoning for many dishes from salads to soups and casseroles. Sometimes 3m (9ft) in height and the breadth of a mature tree if left unchecked. It has elegant foliage and tiny umbelliferous flowers. Plant at the back of the bed.

I have edged Taurus with *Violets,* again herbs of Venus; described by Culpeper as having a mild nature, cold and moist. They were given inwardly or outwardly to cool any heat. Once again they were recommended for quinsy and to dissolve swellings. Violets have certainly treated cancer of the mouth and throat for thousands of years.

In my garden I have mixed sweet violets with the white for their slightly different flowering times. With use in cookery, liqueur, adding colour to pot-pourri and for pressed flower designs; I never seem to be able to grow enough of them.

The remainder of the bed is filled with a variety of mints; gingermint with it's golden striped leaves, the dark black peppermint and fragrant rounded leaves of eau-de-cologne mint. These all tend to be of shorter growth and better visual effect than the *Spearmint* referred to by Culpeper, which he lists as good for many complaints. Those of most application under Taurus being vomits, hiccough, roughness of the tongue and sore gums.

So the bed is filled and we pass on into *Gemini* - May 21st - June 21st, Mercury rules the herbs in this bed which act against diseases caused by Jupiter. The areas of the body under treatment are particularly the shoulders, lungs and nerves. (You may notice that since Aries we are steadily working our way down the body in some aspects).

Again I have placed two herbs which dominate the bed. This time through size, rather than a spreading habit of growth. *Elecampane,* over 1.5m (5ft) tall with huge, velvety leaves and tiny sunflower-like yellow flowers; is a herb ruled by Mercury. Culpeper recommended it to treat coughs and wheezings, as well as fevers and the plague. Chewing the root was supposed to fasten loose teeth and other preparations were used to treat pains in the joints. It has long been associated with treating asthma. I dig the root each autumn to make cough syrup and sweets as a valued home remedy; drying any root left over as a fixative for pot-pourri.

Greek Valerian is the second herb of a similar size, although it's general appearance is far more slender and delicate. Culpeper may mislead a modern reader by referring to Garden Valerian. His description is one of the Greek plant however:- as he tells us the root smells stronger than leaf or flower and the flowers are small and whitish, on stems more than a yard high. He quotes Dioscorides and Pliny on the herb's uses, and states that the root boiled with other herbs is singularly good "for those that are short-winded" etc. He classes it as an expectorant. Nowadays the root is a familiar, evil-smelling ingredient in sleep teas. We may consider this herb as applicable to the nervous system as well as the lungs.

Another, shorter herb of Mercury with thick, grey pretty leaves and round balls of seedheads at intervals on each stem, is *White Horehound.* Culpeper writes the juice of the green herb in honey is good for the short-winded and consumptives. Horehound honey forms part of my winter medicine stores and is, indeed, effective for coughs and colds - see Herbwise Naturally.

The last herb in my Gemini herb bed forms a lovely, fragrant edging. This is *Lavender,* ruled by Mercury and excellent for many nervous symptoms. As a herbal remedy it is famed for treating shock and anxiety, as well as insomnia. The essential oil is also excellent as an antiseptic and healing agent on burns and insect bites. Culpeper warns against the "Chymical Oil - Oil of Spike" - as "fierce and piercing". Modern lavender essential oil is taken from other types of the herb and so is comparatively gentle. Cultivation details for all of these herbs can be found in Herbwise Naturally. With the sweet scent of lavender in our thoughts we leave the astrology garden to consider harvesting and recipes.

Main Harvests - Quick Reference

Agrimony - leaves for wine, or leaf printing. Gather flowering tops for a fawn dye or to dry for pot-pourri.

Angelica - fresh leaves and stems with fish or in rhubarb jam. Candy stems. Fresh leaves for green dye, dried for pot-pourri.

Avens - press flowers, sliced in half.

Betony - dry flowers for flowercrafts. Use leaves for leaf prints.

Calendula - flowers for petal sugar. Ointment. Dry for pot-pourri.

Catmint - dry flowering tops for flowercrafts or to fill cat's toys.

Chickweed - fresh leaves for ointment.

Comfrey - fresh leaves as dye, for ointment or pressed. Make liquid fertilizer and use to protect young plants from snails and slugs. Dry for winter use.

Daffodil - harvest leaves for papermaking or 'rushwork'.

Elder - fresh flowers for winemaking, cordial, vinegar, syrup or to cook with gooseberries. Freeze for cookery. Dry for tea and inhalations. Ointment from flowers or leaves. Poor quality flowers or leaves as dye. Flowers as aphid deterrent.

Fennel - leaves fresh for salads, fish and vinegar. Also dye. Dry for pot-pourri and confetti.

Hawthorn - flowers for liqueur. Press.

Lemon balm - fresh leaves in cookery, wine, liqueur and cordial. Dry for pot-pourri and bath sachets.

Lovage - fresh leaves in salads, soups, stir-fry and vinegar. Dry for winter use. Leaf printing and pressed designs.

Marjoram - jelly. Harvest for drying.

Meadowsweet - wine. Fresh or dried leaves for medicinal tea. Press leaves. Dye from flowering tops.

Mints - gather all mints for drying or freezing before they flower if using for cookery. Jellies. Dry flowering for pot-pourri and flowercrafts. Use applemint fresh, spearmint for vinegar and jelly. Peppermint for syrup, ice cream and buns. Eau-de-cologne mint dry for rose fragrant sachets and bath sachets.

Mullein - flowers as they open for medicinal oil.

Pinks - any early clove pinks for candying, syrup, sugar or liqueur.

Rose - heavily perfumed old fashioned red roses for butter, sugar, honey, syrup, petal jelly, rosewater, vinegar and wine and liqueur. Part-dry for moist pot-pourri. Dry thoroughly for sachets, confetti and dry pot-pourri.

Santolina - harvest flowers for drying as soon as they begin to open as they will open further in the process. Flowercrafts and miniature gardens.

Spanish sage - other sages should not be allowed to flower for the sake of the leaves. Keep this sage for harvesting flowering tops. Cut and hang dry as soon as the flowers open. Foliage is also exceptional for flowercrafts (fresh or dried).

Other Sages -	use green sages fresh in cookery, make vinegar or sage and cider jelly. Dry for culinary seasonings. Purple sage is dried for medicinal needs in winter. Sages can also be dried for flowercrafts. Golden and tricolor are best fresh in flower posies.
Jerusalem sage -	hang dry flowers.
Sweet cicely -	use fresh leaves in cookery. Leaves and some flowering tops dye wool an amazing green. Press small leaves. Leaf-printing.
Sweet woodruff -	hang dry bunches of flowering woodruff to set amongst old books to stop them becoming musty. Use as a fixative for pot-pourri. Fresh woodruff flavours wines and fruit punch and jelly. Press flowering tops. Leaves for leaf-printing.
Thrift -	hang dry flowers of pink or white thrift as they open for flower swags, garlands and miniature gardens.
Thymes -	common and lemon for herb jelly (see Herbwise Naturally). Dry for cookery and flowercrafts.
White horehound -	leaves for honey and cough liqueur.
Wild strawberry -	press flowers as they first open. Press leaves or use for leaf-printing. Eat fruits.

See Herbwise Naturally for bath sachet recipes and Herbcraft Naturally for confetti.

Preserves

IT is tempting at this time of year to spend as much time as possible in the garden. Fine days are also days for harvesting however. The time between 9 and 10 am is often the best to gather leaves and flowers, before the sun draws out essential oils; although roses may need longer to be fully dry. It is also the most comfortable time to be in the garden on really hot days. As the heat increases I make a strategic withdrawal indoors to prepare recipes in the cool of the house.

The few golden weeks when the elderflowers and roses add beauty and fragrance to a herb garden springing to life in all directions, are quite magical. I cannot resist filling the shelves with tangy vinegars, rich syrups, brightly coloured sugars, wines and honeys. There are herbs to cut for drying and freezing as well as simply to enjoy fresh, in salads and sauces.

The rose harvest is always my first priority. Beware of thinking tomorrow will do as you sit back in your garden chair, for if there is a wet and windy period during this time, it often seems to stay for a week or more. Every day which has even a shower of rain can leave the roses with a few drops of moisture amongst the petals, rendering them useless for preserves. Their precious fragrant sweetness can only be captured on dry days when the flowers are newly opened. Full blown roses may still be added to moist pot-pourri, but a close look at the apothecary's rose on it's second day in bloom, will show you how quickly the colour in the petals fades. You may be sure strength of colour, fragrance and flavour are interlinked.

Some of the preserves this month take very little time - the vinegars and most honeys are quick and couldn't be simpler. Preparing roses, or candying stems and flowers takes more patience, but the results are well worth the effort. Once you have experienced having the flower sugars, syrups and jellies to use through the year, you will never want to be without them.

Rose petals can be candied according to the instructions for spring flowers in March-April preserves. Use the red, heavily scented old fashioned rose; such as *Rosa gallica officinalis,* the apothecary's rose. The sweetbriar, *Rosa rubiginosa* can also be used.

The white 'heel' of the rose petals must be removed as this would make the preserve bitter. Take each rose and slice across the base of the flower to remove them. The petals are now released to be floated in cold water to remove insects and quickly patted dry between layers of paper kitchen towel or clean cloths ready for candying.

Note: take especial care never to use roses which have been sprayed with pesticides. This should include consulting your neighbour if the roses are growing along a boundary fence.

Borage flowers may also be candied, along with the enchanting tiny *Heartsease.* Follow the same guidance, removing all green parts. Borage takes a little more skill to candy effectively, but it can be done with practice.

Angelica stems are ready to candy when they are the thickness of your little finger. This may be done in May or June according to the recipe for candying lovage stems in the March-April preserves.

Rose Sugar is made in the same way as the spring sugars of primrose and violet, remembering to cut away the white heels of the flowers, as above, when preparing them. Red roses will give a dark, purplish coloured sugar, useful for decorating cakes, ice-cream and desserts as well as in making sweets. When mixed with egg-white it turns green however, so will not give you pink confections. It is also a useful way to preserve roses for winter rose-petal jelly.

Rose Petal Jelly

I have studied many old recipes which seemed to require vast stocks of roses in bloom to make any quantity at all. The following is my own adaptation from these. You do still need more than one mature rose bush to make it. As you pick so many blooms, remind yourself how wasted they will be as all the fragrant petals fall steadily to the ground if you leave them in the garden.

27 red roses, approx 85g (3oz) petals   Juice ½ lemon
425 ml (¾ pint) cold water   900g (2lb) sugar
100ml (4 fl oz) liquid pectin

Lay the flowers on a chopping board, slicing across the base of each where you see the beginnings of the white 'heels'. With these removed, check for insects, and put the petals into an enamel or preserving pan with the water. Set on a low heat for 30 minutes with the lid on. If the infusion bubbles noisily the heat is too high. It should merely steep. Check at intervals.

Set the pan aside and leave the petals steeping as they cool for 2 hours. At this point you will find they are limp and white, having given all their fragrance and colour to the liquid. Prepare 3 jars as for jellies and keep these warm. Strain out the rose petals, squeezing them well and add the juice of ½ a lemon. Return this liquor to the pan and set it over a low heat. Very slowly dissolve in the sugar, stirring all the time. Turn up the heat and when a boil is reached, stir in the liquid pectin. Boil rapidly for 2 minutes and pour into the ready prepared jars. Seal and label.

Note: if liked, more red rose petals can be added to the jelly after the liquid pectin and left in the finished preserve.

If you do not have so many flowers out at one time, or wish to make more rose petal jelly in the winter, use the alternative recipe below.

Rose Petal Jelly II

The combination of rose water and heavily fragranced sugar makes this a heavenly jelly. Tiny fragments of rose petals will hang in the jelly, colouring it slightly, but you may feel the addition of food colouring will give a necessary finishing touch.

425ml (¾ pint) rose water (if bought from a dispensary, tell them it is for cookery)
Juice of ½ lemon   100ml (4floz) liquid pectin
225g (8oz) rose sugar   few drops red food colouring
675g (1½lb) granulated sugar

Pour the rose water into an enamel or preserving pan. Add lemon juice. If the rose sugar is in quite large granules, grind this first. Add both sugars slowly over a low heat, stirring well. Once the sugar has dissolved bring to the boil and stir in the liquid pectin. Boil rapidly for 2 minutes. Remove from the heat and skim if necessary. Add a few drops of food colouring to bring the pink jelly to a deep red if liked. It is safer to drip the colouring onto a spoon first to avoid adding too much. Prepare 4 jars and pour the cooled jelly into the warm jars. Seal and label.
Another jelly best made at this time is lemon thyme and grapefruit (see Herbwise Naturally).

Peppermint is also at it's best with the tall stems of fresh growth and the flowers still to come. All mints should be harvested for cookery before flowering, as once the strength of the plant is diverted from the leaves, they quickly deteriorate. Gingermint is the only exception. Peppermint syrup is a very useful conserve to have in the cupboard or freezer, it can be used to flavour ice-cream, yogurt, or cakes, or diluted as a refreshing drink which also calms the stomach.

Peppermint Syrup

Approx 12 stems of black peppermint or curled mint - to give 8 heaped tablespoons of chopped herb
1.2 litres (2 pints) cold water
525g (1lb3oz) sugar

Remove any imperfect leaves and wash the herb under the cold tap. Chop the leaves and measure them into a preserving pan. Pour over the cold water and bring slowly to the boil. Turn down the heat and simmer until the liquid is reduced by half.

Strain and measure the liquid. To each 600ml (1 pint) add 525g (1lb3oz) of sugar, dissolving it over a low heat, stirring all the time. Remove from the heat and leave to cool a little before pouring into warm, sterilised screwtop bottles. If you prefer to freeze the syrup leave it to go cold. Freeze in small rigid containers or pour into ice-cube bags. Since you are likely to be using the syrup in relatively small amounts this is most useful. You can then cut away as many cubes as you need, leaving the remainder of the syrup sealed. Syrups do not freeze entirely as they contain so much sugar, they will still be slightly soft and sticky.

Rose Syrup can also be made by steeping the petals as for the jelly recipe and sweetening the decoction as above. This can then be used as a flavouring or drink.

Herb Honeys are made by steeping the chopped, washed herb in honey over a very low heat. About 2-3 tablespoons of herb will be sufficient to add flavour and goodness. Vary the amount according to the strength of that particular herb. Thyme, rose and rosemary give good results. (See Herbwise Naturally.)

Elderflower vinegar is one of the loveliest to make. Unlike the other herb vinegars it is not set on the windowsill. Fill a dark jar with freshly picked, perfect elderflowers which are newly opened. Pour the warm white wine vinegar over them and seal. Leave the jar in the warm kitchen for 3-4 days, shaking it now and again. The perfume and flavour of the elderflowers has now been transferred to the vinegar which is excellent as a salad dressing. Strain the vinegar and return it to the original bottle. Label.

Elderflower cordial is ever popular in our family and I bottle and freeze large amounts, for recipe see Herbwise Naturally.

Other herb vinegars are made by adding the freshly picked herb to a bottle of wine vinegar, and setting it on the windowsill for about 10 days. Amounts of herb vary according to their strength of flavour. One or two long sprigs of rosemary may be sufficient, while several tablespoons of fennel will be needed. Blends of herbs are equally successful;

Bay, Basil and Tarragon has a depth of flavour as well as a spicy note

Tear 3 good-sized bay leaves and push them into the bottle of white wine vinegar, or pour the warmed vinegar over them in a sterilised screwtop jar. Add 6 tops of sweet basil and 4 or 5 good sprigs of tarragon, torn into short lengths. Leave the vinegar on the windowsill in the sun for about 10 days. Open and smell. If the aroma has taken on the qualities of the herbs sufficiently, strain the vinegar and add a fresh torn bay leaf for decoration. Do not forget to label. If you wish to add more flavour, steep a second batch of herbs in the same way.

Herbs to Dry - Methods

1 Bunches of freshly cut herbs must be gathered as they are at their best on a dry day. Tie 6-8 stems together, having stripped away the lower leaves where the stems are tightly bound. Hang them upside down in a clean, dry, warm atmosphere where there is a flow of air to carry away the moisture, but no direct sunlight. (They could be hung in a large airing cupboard or from a line across a spare room.) As soon as the leaves are crisp to touch and the flowers feel thoroughly dry, cut them down and crumble the dried leaves or leaves and flowers to store them in screwtop jars away from the light.

Lemon balm, lemon thyme, sage and marjoram can all be dried in this way. All but lemon thyme should be harvested before the flowers appear. Lemon thyme is cut as the flowers first open for the greatest flavour.

2 Some herbs such as lovage and sweet cicely, rose petals and dill, dry better as single leaves or individual petals scattered over clean muslin stretched over a frame; or a nylon jumper dryer, set in the airing cupboard. Rose petals can also be hung in large muslin bags in a warm, dry atmosphere, so long as you check their progress at regular intervals and keep turning them.

3 Alternatively, if you have no space to hang dry herbs or set them on racks, they can be dried in most microwaves. Check the manufacturers instructions for confirmation before experimenting as some are unsuitable. Lay the leaves between sheets of paper kitchen towel on the turntable. In my microwave full power for 1 minute draws out most of the moisture. Remove the paper and herb and flip it over, laying it with the dry paper underneath, back on the turntable. Remove the wet paper from on top of the herb and replace with dry. Set again for 30-60 seconds as necessary. When the herb is crisp, crumble into jars as before. I prefer the first two methods as this involves a great deal of paper kitchen towel to produce a jar of dried herb. It is also comparatively labour intensive.

4 An exception to these methods is made for drying calendula petals. The flowers are carefully pulled apart and the centres discarded. Lay the washed and dried petals (if for culinary use) on a large plate one layer deep. Set in the oven with the lowest setting (no higher than 50°C) and the door ajar. When crisp store in dark glass jars.

5 Wash the herbs under the cold tap and place in freezer bags in small amounts. Evacuate the air from the bags, seal and freeze. Chopping can be saved by crumbling the frozen herb before thawing. This is especially useful with mint. Always label frozen herbs properly.

Herbs best frozen rather than dried - Basil, mints, chives, parsley, chervil, elderflower, fennel.

Frozen elderflowers can be added to gooseberries as these are taken from the freezer later to be cooked.

ALWAYS STORE DRIED HERBS IN SCREWTOP DARK GLASS JARS
AWAY FROM DIRECT LIGHT All should keep for up to 1 year.

Herb Teas

FRESH teas are perfect at this time of year. On hot days an iced herb tea can be wonderfully refreshing and soothing.

Herbs at their best include peppermint, lemon balm, borage, thymes, fennel, dill and chamomile. Of these, peppermint is helpful for travel sickness, or simply to settle your stomach after a rich meal - as well as filling a role of refreshment.

Lemon balm is beautifully soothing as a gentle tranquilizer after a hot, hard day. It can also help to settle mild period pains and headaches.

Borage contains a high proportion of potassium and should be avoided by anyone with kidney problems for that reason. The potassium does however help to cool you in hot weather.

Thyme teas can be helpful against headaches, summer colds and, possibly, an overactive mind at night.

Fennel and dill both have an aniseed flavour and are useful diuretics in addition to soothing indigestion.

Chamomile tea has always been known as a relaxant but the flavour is not to everyone's taste. Only leave to stand for 3 minutes, no more. Double chamomile flowers are better for you if you take the tea regularly.

Fresh herbs can be blended to make tea. You may like to add a sprig of lemon thyme to a pot of lemon balm tea to intensify the flavour, or add a little borage to other teas.

Pick 2 young tops of green herb, or 4 sprigs of flowering thyme, or about 5 chamomile flowers per cup, and add another for the pot. Warm the teapot which should not be metal and pour boiling water over the washed and torn herb. With the exception of chamomile, leave to stand for about 4-5 minutes. Strain and drink the tea as it is, or sweetened with honey. All herbs are potentially medicinal as teas and you should not drink a herb tea regularly more than once a day, unless you wish to experience therapeutic effects. Several cups of fennel tea a day for instance could have you making extra trips to the toilet.

Cold tea left in the pot can come in handy - chamomile tea will also be appreciated by plants, especially in a greenhouse. Peppermint tea can be poured away where you wish to discourage ants. Cold fennel tea makes an excellent eyewash, and cooling thyme tea is an antiseptic for cuts and grazes.

Making rose-petal jelly

(Below) *Honeysuckle and jasmine arch*

Entrance covered way

(Below) *Posy*

May - June

(Top right) *Ringlet on ragwort*

(Far left) *Mullein moth caterpillar*

(Left) *Painted lady on Greek valerian*

(Lower left) *Hedgehog*
(Below). *Bee on Elecampane*

Cancer   (Top) *Astrology beds Aries - Virgo*   *Leo*

May - June

Harvesting flowers, making hypericum and verbascum oils

(Left) *Stem basket -before trimming* (Below) *Moist pot-pourri*

Wines and Liqueurs

Agrimony and Ginger Wine

SINCE agrimony is good for the liver, I thought it would be a healthy choice to make wine with the herb. A very old recipe for treating summer colds using agrimony in a lemonade type infusion spiced with ginger, gave me the idea for combining these ingredients. Heavily flavoured with ginger, the wine is just ready in time for Christmas when it is a favourite warming tipple.

You will need:

4 cups of washed, chopped agrimony leaves (gathered as the first flowers open)
50g (2oz) fresh root ginger, coarsely grated

1.35kg (3lb) sugar	25 g (1oz) fresh bakers yeast
3 tablespoons chopped raisins	1 slice bread, toasted
4 lemons	4.5 litres (8 pints) water
1 orange	

Add 2.8 litres (5 pints) cold water to the leaves and ginger in a large preserving pan. Bring slowly to simmer and keep simmering for about 20 minutes, when the liquor will have turned a darker colour.

Thinly peel the rind of the lemons and orange (no pith) into the fermenting bin. Add the sugar and juice of the fruits. Strain and measure the agrimony decoction, pouring this over and stirring to dissolve the sugar. Make the quantity of liquid up to 4.5 litres (8 pints) with boiling water. Stir and cover. When the must has cooled to bloodheat, float the yeast on toast on the top and leave, covered, for 24 hours. Remove the toast and yeast and stir. Add the chopped raisins. Keep in a warm temperature 21°C (70°F). Stir night and morning for 10 days. Strain or syphon into a sterilised demi-john. Set the labelled demi-john in a warm place until it stops fermenting. Bottle the wine.

IN the garden hedgerow I have left several hawthorn bushes to mature into trees. These screen the compost heap and also provide a harvest of delicate hawthorn flowers in early summer, and hawthorn berries in the autumn.

A plentiful supply enables me to pick sufficient flowers to fill a small bottle of brandy for a traditional treat.

Hawthorn Liqueur can then be used to flavour cakes and desserts. For the full recipe see Herbcraft Naturally. Other liqueurs in Herbcraft Naturally for this time are Melissa, and Peppermint. Also in the wine and liqueurs section you will find recipes for Lemon Thyme and Lemon Balm, a much appreciated wine made every year since I first invented the recipe. Elderflower and Kiwi, and Strawberry and Rose petal wines.

In the Home

AS in the March-April section, I have chosen recipes for personal as well as household use. Such a wonderful selection of ingredients are available that I have kept in mind the number of preserves to be made at this time. The following recipes are those which take a short time to make and are spread over more than one day.

Ointments

The most versatile and valued ointment for everyday family use is surely calendula. Even in this day and age it is well-known and widely recommended for everything from preventing and treating nappy rash, to healing grazes and minor injuries.

Calendula flowers can be picked for this recipe throughout the summer and early autumn, alternating ointment making with culinary recipes, according to the number of flowers open at any time.

Making ointment is very simple. All you need is sufficient herb to macerate in the oil, and beeswax.

Calendula Ointment

600ml (1 pint) oil   50g (2oz) beeswax
Calendula petals

Although other base oils can be used, sweet almond oil is gentle and enriching for the skin and gives good results. You can buy it in bottles of 250 or 500ml in wholefood or healthfood stores or a litre at a time from herb suppliers. Pick the calendula flowers as they are newly opened on a dry day before the sun is high in the sky. If they are clean and free of insects, they can be added straight to the oil in a dark screwtop jar. If there are insects between the petals, pull the flowers apart washing petals and centre quickly in cold water before patting them completely dry with a clean cloth or paper towel, and adding to the oil.

Leave the flowers in the oil, adding more on another day until the jar is absolutely full of oil-covered flowers. Be sure the topmost flowers are completely submerged. After several days the oil should have taken on a rich egg-yolk colour from the calendula. If you are not satisfied of this after 7-10 days, strain the oil through fine muslin or coffee filter paper and add more flowers to repeat the process.

Set the jar of prepared, strained macerated oil in a deep bowl or large jug of very hot water, to heat it gradually through. Put the beeswax into a strong oven-proof bowl on a very low heat, or into a double pan with boiling water beneath. Steadily melt the beeswax. When it is ready, having checked the oil is warmed through, gradually add the melted beeswax to the oil stirring all the time. With the two combined, pour the liquid ointment into clean, sterilised prepared jars or pots with screwtops. Seal and label. Use as required.

Other herbs which make useful ointments are elderflower, comfrey and chickweed. For these the method is slightly different.

Elderflower Ointment - for scratches and bruising, and inflamed itchy skin.
Pick the elderflowers on a dry, sunny day in late morning, choosing only those which smell sweet and are in perfect condition - having newly opened. Elderflowers of poorer quality can be useful for dyeing wool or silk - see Craft.

Pour 250-500ml of sweet almond oil into a glass, pyrex or enamel pan. Remove the thick stems from the umbels and push as many florets of the elderflowers under the surface of the oil, as you can.

Leave the pan on the lowest heat possible for 2-4 hours, until the oil has changed colour, taking on a greenish tinge and smelling strongly of elderflowers.

Melt the beeswax, following the same proportions of 50g (2oz) beeswax to 600ml (1 pint) of oil to give a fairly stiff ointment. Adding less beeswax will give a creamier consistency. This is fine in winter, but in hot weather the oil may separate out. If this should happen, simply reheat and melt the two together again. Add the beeswax to the oil, stirring briskly with a glass rod or wooden spoon handle. Pour into prepared, sterilised pots or jars as the ointment is cooling. Label.

Comfrey Ointment is made by macerating torn fresh young comfrey leaves in a pan of oil for 4 hours over a low heat, and blending with beeswax as above. Add 3 drops essential oil of lavender before pouring into the jars. It is excellent for torn ligaments, broken bones, healing clean cuts and joint pains.

Although looked upon by most gardeners as a weed rather than a herb, chickweed is a valuable harvest. If you have been careful to avoid growing it, a friend may well be glad to have some weeding done. *Chickweed Ointment* is made in the same way as comfrey, putting as much green leaf into the oil as possible. The maceration is deep green, giving a measure of it's medicinal properties. Make to treat skin rashes and sores resulting from mild eczema or psoriasis and like complaints. Medical advice should be sought if the conditions persist.

Moist Pot-Pourri

When the roses are in bloom and the rich, heady perfume hangs in the still, summer air, there is a strong temptation to try to hold on to such perfection. Most pot-pourri is made up of fully dried ingredients. The older method which prompted the name pot-pourri - literally, 'rotten pot', gives a far superior result. The main ingredients are partially dried, fragrant rose petals and coarse sea salt. Together these produce a sticky 'Cake', which is broken up and mixed with other partially or completely dried herbs, spices and roots. Essential oils and brandy are the final ingredients in a recipe which may be freshened as years pass - in fact, over a lifetime - for a good moist pot-pourri can last for 60 years. A different concept altogether from the modern mixes which are sold under the name of pot-pourri. All it requires is a tall, straight sided earthenware or china container with a lid.

The following blend is my own, based loosely on a very old recipe. Months later the perfume is delicious. If you do not have all the ingredients you too can adapt it using different herbs and flowers. All that should remain basically the same is the relationship of the quantities of rose petals, salt and fixative roots. The brandy stirred in at the end of the recipe is to ensure the mix remains moist as it should be.

Method

Firstly, pick fragrant roses as they open, discard the centres, spreading the petals on a rack covered in muslin to begin drying. The heavier the fragrance is, the better the final result will be. The colour of the petals does not matter as the salt will act as a bleaching agent, removing their beauty as the pot-pourri is prepared. I like to mix **Rosa mundi** and the York and Lancaster rose together with fragrant white blooms, saving the red roses for cookery. The rose petals should be dried away from direct sunlight in a warm, airy environment. Remove them from the rack and layer with salt in the container as soon as they are leathery. If they become crisp they have dried too far for this recipe. A few petals at a time can be dried by hanging them up in a muslin bag.

As the roses open, pick them preferably in mid-morning, being careful to do so after any rain or dew has dried. Mould can be the result of using damp roses. The amount of rose petals available to you may decide the quantity of pot-pourri made. You can make more or less than this recipe so long as you follow the ratio of roses, salt and fixatives.

Simply layer salt, then rose petals which are part dried, and salt again, in your straight sided container. Add more roses and salt until the rose season is finished, or you have sufficient. Between additions and for 2 months afterwards, keep the rose petals and salt pressed down in the jar with a heavy weight, and cover the jar. Check the mix occasionally.

After 2 months remove the lid and weight and break up the sticky top layer of caked roses and salt. Stir in the dried ingredients, herbs first - and then the ground dried fixative roots. Flake the cinnamon stick over the mix and slice the vanilla pod into 8 short pieces before adding. Carefully drip in the essential oils. Lastly sprinkle over the brandy and toss the pot-pourri as you would a salad. This powerful pot-pourri uses ingredients which may be unsuitable for anyone with respiratory problems.

Ingredients:

Approx 2.8 litres (5 pints) of rose petals, partly dried
Approx 1.7 litres (3 pints) of coarse sea salt or bay salt
1 cup lemon verbena leaves

½ cup eau-de-cologne mint	1 heaped tablespoon ground orris root
½ cup jasmine flowers (optional)	1 heaped tablespoon ground angelica root
½ cup lavender	1 dessertspoon ground frankincense
1 sliced vanilla pod	1 dessertspoon brandy
1 flaked cinnamon stick	5 drops essential oil Benzoin res.
2 teaspoons freshly ground cloves	6 drops essential oil Bergamot
2 dessertspoons star anise	5 drops essential oil Rose Geranium

This amount fills a large sweet jar. Store sealed for 2 months before opening occasionally in a warm atmosphere. Do not leave open for more than 30 minutes at a time. More ingredients can be added the following year if liked. A lid with small holes is best. The rose geranium or bergamot may be left out and another oil substituted if the herb ingredients change. One of them should be present to enrich the rose, however. As long as ground benzoin is substituted for the angelica root or frankincense, sandalwood or frankincense essential oil may be substituted for benzoin oil.

Craft

Elderflower Dye

DYEING with elderflowers has become part of my general harvest. I have already gathered the umbels of delicate white flowers for making cordial, ointment and so on. As I prepare the culinary and medicinal recipes, I simply sort out those umbels which are not quite perfect - either with unopened florets or some tinged brown and too far gone. These are laid together in a separate bowl and generally I have sufficient for dyeing - about 100g (4oz). This will give really wonderful results with 1m (1yard) of pure silk or 50g (2oz) of wool. The elderflowers are added to 2.8 litres (5 pints) of water in a dyepan and simmered for 40-50 minutes. Strain out the flowers.

Prepare your wool or silk as on pages 26-27 mordanting with alum. Enter the wool into the elderflower dye liquor at a temperature of hand-hot and simmer for about 50 minutes. Leave to stand overnight. Rinse thoroughly in cold water and drip dry. With silk enter this into the liquor when it is cool and bring the heat slowly to just below simmering point. Leave the silk to soak in the dye in a suitable container where the dye can reach all the fabric evenly. Lift the silk out of the dyepan, smoothing any ridges where dye might collect, at regular intervals. When the silk has reached the colour you require (2-4 days) remove it from the dye, rinse thoroughly in cold water and drip dry. This can be a beautiful, fast, light gold. I have washed silk dyed with elderflower many times without colour loss.

Elder Leaves

The same dye process can be repeated with elder leaves gathered just before the flowers open, or at the same time. An alum mordant with silk will give a deep old gold which is wonderfully rich. The addition of a hint of iron to the dyebath as the silk is being heated (silk must be lifted out meanwhile until the iron is stirred in) produces shades of green.

Other good greens can be obtained from angelica and comfrey as detailed in Herbcraft Naturally.

Sweet cicely

Leaves gathered along with a few of the flower heads as they first open at the beginning of May, may achieve an astonishing lime green when the wool is mordanted with copper sulphate. To prepare the mordant, dissolve one teaspoon of copper sulphate (available from dye suppliers) and ½ teaspoon of cream of tartar in a little boiling water. Add this to 2.8-3.4 litres (5-6 pints) of water in the dyepan. Enter the pre-washed and soaked wool as before, when the temperature of the water reaches hand-hot. Keep the wool at a very low simmer for about 50 minutes. Cool and squeeze gently before entering into the dye liquor.

To prepare the dye gather about 100g (4oz) of leaves and flowers to 50g (2oz) wool. Tear the leaves into the dyepan with 2.8 litres (5 pints) of water. Bring to a fast simmer and keep simmering for 1 hour. Strain out the herb. Cool to hand hot, enter wool and maintain a low simmer for another hour. Remove from the heat, leave to stand overnight. Rinse thoroughly and drip dry.

Agrimony

Flowering tops and leaves are used, and again double the weight of herb to wool for quantity. Simmering the agrimony for almost an hour produces a rich, reddish liquor. Wool pre-mordanted with alum is entered after the herb has been strained out, giving a lovely soft fawn colour. Simmer for 1 hour and leave overnight before rinsing. Silk pre-mordanted with alum takes on a much deeper colour over 3-4 days soaking in the dye liquor. Treat as the silk in the elderflower recipe.

Flowers and Foliage to press

SUMMER bounty has now truly become available as the swelling list of popular leaves and flowers below, shows. More and more seem to ambush you for a place in the album as you wander up the garden. Some are fleeting and are best gathered as soon as conditions are right - forget-me-nots, elderflowers and sweet woodruff; while others, such as the wild strawberries, greater celandine, heartsease and avens, flower on and on.

Herb Robert produces brilliant red foliage in very dry weather, far more impressive than the green leaves. Honesty tops are more effective when harvested with a few seedcases forming below the topmost flowers. Umbels of elderflowers appear as trees when pressed. Small rosebuds can be pressed successfully if they are first sliced in half with a knife while still tightly closed. Ajuga, also known as bugle, may be sliced if necessary but this is more difficult. Press double pink flowers as separate petals.

Flowers	Foliage
alehoof	alehoof
aquilegia	fennel
avens	golden hop
bugle	Greek valerian
catmint	herb Robert
dyer's woodruff	jasmine
elderflowers	lady's mantle
forget-me-nots	lovage - small individual leaves
fumitory	meadowsweet
greater celandine	salad burnet
heartsease	sweet cicely
herb bennet	
herb Robert	
honesty	
pinks	
rose - small buds	
Spanish sage - flowering tops	
sweet cicely	
sweet woodruff - flowering tops	
thyme	
viper's bugloss	
wild strawberry	
woad	
yarrow	

Midsummer Posies

HERB posies are a true delight. The wide variety of colours, forms and textures in the flowers and foliage, coupled with their heady perfumes, makes them outstanding. Whether you prefer to set posies of herbs about your home in old-fashioned posy bowls, or plan to take them as gifts when visiting friends, they will surely be appreciated.

The central flower in a posy is traditionally either a rose with the bud just beginning to open, or a dramatic pink or carnation. Around this stem are placed concentric rings of alternating foliage and flowers with contrasting textures and either shades of the same colour, or contrasts. The posy is always surrounded and framed by foliage with large, evenly shaped leaves to add the finishing touch.

In preparing the posy, the stems should be cut at about 18cm (7ins) long and the lower leaves removed for setting in water or tying together to be enclosed in a posy holder. Posy holders can be bought in florists or at bridal accessory counters, and consist of a plastic holder with a lace effect top. One can easily be made using a cone of stiff lace, or a paper doily with a hole cut in the centre for the stems to pass through. Tied with ribbon this can look lovely.

Each circle of herb is tied in place around the central rose or pink, so that the whole is fixed neatly and securely. The posy holder completes the effect for presentation. Alternatively, the flowers and foliage can be set into a wire frame inside the bowl for a display in the house. In deciding which herbs to use - the language of flowers may be a source of inspiration for a special occasion - see Herbcraft Naturally. I often like to wander around the garden picking different stems and trying them together before coming to a final decision. At this time of year the following are particularly lovely;

chamomile	lemon scented geranium	santolina (silver or green)
eau-de-cologne mint	peppermint	sneezewort
golden marjoram	pineapplemint	southernwood
golden, tricolor and		
purple sages	pinks	thrift
Jerusalem sage	roses	thymes
lady's mantle	rosemary	yarrow
lemon balm (variegated too)	salad burnet	

Midsummer is a magical time and traditions honouring the Solstice and power of the sun are very ancient. Christian festivals overlaid the older feasts and June 24th, St John's day, became a favourite time to pick a protective posy. It was traditionally hung in the house to dry and kept there to drive away all manner of evil until the next year. On this day the power of the sun is at it's height and the power of the herbs, may, in truth, be strongest. We should not forget the grain of truth at the centre of many old instructions for gathering herbs. The chemical balance within the plants is, indeed, affected by climate, phases of the moon, etc.

Protective posies were also picked on the Eve of the Assumption, August 14th, originally the day of the Mother Earth. They might contain 7, 9 or 15 herbs and often reflected a perception of the relationship of the sun and planets. If you have planted an astrology garden it will be easy to gather such a posy. Here are some suggestions of herbs to combine for a 7 herb posy.

Generally a protective posy has a flower of the **Sun** at the centre. Choose from: a sunflower bud or mini-sunflower, St John's wort, calendula, chamomile. Around this cluster of flowers or central bloom set a herb foliage dedicated to **Mercury.** Choose from: fennel or dill, calamint, horehound, southernwood. Next flowers of **Venus.** Choose from: lady's mantle, self-heal, thyme, alkanet or yarrow. In place of the earth I have set a herb ruled by the **Moon.** Choose from: clary sage, adders tongue or orache foliage. Next in relation to the Sun we set a herb ruled by **Mars.** Choose from: blessed thistle, basil, wormwood, butcher's broom or a red hawthorn in flower if you can still find one. Herbs of **Jupiter** offer some exceptionally elegant foliage as well as flowers. You may wish to set two circles of flowers together to end with foliage. Choose from: agrimony, costmary, herb bennet, roses or clove pinks. Lastly enclose the flowers and foliage with a circle of herbs ruled by **Saturn.** Choose from: woad, mullein, or comfrey. Perhaps the sympathetic magic of imitating the order of the universe will work for you

Stem Basket

A T a time when herb hedges are trimmed and your harvest of santolina, thyme, winter savory and the hyssops is just beginning; it is good to have a project in mind for the dried cut stems. The subject of making stem baskets has been detailed in Herbcraft Naturally. However, this basket offers a new approach in design.

A basket for sitting on the side rather than carrying about, it has a very different handle. While being practical, this also offers a central decorative feature. **You will need;-**
A wooden base - the one illustrated is a slice of tree trunk, 2.8cm (11ins) in diameter and 2.5cm (1in) thick.
3 short lengths of thick dogwood or other shrub -2 x 11cm (4½ins) long and the 3rd 8cm (3¼ins) long
1 thinner length of dogwood for rim
1 length sturdy dogwood with a forked top 28.5cm (11ins) long
Panel pins 1.5cm (⅝ins)
4 screws 3cm (1¼ins) No 8
Crochet cotton or raffia
Approximately 55 bundles of winter savory, santolina, thyme and/or hyssop as available.

To begin:
First, clean and smooth the base. Hammer in the panel pins in 2 staggered rows around the edge of the base, with the pairs approximately 2.5cm (1in) apart. Drill holes through the 3 rim supports where they will be attached to the sides of the base. Drill corresponding holes into the base sides. Drill a hole through the centre

of the base ready to attach the handle. Screw the rim supports in place. Fix a screw through the base and into the bottom of the handle. Coil the thinner length of dogwood to form a rim with the same diameter as the base. Tie in several places to secure. Tie again with raffia to each of the rim supports.

Lay bunches of herb ready to work. Tie the crochet cotton or a long length of strong raffia to the lower of 2 panel pins on the right of a rim support. Take the thread up and around the panel pin above and while keeping the thread taut, lay a bunch of herb to fill the space between the pairs of pins. Adjust the stems to fit, leaving any bare area below the base, with sufficient length to take the bunches at least 5cm (2ins) above the rim. Bring the thread tightly across the bunch as in diagram 1, to the next lower pin and make a figure of eight movement around this and the upper pin. Repeat until you reach the next rim support.

Bring the thread back from the top panel pin of this pair across the last bunch and down to the bottom pin on the other side. Continue, reversing the movement until you have returned to the first rim support. Tie off securely and cut the thread. Each bunch will now have a cross of thread holding it securely. Repeat between the other stem supports.

Thread a large needle with a long thread of crochet cotton. Tie the other end around a rim support with a clove hitch knot. Stitch the bundles to the rim by bringing the thread out under the rim half way across a bundle of herb and back over the rim, then out again half way along the next . See diagram 2. Tie end securely.

1

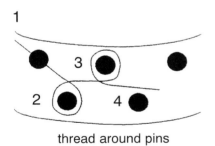

thread around pins

2.

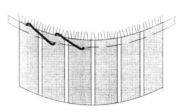

stitching herbs to basket pins

75

July - August

Soothing mints, refreshing lemon flavours,
iced herb tea in perfumed shade.
Butterflies mob oregano - gatekeeper
and comma dance. Bees hang laden,
near exhaustion on the leaves of motherwort.
Harvest, harvest, rich abundance -
flower-filled baskets are kitchen bound.
Wines and jellies, syrups, sugars,
dyes and fragrance stock the shelves.
Another year will be supplied.
Peace, as dusk falls.
Bright colours fade, red bergamot,
clove pinks, are hushed. Marigold closed.
Blue hyssop softens, the scene is set
by dreaming towers of clary sage.
Serene with evening primrose glow,
we sip the nectar of the garden.
Moonlight touches santolina, lovingly awakens beauty.
Seedheads whisper in the silence; awed,
we gaze in meditation.

In the Garden

ONCE again harvesting is the key task/pleasure during the summer months. While other gardeners are busy 'dead-heading', the herb gardener may consider 'live-heading' as the order of the day. Roses, clove pinks, chamomile, lavenders, St John's wort, bergamot, golden rod, and many more, provide a continuous flower harvest for cookery, remedies, wines, fragrances, dyes and flowercrafts.

As basket after basket of herbs is gathered, you will need to leave sufficient flowerheads for the seed harvest yet to come. This will also ensure each shade of the rainbow of herb flowers is represented in the garden for its full time. Many herb flowers open one after another on the plants, giving a harvest period of several weeks.

With some, the seed is the awaited harvest. Coriander, caraway, dill, fennel and anise are the most valued. Lovage, angelica and sweet cicely are also used in recipes. Remember to check the tall lovage stems regularly for ripe seedheads.

Harvesting Seeds

CUT seedheads on some stem as the seeds turn from green to grey, or light brown. (Sweet cicely can be left longer.) Hang bunches of seedheads upside down indoors over a tray or cloth, allowing the seeds to fall as they ripen in the sun. This can avoid insect infestation which may happen if they are left outside. As with herbs for drying, cut them on a dry day, preferably two or three days after rain.

With sunflowers, cut a length of stem with the seedhead, when the back of the head turns yellow and it bends forward. These can be stood in a summerhouse or conservatory, with a cloth to catch the seeds. Generally they need a little help to clear them from the seedhead. In some areas where many are harvested, a round piece of wood with nails or hooks set into it, is pushed into the seedhead and turned, to bring them out quickly.

Do remember the birds in your garden are keeping a close eye on the seed harvest too and leave them a share of their real delights. Finches enjoy angelica seeds, eating them as they fall. Later in the year, I have often seen sparrows fighting over a ripening sunflower head. Willow warblers dart among the tall, waving fennel, and the bullfinches and other small birds will come for the evening primrose seeds and teazles.

Other seeds can be gathered to re-sow annuals and biennials, or increase stocks of perennials. Basil, borage, biennial clary sage, calendula, *coreopsis tinctoria,* dill, flax, mullein, tagetes and weld; could all be saved for the next season. Angelica should be left to seed itself, as this is more successful.

The following seeds will all be ripening in late July or August:

betony	dyer's chamomile	honesty	santolina
borage	flax	hyssop	self-heal
calendula	goat's rue	lady's bedstraw	sweet cicely
chamomile	greater knapweed	lady's mantle	sweet rocket
coreopsis	Greek valerian	lovage	thrift
cowslip	heartsease	meadow clary	white horehound
dill	herb bennet	motherwort	weld

Test for ripe seeds by shaking over a dish. If some fall readily, set a large bag beside the bush and cut the stems, turning their heads down into the bag. Shake the seeds free with the bag held closed. Dry on a labelled dish in the sun, then take this outside, blowing gently over the surface to remove any fragments of seedhead and insects. The dry seeds can be stored in plastic screwtop containers, or sealed envelopes, until spring. Always label the containers immediately, adding the date. Store in a warm, dark cupboard.

Dyer's broom uses the sun's heat to trigger the seedpods to open in dramatic explosions. To save the seeds you will need to set the pods on a table in front of a sunny window, with a large cloth spread out to catch them. The loud cracks heard as the pods burst, herald a display worth watching.

Attractive seedheads

For flower arrangers the seedheads may have more interest than seeds. The herb garden offers a fascinating selection;

angelica -	spray to hold seeds.
blessed thistle -	elegant bonnets filled with down.
cowslip -	simple yet attractive.
elecampane -	a later harvest, perfect sprayed gold.
fennel -	can be pretty sprayed silver, or left natural.
golden rod -	a later harvest, lovely sprayed silver or gold.
greater knapweed -	feather light 'fairies bonnets'.
herb bennet -	spiky and striking for miniature work.
honesty -	needs no introduction.
Jerusalem sage -	left until late autumn these have a natural bronzed look.
milk thistles -	long spines, elegant.
motherwort -	vicious but attractive.
poppy -	lovely sprayed, or left natural.
sea-holly -	both the true herb and smaller planum are lovely.
St John's wort -	abundant clusters, pretty sprayed silver.
teazles -	sharp but ever attractive.
white horehound -	pretty, do not gather when wearing a jumper.
wild basil -	similar to horehound, but softer.
woodsage -	elegant

Preparing hedges for Autumn

KNOT gardens and small herb hedges need to be trimmed about every 3 weeks throughout the summer. Especial care must be given in late August to lavenders which will have been left to flower. Cut the lavender as the first flowers are opening on each stem, taking the stalks right back to the previous year's growth. Leave neat, compact bushes. These will then have time to produce a little growth before an early frost may halt them.

Some lavenders flower late, and these are simply taken in their turn as the first flowers open. Do make sure however, that they are all cut back in early autumn. Without this cut, the bushes will become leggy and unwieldy, and you will be left with unwanted woody growth.

Southernwood is another herb which needs to be cut right back at the end of August. Cut it by two thirds to leave a compact bush, or you will find you have growth in the spring which looks like a lot of shaving brushes on long bare stems. Treated in this way, southernwood can be a most attractive bush. It can stand polluted air in roadside front gardens better than any other herb.

Watering

IF, as is often the case in recent years, there are many more dry harvesting days than refreshing showers for the herbs, you may need to water. I have always kept watering to a minimum.Plants can too readily be encouraged to seek surface water, rather than sending roots down to underground moisture. Most perennial, and generally, also biennial herbs, will cope with excessive heat and lack of rain for several weeks. The only herbs which will suffer, particularly from hot sun, are those which would naturally grow in damp situations. Mints are the most vulnerable.

Water any herbs in pots or tubs. Also new additions to the garden. If herbs have wilted on an exceptionally hot day, add 4 drops of Bach Rescue Remedy and 2 drops of Willow remedy to their water for a better recovery.

Bach remedies can also be helpful with any foliage problems appearing in the summer. I have used the Crab Apple remedy in combination with Rescue - 8 drops of Crab Apple to 2 of Rescue in a filled watering can.

With plants cautiously watered in dry weather and supported by natural twigs and branches as they grow taller and heavier with their harvests; you will have time to bask in the sunshine.

Butterflies

IF you have cut back one third of your nettle patch in early June, one third in July, and one third in early August; the butterflies may have been encouraged to lay eggs there. They like a nettle patch in a sunny south-facing hollow. Check both sides of leaves for eggs. Small tortoiseshell and peacock eggs will be on the under surface. If the leaves are rolled up they may contain eggs of the red admiral, and eggs on the upper surface in webs are likely to be either red admiral or those of the comma butterfly.

Herbs such as oregano will bring as many butterflies as a buddleia. Peacock, red admirals, gatekeepers and commas all find delight in the purple flowers. Small whites, yellows and skippers settle on lavenders, while the comma and small copper also enjoy sorrel and yarrow. The tall elecampane flowers form perfect landing 'dishes' for red admirals, tortoiseshells, clouded yellow and the painted lady, which is also to be seen basking on variegated lemon balm leaves.

With butterflies flitting about the flowers, bees buzzing and birds eating the honeysuckle berries; we turn to considering the astrology beds ……..

The Astrology Garden

THE **Cancer** sign begins at midsummer, June 21st-July 21st, which might lead you to think it should be ruled by the sun. However, Cancer, with the symbol of the crab, is ruled by the moon. Those herbs ruled by the moon have cool characteristics, either being almost succulent in leaf, as with purslane and stonecrop; ferns - as with adders tongue and moonwort; or having white flowers or watery associations - white lilies, white roses, and yellow water lilies.

When making the garden, I was faced with the problem that most herbs ruled by the moon would not thrive on a sunny, south-facing bank. Reading Culpeper with care, I kept those parts of the body affected by Cancer in mind. He gives the brain, the left eye of a man and the right eye of a woman, and some further reference to the stomach. I made the following choices.

Culpeper writes that although **Agrimony** is under Jupiter, the herb is also under the sign of Cancer, removing disease in the parts under the sign by sympathy. Agrimony has long been associated with treating the eyes, its very name possibly referring to 'argemoney' or white specks in the eye. He also tells us the **Hyssop** "strengthens all the parts of the body under Cancer and Jupiter." He recommends it for purging gross humours and helping falling sickness. In my garden hyssop supplies a tangy flavouring, is included in the rum honey cough liqueur and much appreciated in flowercrafts. He places **Lemon balm** under the sign for its ability to lift melancholia and emotional troubles, removing obstructions to the brain. We can still appreciate the gentle tranquillizing effect of lemon balm tea today.

Where agrimony cures eye problems and strengthens the eye by sympathy, **Wormwood** cures by antipathy. Being a martial herb, the heat of wormwood counteracts the coolness of the moon's influence. Planted in another situation, perhaps near a pool, wormwood could be very effective beside white lilies, or surrounding white roses. This is a combination I have planted in the shadiest corner of the wine and liqueur garden.

To the agrimony, hyssop, lemon balm and wormwood, I have added two lunar herbs. The first is **Biennial Clary Sage.** The seed of this herb set in water produces a mucilage which was used to take down swellings and draw out splinters. I can only presume that the mucilage is meant when Culpeper refers to the seed being put into the eyes to clear them from "things gotten within the lids to offend them, as also clears them from white and red spots on them." The powder of the dried root was used as snuff, to purge the brain of "much rheum and corruption."

In modern use clary sage is appreciated for beauty and the powerful perfume, which acts directly on the brain, to lift your mood. Larger doses have an aphrodisiac quality, but beware of the headache which can immediately follow too large a dose. Treating pain is the work of our last herb, the **Poppy**. Its action on the brain when administered as opium is well known. A lunar herb, poppies end our exploration of Cancer.

With the next sign, **Leo,** July 21st-August 21st we come into the realms of the Sun. With the symbol of the lion and the position of the sun in the universe, it is not surprising that it rules the heart. We should add to this the right eye of a man and the left eye of a woman.

Cold Saturn is in opposition to the Sun's heat. Culpeper recommends **Bay** to work against Saturn's influence, which he believed produced rheumatic distillations from the brain to the eyes. Bay remains an important herb and decorative evergreen in every kitchen garden.

Angelica towers above the young bay in the astrology bed, listed in Culpeper's herbal as "In all epidemical diseases caused by Saturn, that is as good a preservative as grows." He also directs the juice or water to be dropped into the eyes for dimness of sight. A painful remedy I suspect, not to be tried. Under this herb he gives details of the best astrological aspects for gathering angelica, herb of the Sun. The warming and comforting qualities of angelica are still used in herbal medicine. In the kitchen it is invaluable.

The Sun also rules a favourite herb of mine, the **Pot Marigold** or **Calendula.** Who could look at the cheery orange flower, so like an image of the sun and not make the association? The calendula remains a herb to strengthen the heart. Culpeper tells us of its use as a substitute for the more expensive saffron, in treating measles and smallpox. As a colouring, flavouring, and soothing compress and ointment, the pot marigold is one of the most useful herbs.

Its partner at the front of the bed is hardly less appealing. **Borage** is also cheering, and was, even then, a long-established cordial to the heart. The distilled water of borage was applied to the eyes to relieve inflammation. Although we are unlikely nowadays to give the root to defend the heart in pestilential fevers; we may still enjoy candying the flowers.

The last herb, **Motherwort** is ruled by Venus, placed by Culpeper under the Sun, and is a cardiac herb which remains in use. He tells us there is none better to "take melancholy vapours from the heart, to strengthen it, and make a merry, cheerful, blithe soul...." What better tea than this for difficult times.

Cultivation details for angelica, bay, biennial clary sage, borage, hyssop, motherwort and pot marigold can be found in Herbwise Naturally. Those for agrimony are in Herbcraft Naturally. Details for poppies and wormwood are in the Cultivation Section.

Main Harvests - Quick Reference

Agrimony -	continue harvesting for dyeing, pot-pourri or wine.
Bergamot -	flowers and leaves in tea and jelly. Dry for pot-pourri and flowercrafts.
Betony -	dry flowers for flowercrafts. Use leaves for leaf printing.
Biennial Clary Sage -	dry for flowercrafts. Press flowers and bracts.
Calendula -	petals for sugar, wine, ointment. Dry to add colour to pot-pourri.
Chamomile -	gather as flowers open. Dry for shampoo, tea, pot-pourri and fragrant pillows for stress.
Chives -	salad herb.
Coreopsis -	flowers for dye. Fresh or dried.
Coriander -	seeds for cookery, liqueurs and pot-pourri.
Clove Pinks -	sugar, candy flowers, syrup, wine, liqueur, conserve.
Dill -	flowers for pickling, dry seeds for seasoning and medicinal use.

Dyer's chamomile -	flowers, fresh or dried for dyeing.
Fennel -	seeds for pickling and seasoning. Dry for culinary and medicinal use. Also flea deterrent for dogs.
Gall nuts -	gather as they fall from oak trees, for making ink and dyeing wool and silk.
Germander -	dry flowering stems for miniature gardens and flowercrafts.
Golden rod -	flowering tops for dye. Flowers for wine.
Hyssop and rock hyssop *(Aristatus)* -	dry flowering stems for stem baskets and flowercrafts. Dry leaves for flavouring and fragrance. Fresh in fruit puddings and liqueur. Press flower spikes.
Lady's mantle -	press flowers and small leaves. Leaf prints. Dry flowering stems for flowercrafts.
Lavender -	dry for posies and pot-pourri. Flowering stems for decorative favours, fans, fringes and mobiles. Vinegar. Addition to tea.
Lemon balm -	last cut to dry or freeze.
Lemon verbena -	leaves for jelly. Dry for tea or fragrances.
Lovage -	seeds for cookery.
Marjoram -	dry for seasoning. Fresh in jelly.
Meadowsweet -	flowers in wine and dye.
Mints -	last harvests of new growth of leaves for tea, jelly or freezing. Dry flowering eau-de-cologne mint, peppermint, pineapplemint, spearmint and buddleia mint for flowercrafts.
Motherwort -	leaf printing.
Mullein -	flowers in oil for medicinal use. Flowering tops for dye.
Nasturtium -	flowers in vinegar.
Oregano -	dry flowers for miniature gardens and flowercrafts. Fresh as dye.
Roses -	harvest continues in July. Combine with clove pinks in liqueur. Add to moist pot-pourri.
Sage (purple or green) -	dry for cookery and medicinal tea.
Sneezewort -	dry flowers as they open for flowercrafts.
Soapwort -	leaves and stems fresh for washing.
Southernwood -	dry for moth sachets and flowercrafts.
St John's wort -	flowers in oil for medicinal use. Fresh tops for dye. Dry for flowercrafts.
Sweet cicely -	leaves for wine, sweetening. Press. Dry for cookery.
Tagetes (lemon and tangerine gem) -	fresh or dried flowers for dye.
Tansy -	flowering tops for dye. Dry flowers for miniature gardens and flowercrafts. Dry leaves for moth sachets.
Thrift -	hang dry flowers as they open for miniature gardens and flowercrafts.

Thyme -	last cuts for seasoning, pot-pourri and sachets. Longer stems dried for stem baskets.
White horehound -	younger leaves in honey or dry for medicinal use. Also in rum honey cough liqueur. Dry flowering tops for miniature gardens and flowercrafts.
Winter savory -	dry when first flowering for seasoning. Dry long stems for stem baskets and flowercrafts.
Wormwood -	dry on stems for use as insect and rodent deterrent.
Yarrow -	dry flowers for medicinal tea, confetti and sachets. Press. Dry flowering stems for flowercrafts.

Preserves

IF you did not have time in May or June to fill your cupboards with all the herb vinegars, honeys, syrups or jellies you would have liked, many of them can still be made. Drying and freezing herbs also continues. Wherever you have gathered herb foliage over past weeks, you will now be rewarded with fresh growth for a second harvest. Heartsease and borage flowers can still be candied alongside the delicious clove pink petals which will be ready through July. Clove pinks are as important in the culinary flower harvest this month, as roses were in June. Only clove scented *Dianthus caryophyllus* should be used.

The spicy seeds should not be forgotten. Lovage, coriander, caraway, angelica, dill, fennel and anise are available to include in pickles and vinegars, or store dried for winter use.

The rose harvest may have had to be taken in quite a short period.The gathering of clove pinks as they open successively on the plants, can stretch over several weeks. All of the recipes can be made simply by processing however many flowers are available on that day. It will not matter if 2 or 3 days of rain interrupt the pattern. Just a few minutes spent picking and grinding them with sugar, or layering petals in sugar or brandy, will be all that is necessary. Always pick the flowers on a dry day, in mid-morning if possible.

Clove Pink Sugar is made in exactly the same way as rose sugar; taking each flower and cutting away the white 'heel' at the base of the petals, before washing them. With pinks several flowers can be sliced through at once. For the herb flower sugar recipe see March-April preserves. This sugar is bright pink and strongly clove flavoured. It is perfect for sweetmaking.

Calendula sugar may have been made earlier. If, however, you needed all your flowers for medicinal recipes in June, you can now harvest flowers for cookery. Take each calendula flower apart, discarding the centres, before making the sugar to the same recipe.

Clove Pink Conserve is a very special treat, bordering almost onto a liqueur. I found the recipe in a book over 200 years old and could not resist trying it. Once tasted, it is sure to become a regular favourite.

Take the flowers and slice away the white 'heels' at the base of the petals. Wash the petals in cold water and pat quite dry between clean teatowels or paper kitchen towel. Layer the scented petals with finely ground white or brown sugar, in a sterilised screwtop jar. Keep on layering petals and sugar until you run out of petals, or come to the neck of the jar. Pour a little red wine over the flowers. If the jar is filled, bring the level of liquor up to the top. I have used my blackcurrant and curled mint wine in this recipe with great success.

The conserve is ready to taste immediately. Add a spoonful or two to fruit salads, trifles and yogurt. Alternatively, pour over ice cream or into a sponge flan base before adding the fruit and glaze. See November-December preserves for a gift idea.

Clove Pink Syrup

GATHER sufficient clove pinks to weigh approx 50-85g (2-3oz). Slice away the white 'heels' as before and set them in a bowl. Pour 600ml (1 pint) boiling water over the petals and leave in the covered bowl overnight. Next morning strain and pour the infusion into a thick bottomed pan. Slowly dissolve in 450g (1lb) of sugar over a low heat. Bring to simmer until a syrupy consistency is reached. Pour into sterilised jars or bottles. Keep in the fridge once opened. Alternatively, freeze in ice cube bags for drinks. The syrup can be diluted as a delicious drink, added to jellies or fruit punch and fruit salad recipes.

If you have only a few clove pink flowers then you may like to:

Crystallise clove pink petals in the same way as the roses, cutting away the white 'heels' to avoid bitterness. They candy well as individual petals to decorate cakes, desserts and chocolates.

Savoury recipes abound in July and into August. The two below may set you experimenting with more herbs. The first is invaluable to flavour or accompany fish.

Fennel Orange and Lemon Jelly

3 cups sugar	100ml (4 fl oz) liquid pectin
Juice of 1 lemon	Pure orange juice
½ cup herb infusion	

Pour 1 cup of boiling water over 4 tablespoons chopped fennel leaf in an enamel pan. Simmer gently for about 10 minutes, until the liquid is reduced by half. Meanwhile put the sugar into a preserving pan and pour the juice of a good sized lemon into a cup. Fill the remainder of the cup with pure orange juice and pour the mixed fruit juices over the sugar. Add the strained herb infusion and set on a low heat.

Prepare 2 jars by sterilising them and keep these warm, while stirring the jelly until the sugar has dissolved. Bring to the boil and stir in the liquid pectin. Boil rapidly for 2 minutes. Skim if necessary. Cool a little before pouring into the warm jars. Seal and label.

Another tasty and useful jelly is made at this time, gathering the winter savory as it comes into flower. This jelly can be added to bean casseroles, meat or fish dishes.

Savory and Grapefruit Jelly
3 cups sugar 100ml (4fl oz) liquid pectin
1 cup grapefruit juice
½ cup herb infusion made with 4 tablespoons chopped winter savory
Make the jelly as for fennel, orange and lemon, above.

Vinegars

PICKLING vinegars have been popular over the centuries. In earlier times they were a very necessary way of preserving vegetables for the winter. The choice was not restricted to mushrooms, onions, beetroot and mixed vegetables as it often is today. Sweet cicely and nasturtium seeds were picked green and having been soaked in brine, drained and dried, were covered in hot, spiced vinegar. These, alexander buds, elder stems and numerous edible flowers, were pickled to add flavour or colour to winter salads. Violets, cowslips, clove pinks, elderflowers, borage and rosebuds were among the most commonly used.

Even the vinegar might be made in a variety of ways. Consulting the **Secrets of Arts and Trades,** published in the 18th century, I found a variety of ingredients used to change wine into vinegar. These ranged from red beet, which could achieve the effect in less than 3 hours, to a drachm of hare's marrow. I'm not sure I would wish to use the resulting vinegar from this, or recipes which added yew wood and 'cyprus'. Roses, toasted acorns, damask raisins and wild pear tree leaves seem tasty by comparison.

White wine or cider vinegar are commonly used in modern recipes. Perhaps the most famous combination in a herb pickle, is one of dill flowers and cucumbers. The cucumbers are first soaked in brine, drained and dried, before the hot, spiced vinegar is poured over them. In Russia, vodka is used instead of vinegar, an interesting variation for a tipsy salad.

Herb seeds which can be pounded and added to flavour pickles are coriander, dill, anise, caraway and cumin. Lovage seeds could also be added for their powerful, spicy flavour.

One of my favourite herb vinegars with a hot flavour can be made in July or August.

Nasturtium Vinegar
The herb has wonderfully decorative flowers in shades of yellow, orange and red. I grow the plain nasturtiums for cookery and use mainly red flowers. These turn a white wine vinegar a lovely deep red. Having almost filled the bottle or jar of vinegar with flowers, I add a couple of torn nasturtium leaves, half a teaspoon of pounded lovage seeds, and/or a slice of red pepper, to give a really spicy vinegar. It is then set on the windowsill for about 10 days before testing. If you require a stronger flavour, strain out the herb, add fresh, and repeat. When ready, strain the vinegar and be sure you have labelled the bottle. Some flowers can be left in, if wished.

Wines and Liqueurs

Golden Rod Wine

The brilliant sprays of yellow flowers seem to call out from the flower bed to be noticed and used. Gather them as soon as they open, cutting sufficient flowers from the main flowerheads to fill a 600ml (1 pint) jug. This measurement is taken, as with the cowslips and primroses, with the flowers loosely dropped into the jug, not packed down.

Ingredients:

600ml (1pint) Golden rod flowers	4.5 litres (8 pints) boiling water
2 large oranges	25g (1 oz) fresh yeast
1.35kg (3lb) white sugar	1 slice toast
2 Campden tablets (optional)	225g (8oz) Muscatel raisins

Put the flowers in the fermenting bucket with the sugar, thinly peeled rind, and juice of the oranges. You may wish to add the crushed Campden tablets before pouring on the boiling water, and stirring to dissolve the sugar. If you are using the tablets add only 2.8 or 3.4 litres (5 or 6 pints) of boiling water. Add the remainder after leaving the wine covered for 24 hours for the Campden tablets to kill the natural yeasts in the flowers. This will bring the wine up to blood heat, ready to float the yeast on toast on the top.

If you are not using the Campden tablets, simply add 4.5 litres (8 pints) boiling water and leave to cool until blood heat is reached. Add the yeast on toast.

Leave the yeast on the wine surface for 24 hours, then remove carefully, stir and add the chopped raisins. Stir night and morning for 8 days, and then strain into a prepared demi-john. Seal with a fermentation lock. Label with content and date. Leave in a warm place (about 21°C, 70°F) until fermentation ceases. Bottle. The wine can then be drunk after 6 months, but will be better if kept for a year.

See Herbcraft Naturally for more details on winemaking and the following summer recipes:-
Redcurrant and Pinepplemint - a light, sparkling rosé (good dessert wine).
Blackcurrant and Curled Mint - a rich red wine with minty after-taste.
Pot Marigold and Peach - rich and fruity with a wonderful golden colour.
Rum Honey Cough Liqueur - a must for the winter medicine cabinet. This liqueur is ready to drink in a fortnight. One small tot at bedtime will ease your cough and help you sleep soundly.

In the Home

Soapwort Cleanser

Soapwort, with its mass of pink flowers in late summer, makes a pretty addition to the herb garden or flowerbed. A patch 1m (3ft) square will give you a plentiful supply for washing wool and silk, and use in shampoo recipes. (see March-April In the home section). The plant is naturally rampant, needing harvest to control the spreading rhizomes in spring or autumn.

From midsummer through July the highest content of saponins may be available, coinciding with the time of harvest for drying. It is also the beginning of the busiest dye season for wool and silk.

Soapwort has been particularly associated with washing raw fleece and was used in past centuries at the fulling mills. It is still relied upon to cleanse and restore natural dye colours and fibres in old tapestries and fabrics. The herb's gentle cleansing action is due to its neutral rather than alkaline suds. This also recommends it for washing silk. Used in early laundries, soapwort produces far fewer suds than a modern cleanser, but this does not restrict its effectiveness.

When drying the herb, it may be cut before, or during flowering. All parts - stems, leaves and flowers are hung - dried in bunches, chopped and stored. The rhizomes are dug, cleaned, chopped, then dried in a warm oven. Store in glass jars for winter use.

Stems and Leaves

To wash 50g (2oz) of wool or silk in readiness for dyeing, gather about ½ cupful of fresh leaves and chopped stem. Soak them in 1.7 litres (3 pints) of warm water for 15 minutes. Give a brisk stir. Strain into a basin with the hot tap running to bring the temperature to the desired heat. Enter wool or silk and wash. The water will have a greenish colour which rinses out of the washed articles.

With dried stems and leaves, one cupful can be steeped in 1.7 litres (3 pints) of water in a large pan over a low heat for 20-30 minutes. Stir briskly and strain into the basin, adding some water as before. This time the water will be yellowish. Again the colouring washes out.

Rhizomes

¼ cupful of fresh or dried rhizomes should be soaked in 1.7 litres (3 pints) warm water for about one hour before straining into the basin as before. Dried rhizomes give even better results if heated gently, as with the dried leaves and stems. In general the rhizomes give more suds. Use as before.

When cleaning needlepoint pictures, stools and items which cannot be thoroughly rinsed, I prefer to steep the rhizomes to prepare the cleanser. Use a sponge to draw up the sudsy water, and dab gently over the area to be cleaned. Follow this with a second sponging of clear water. Dry, still stretched to shape, in a warm atmosphere. Do not put in full sun.

Verbascum Oil

Simple to make, verbascum oil is beneficial when applied to dry eczema. One or two drops in the ear can also relieve earache due to a mild infection or inflammation. Naturally, if the earache persists, or is severe, a Doctor or medical herbalist should be consulted. The verbascum, better known as mullein, comes into flower over a period of weeks. The individual flowers open a few at a time on the tall spire of buds. The bright yellow flowers are picked as soon as the dew has dried, and not later than mid-morning, when they are in perfect condition. Hot sun will quickly affect them. Put the flowers (insect free) straight into a glass bottle of pharmaceutical quality olive oil. (Available in glass bottles from some chemists).

If a very small quantity of oil (about 2 teaspoonsful) is poured out of the bottle first, then you will be able to keep pushing flowers into the oil until the bottle appears to be full of them. Push as many as possible beneath the surface of the oil, using either a clean cocktail stick or part of one of the mullein leaves.

Seal the bottle and set it on the windowsill in the sunshine. Over a period of days the flowers will turn dark brown, until the oil itself appears to be very dark in colour. Depending on the weather, this may take 2-3 days, or 2-3 weeks. When the dark colouring is even at all levels, strain out the flowers and pollen by pouring the oil through a very fine muslin, or coffee filter paper.

Wash the bottle thoroughly and sterilise it with boiling water. Leave to dry and refill with the oil.

Hypericum Oil is made from the flowers of perforate St John's wort in the same way. If the flowers are examined closely you can see tiny red dots at their edges which mark the presence of the oil glands. Set perfect flowers in olive oil in a glass bottle on the window sill. In this case the oil will steadily turn a deep, blood red, as the heat of the sun draws out the hypericum.

Once the colour is obtained, which may be in 3 days, or 3 weeks, as before; filter the oil, returning it to the sterilised bottle. Hypericum will act as a preservative to the oil and so this medicinal oil keeps indefinitely. It is best stored in a cool dark place however. Always label the bottle. Use Hypericum oil externally only on minor burns and scalds after they have been cooled, to assist healing and reduce scarring. Also on deep bruising and all nerve injuries and inflammation such as shingles, (after the initial treatment from a qualified practitioner).

Craft

Golden Rod Dye

I have always considered July-August to be the most important time of year for dyeing. The bright sun quickly dries dyed wool and is an excellent first test for light fastness. There is always such a profusion of dyes ready for harvest in these months that I have plenty to dry for future use. The choice offers almost every colour;

Flowers	Roots	Flowering tops	Leaves
calendula	meadowsweet	agrimony	angelica
coreopsis		burdock	comfrey
dahlia		dyer's broom	fennel
dyer's chamomile		golden rod	gypsywort
elecampane		oregano	horseradish
St John's wort		ragwort	purple sage
sunflower		tansy	weld
tagetes (lemon and tangerine gem)			yarrow

Recipes for coreopsis, dahlia, dyer's chamomile and tagetes (calendula flowers are best mixed with tangerine gem), are to be found in Herbcraft Naturally. Also those for meadowsweet root, oregano, tansy, angelica, comfrey, gypsywort, purple sage and weld. Agrimony was detailed on page 72 in May-June. Amongst the other dyes listed, my best results have come from the sources below.

Over the years I have found that gathering golden rod flowers for dyeing is best done when they are fresh and newly opened. If the harvest is left until the flowers have been enjoyed in the garden for several days first, the results do not seem to be as strong.

Dye Recipe:
Gather 100g (4oz) of flowerheads - about 15cm (6ins) stem also included to dye 50g (2oz) of wool and add these to 3.4 litres (6 pints) of water in the dyepan. Simmer for 1 hour and strain out the flowers.

Alum Mordant
Prepare the wool and mordant as on page 26. Enter the wool for 45 minutes at just simmering for a clear, fairly strong yellow from the dyebath.

Iron
¼ teaspoon may be added for the last 15 minutes in the dyebath, as with the bramble-tip recipe, for shades of green.

Chrome Mordant
A number of August and September flower harvests such as golden rod, dahlia, tagetes and *coreopsis tinctoria* will give deeper, brighter colours with a chrome mordant. Chrome is particularly toxic and not all dyers wish to use it, however steps can be taken to reduce the burden on the environment and ensure personal safety.

I have discussed methods of disposing of chrome mordant at some length with other dyers. Pouring the mordant liquor into garden soil is definitely not recommended, as a future owner of the house may grow vegetables there with no knowledge of the toxic residue in the soil. If it is poured down an outside drain it may be flushed away and diluted with plenty of water, but will eventually cause pollution somewhere. It can be treated chemically, but so long as you have a safe place to keep a toxic substance, it is probably best to re-use the mordant liquor.

When the wool has been removed, allow the mordant to go cold and take it outside to pour from the pan into bottles. Use a funnel which should be kept just for this purpose. Label carefully as toxic mordant and keep well away from children. When you wish to dye with a chrome mordant, re-use the liquor, adding more chrome and a little extra water.

To mordant wool successfully with chrome, it should first be washed and soaked as in the previous dye recipes. Prepare the mordant by adding a generous ¼ teaspoon to the 3.4 litres (6 pints) of water in the dyepan. Stir the orange powder in with a glass rod or stick which you can burn later. The mordant must be kept away from the light when in storage and use. It is also a sensible precaution to wear rubber gloves and keep the room well ventilated. Some people like to wear protective glasses - sunglasses will do, just in case of splashes. Entering and removing the wool carefully, and pouring the liquor with care, should avoid accidents. Do not re-use the measuring spoon to stir your tea.

The lid should be placed on the dyepan while the liquor is brought to hand-hot, and only removed briefly to enter the soaked wool at this point. If you have a bright light over your hob, turn this off while you have the lid off the dyepan. Keep the wool just simmering for about 50 minutes, stirring it round and making sure it is fully immersed at intervals.

The wool is then entered into the dye liquor at a hand-hot temperature, having squeezed the mordant gently into the pan. Cover the wool once again while in the dye liquor. Heat for about one hour, then leave to stand overnight. A strong colour can be obtained with silk also, by adding warm, alum mordanted fabric when the dyepan has been removed from the heat. Leave this in the dye for several days. Wool mordanted with chrome and dyed with golden rod can become a wonderful, rich, ginger-brown.

Dyer's broom

A dye which has been used extensively. The flowering tops of this herb give a brilliant vibrant yellow. It was also once overdyed with woad to obtain "Kendal green". For the yellow, I simmered 100g (4oz) of herb for 1 hour to dye 50g (2oz) of wool pre-mordanted with chrome. The wool was also heated for 1 hour in the dyebath. Silk pre-mordanted with alum gave an equally vivid result.

Ragwort

Double the quantity of flowering tops to wool are simmered for 1 hour. A deep mustard-gold is achieved with a chrome mordant.

Yarrow

For this dye I picked the flowering tops with more leaf and stem included than flowers. These, when simmered for about an hour, produced a liquor which looked encouragingly dark when strained. I used twice the quantity of herb to wool. Having mordanted the wool with copper sulphate, I was disappointed with the pale result after simmering for 50 minutes. Adding ¼ teaspoon of iron for the last 15 minutes gave a rather lovely, soft greenish grey after steeping overnight.

St John's wort and **Elecampane** flowers both produce pretty yellows with alum or chrome as a mordant. I have tried for years to gain the red from the perforate St John's wort, but still without success. **Horseradish** leaves give a pretty yellow on silk mordanted with alum, (soaked for 2 days), but I have not found them worthwhile in dyeing wool. **Burdock** tops and leaves gathered immediately after flowering also offer a better result with silk. A good ginger was obtained after soaking for 2 days. With a copper sulphate mordant on wool, it needed iron to give a good mid-green, similar to that from comfrey. Both bronze and green **Fennel** result in pale green on copper sulphate mordanted wool. A light tan is the rather disappointing result with alum.

Clove pinks

(Right) *Clove pink conserve*

(Below) *Agrimony*

July - August

(Top) *Lavender Fringe*

(Left) *starting star mobile*

(Below left) *"rays" to mobile*

Completed leaf mat

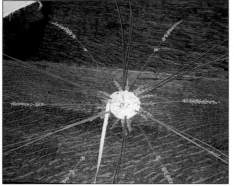

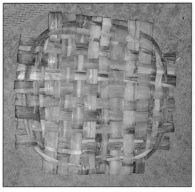

View from serenity

(Below) *Alpha in the serenity*

July - August

Knot in summer

Flowers and Foliage to press

THE bountiful harvest continues, but in August we are reminded the summer will not last for ever. It can be a lovely project to make special envelopes to contain seeds you will later gather for friends. It shows special thought if you not only write a little information on each herb's needs and harvest on the envelopes, but add the pressed flower or leaf of the herb. A selection of these can make the most attractive Christmas or birthday presents.

The flowers or young leaves available during these two months are particularly useful for decorating seed packets.

betony
biennial clary sage
borage
dyer's broom
elder leaf (variegated)
fennel
gingermint
golden hop
golden rod
heartsease
herb Robert
honeysuckle
hyssop
jasmine

lady's bedstraw
lady's mantle
mallow and marshmallow
meadowsweet
motherwort
mugwort
oregano
pinks
salad burnet
self-heal
St John's wort
sweet cicely
viper's bugloss
winter savory
yarrow

Lavender Mobiles

LAVENDER cut straight from the bushes can be used in many imaginative ways. In Herbcraft Naturally I explored using traditional corn dolly patterns, producing a beautiful Welsh fan design to display the decorative flowerheads. The small project of lavender favours offered the option of weaving the finished item.

The fringe and star designs below are intended to be hung as mobiles, although the fringe could be fixed to a mirror. Many people have chosen to do this with the Welsh fan, to brilliant effect. As a mobile hanging in a flow of warm air, the lavender will also fragrance the room. Both mobiles are simple and need no previous experience with weaving them.

Lavender Fringe

You will need; fine crochet thread, lavender stems in any multiple of 3.
The size of the fringe can be extended, according to the length of lavender stems available. Dark flowered lavenders tend to be most effective, but these often have shorter stems. The longest can be 1m (3ft), whereas the Munstead I have used, will only offer stems of 17.5-25.5cm (7-10ins).

1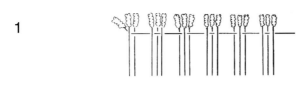

2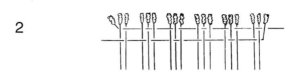

3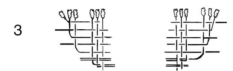

The fringe illustrated is 17.5cm (7ins) at its widest point. For this, I cut 18 stems of lavender and tied them in bunches of 3: with the ties just below the flowerheads. The lavender must be worked immediately, before the stems dry out.

To Begin

Lay the bunches of lavender approximately 2.8cm (1¼in) apart on a table or flat surface. Take the outer stem on the left and weave it under and over all the other stems in turn, until it reaches the other edge. Leave the end sticking out just beyond the last stem, (see diagram 1). Kink the outer stem on the right gently, a little way down, and take it carefully under the next stem and continue in the same way back across. This stem should be about 1.3cm (½in) below the first stem woven. Leave the end sticking out just beyond the outer stem as before, (see diagram 2). Continue, alternating the next outer stem at either side.

When you reach the stems from the second bunches, you may need to start laying every second stem alongside the last to be woven, (see diagram 3). Otherwise the last stems to be worked will not be long enough. The 2 central stems are left straight and tied together to make a hanging rod or handle.

The fringe could be decorated by slotting long, tubular beads over the bunches of 3 stems, to cover the ties below the flowerheads.

Star Mobile

YOU will need; 2m (2⅓ yards) of silk ribbon. 7cm (¼in) wide, crochet thread, needle and cotton. At least 18 lavender flowerheads with long stems, preferably with dark flowers. At least 6 shorter stems of flowering lavender.

To Begin

Choose 18 lavender stems with dark flowerheads of about the same size. Lay them on a table in groups of three. If there are some slightly longer flowerheads, set these in the centre of each group or bunch. Tie the bunches together just below the flowerheads.

You now have 6 bunches of 3 stems each. Lay 2 bunches with one on top of the other and the flowerheads pointing in opposite directions. Twist the stems of the second bunch slightly, to lay them beneath the other flowerheads, (see diagram a). Next, lay 2 more bunches at right angles to these: again with 3 flowerheads pointing in one direction and 3 in the other.

Using the stems, pull the flowerheads close together to form a cross. Tie just below the flowers, to hold them in position. You now have 4 groups of 3 flowerheads with the stems of the flowers opposite pointing straight outwards, beneath them (diagram b). Think of the flowerheads as at 12 o'clock, 3 o'clock, 6 o'clock and 9 o'clock.

Lay the next set of 3 stems beneath the other stems, with the heads filling the gap between 9 o'clock and 12 o'clock. Lay the last set of 3 stems beneath the others, with the heads filling the gap between 3 o'clock and 6 o'clock. Adjust the stems so that the flowerheads are equally spaced in a circle; with small gaps between each set of 3. Tie again, (diagram c).

Take the length of ribbon and fold one end tightly around any group of 3 stems, behind the flowerheads, and stitch in place. Next, take the ribbon under and over the following groups of 3 stems in order. Keep the ribbon behind and beneath the flowerheads. On the next round, go in front of the next group of flowerheads, behind 3 bare stems, in front of the next group of flowerheads, behind the stems and so on, (diagram d).

After this round, weave the ribbon around the stems only. Keep it behind the flowerheads. At every other round you will need to pass the ribbon under or over 2 groups of stems, to cope with the even number of stem bundles.

During the 3rd round, insert an extra shorter stem of lavender with a long, possibly lighter coloured, flowerhead. This will stand out as a 'ray' from the central star, between 2 groups of flowerheads, (see diagram e). Adjust the length of the stem, cutting it shorter if necessary.

The 'ray' may reach out for several inches beyond the central star of flowerheads, or end with the lower pair of flowers, in line with outer edge of the central star.

Stitch the end of the stem into the ribbon at the centre back, and cut the thread. Remember to protect the flowerheads by laying them on a soft pad whenever you need to lay the star down as you work.

Continue weaving, adding a second stem in the same way, opposite to this one. Add the 3rd and 4th stems in the next round, and then the 5th and 6th. Weave on until you are satisfied with the appearance of your mobile. There should be a minimum of 8 rounds. Stitch the end of the ribbon neatly, having cut it to length.

The groups of 3 stems may be left long, or cut shorter, as you please. Hang from a loop of thread or ribbon stitched to the ribbon back.

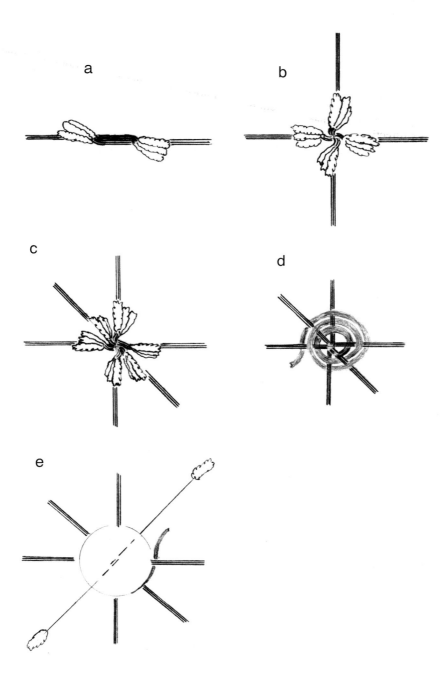

a

b

c

d

e

94

Leaf Mats

RUSHWORK is one of the oldest crafts. Where most people no longer have ready access to rushes, daffodils and irises are a common feature in many gardens. Working the beautiful shades of these dried leaves into mats and baskets has always appealed to me. Quick and simple, the pattern below may encourage you to try more complex projects.

The leaves are gathered and dried after the plant has flowered. Do not wait until the leaves have deteriorated before pulling or cutting them and laying to dry in a warm atmosphere. In good weather this is best done outside on a rack. Cover the leaves with a layer of netting or muslin to stop them from blowing away as they dry. This will also keep them from curling up and becoming damaged.

When they are completely dry and crisp to touch, store them in a flat box. Add a sachet of silica gel crystals, if you have one, to maintain a dry atmosphere,.

Preparing to work

Set the dried leaves to soak in a bucket or bath of cold water. Leave for 3-4 hours. Pour away the water and lay the leaves on a damp towel. Set another towel on your working surface.

Choose 16 strong leaves of a good length and colour. If some are much wider than others, alternate these as you use them. Very wide ones might be folded. Wipe them clean and lay 8 side by side on the towel. Alternate narrow and wide ends of leaves at top and bottom.

Centre weave

Lay one hand across the leaves, about one third of the way down their length. With the other, lift the 2nd, 4th, 6th and 8th leaves, folding them back over your first hand. Lay a fresh strong leaf over the leaves laid down, so that it is centred across them. Bring the other leaves back down.

Now raise the 1st, 3rd, 5th and 7th leaves. Fold them back against the edge of the leaf you have just laid across the others. Lay a second horizontal leaf over those still laid down, (see diagram 1).

Repeat until you have laid 8 leaves to form a checkerboard pattern. If some leaves are different shades to others, try to lay these to best advantage in the design.

Edge weave

With the centre weave complete, choose the strongest, long, thin leaves as weavers. Set one behind any leaf at the edge, tucking the end down into the weaving, (see diagram 2). Bring this weaver in front of the next leaf and behind the one following. Continue in front of one, behind one, around until you are almost back to the start. If you run out of weaver before that, tuck another leaf into the weaving and weave the two together for a little to give added strength. Leave all ends beneath the mat. Shape the corners as you pass the weaver from one side to another.

When you reach the edge leaf before your starter, push another long weaver into the weaving and take this behind and in front of the edge leaves, working round as in the diagram. This is called pairing. After one row, cut all the edge leaves to the length of the shortest one. Work 3 or more rows in this fashion until your shortest edge leaves are only 58cm (2-3ins) long. Tuck the end of the last weaver into the weaving.

Border

Turn the mat over and fold each edge leaf in half, bringing the end over the last row of pairing and tucking it in to an earlier row. If you have only worked 3 rows, every other edge leaf can be threaded behind a square of the checkerboard pattern.

Allow the mat to dry first on the towel and then hung in a warm, dry atmosphere.

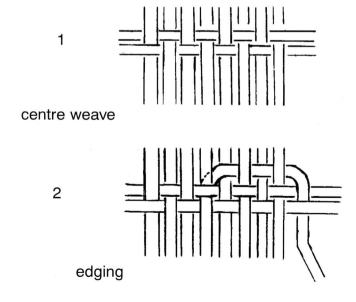

1

centre weave

2

edging

September - October

Plump fruits darken, rich and luscious,
nature's larders stocked for winter.
Birds rejoice in berries, seeds;
leaving feathers on the teazles
grasped as payment for their fill.
Misty mornings, dew-soaked grass.
Jewelled webs hang from the fennel,
kissed by sunbeams into life.
Yellows, mellowed, earth's rich beauty
feeds itself - death brings no loss.
Frost seems first to deepen glory.
Golden trees tinged red as fire.
Seedheads white-topped,
outlines softened, by sharp ice.
Cold and heat yet tilt the balance.
Frost-touched nights and sunlit days -
drawing from us deep thanksgiving.
Now we yield imagined power
to the source of all we gather.
Sacred is our paradise.

In the Garden

IN recent years these have been truly golden months when the weather has been glorious. We have enjoyed summer temperatures even in October. The red admiral has basked on brambles and herbs, and the swallows have remained a week or so longer. Then the season of mists and mellow fruitfulness has fully lived up to its name.

Harvest continues at the centre of gardening tasks in September, while 'putting the garden to bed' for the winter, follows naturally. Amid the richness, there is always a sense of working against the clock as the nights grow colder. The chance of a single frost at the end of September remains, and must be prepared for.

Hedges

The shorter hedges of germander, winter savory, santolina, box, hyssop and thymes should all have been clipped during the last month. If the weather remains warm however, and there is some rain, they may produce several inches of growth in September. If this happens, it is better to clip them again when the forecast is good for several days. Do not leave unwieldy growth which will be a real problem in spring.

Rosemary, lavender and sages should also receive attention. If the rosemary has grown considerably since the spring harvest, cut it back by one third at the beginning of September. Cut late flowering lavenders back to the previous year's growth as the flowers open. Take any cuttings of all hedging herbs at the beginning of September. These can be established in pots before the cold weather, and spend the winter in a cold frame or greenhouse. Plant out in the spring. Harvest sage and either dig out old bushes now, setting cutting in their place, or earth up the old bushes next spring to produce rooted cuttings 'in situ'.

Trim back curry plant. Set cuttings of this and winter savory where next year's pea and bean rows are to be. Add a mulch rich with chopped comfrey to retain moisture around them and feed the soil.

Sowing

Seeds of perennials, or biennials such as foxglove, biennial clary sage and mullein, can be sown now rather than in spring. Those which need frost to germinate - cowslips and sweet cicely, for instance, are better sown in autumn. Angelicas will have sown themselves. Dyer's bistort is unlikely to ripen seeds before the cold weather. This can be potted up and taken indoors to flower and produce seeds in readiness for spring. If you wish to harvest caraway next year, then sow it now. Garlic cloves may be set in the earth about 5cm (2ins) down with the pointed ends upwards ready for next year.

Cutting Back

As you go about the garden harvesting seeds, (see table at the end of this section) and/or seedheads, cut down those dead stems which will be unsightly. Stems of nettle, sunflower, mallows and hollyhock can all be laid under a shady hedge to rot for papermaking, or spinning the fibres. Also cut dying leaves which will become a soggy mess in autumn rain. These include elecampane and angelica. Harvest comfrey back to the ground, chop the leaves and stems and add to the compost. Spread this thickly over the beds. Pile compost or well rotted manure around roses, and heap extra compost around and over mints, Greek valerian, angelica, mugwort and bay. An extra covering of compost should also be given to angelica, elecampane, bergamot, marshmallow, sweet cicely, lovage and soapwort, after you have completed root harvest or division of these.

Leave some seedheads and stems, both for the benefit of wildlife, and for interest and beauty in the frosted winter garden. The birds' particular appreciation of teazle seedheads can be seen from the feathers left behind as they struggle to escape the plant's spiny grip. Finches and tits love yarrow and evening primrose seeds. They will be a joy to watch perching precariously on the stems, leaning over to eat the seeds, while swaying dangerously. Seeds of lemon balm and fennel are also enjoyed, along with many berries, hips and haws.

This upper protection of stems and dead materials also provides windbreaks and shelter for the fresh growth of plants in warmer winter periods, and for helpful insects such as ladybirds.

Preparing for Frost

It will save worry if the less hardy herbs are potted up with compost as early as mid-September. Scented geraniums, lemon verbena, small bays, pineapple and tangerine sages, and less hardy variegated or prostrate rosemary and lavenders, are all in this category. You can then set them in their pots into the ground and leave them in the beds until frost threatens. At this point it is easy to lift them and move into a greenhouse, or take indoors. While the scented geraniums and lavender thrive well in the house, rosemary will often die in January or February, and the sages and lemon verbena can also suffer.

Putting the pots out of doors in a sheltered position on good days will help them through the winter, especially if they receive rain rather than tap water. If your garden is reasonably sheltered, you may be able to leave all but the scented geraniums outside. I have been successful in keeping tricolor sage healthy, set in the serenity knot with a double thickness of net curtain over the surrounding area. Pinks in exposed conditions will appreciate such cover during hard frosts too.

Root Division and Harvest

The harvests of lovage, sweet cicely, marshmallow, elecampane, soapwort and meadowsweet, will ensure these herbs are regularly controlled. If you are growing madder for dyeing, the roots are harvested after 3 years. They grow best, producing more alizarin pigment, if the soil is composted well and lime added. Give extra compost every year. Bergamot needs to be dug up every other year and the new root growth around the edges broken away from the dead centre and re-planted. Cover all these with a thick layer of compost afterwards.

Other spreading herbs such as tansy, mints, lemon balm, comfrey and yarrow may be divided at this time, or left until spring. Golden rod, periwinkle and Russian tarragon can quickly take over a whole bed if left to themselves.

With the roots divided, seeds gathered and beds tidied, any weeds should be removed. Some wild strawberries and young forget-me-not plants may usefully be left to act as ground cover, until annuals can be planted out next spring. As you remove wild strawberries, you may wish to collect the longest runners and wrap these in wet towelling to keep them supple for basketry. Retiring to a shady corner of the garden immediately after a session of weeding, you can make a charming miniature basket in a short time. See Herbcraft Naturally.

Paths
These should be weeded at the same time and bark paths topped up with an extra layer as necessary.

Pruning Shrubs and Trees
Honeysuckle, dogwood, brambles, hazel, balsam poplar and elders, can all be pruned in October. The thinner stems may be used immediately for basketry, or prepared by 'fading' under a hedge for several weeks. See basketry section in Herbcraft Naturally. Generally, thin stems are pliable when first cut, although all except honeysuckle will still need to be soaked first.

The golden hop in my garden provides an annual basketry harvest. The plant should be cut right down to ground level in October, for its own benefit. I cut it as I need more stems, during weaving. It is a joyous experience to sit in the garden weaving in the warm autumn sunshine. Meanwhile the delicious perfume from the white flowers of the ***Rosa moschata*** wafts from the covered way. This old rose can flower on into November until the hard frosts.

Thicker stakes have been taken from the hazel tree in some years to use as supports for the roses. They give strength with a natural beauty.

Every harvest should, in itself, be a preparation for the following year. If carried out in a spirit of thanksgiving and respect for all life in the vicinity, it cannot fail to improve the quality of the garden.

Seeds to Gather

agrimony	echinacea	milk thistle
alecost	elecampane	motherwort
anise hyssop	evening primrose	mullein
aquilegia	fennel	nasturtium
basil	French parsley	oregano
betony	golden rod	salad burnet
biennial clary sage	greater knapweed	salad rocket
borage	gypsywort	sea holly
calendula	hyssop	soapwort
chamomile	lady's bedstraw	St John's wort
clove pinks	lady's mantle	sunflower
coreopsis tinctoria	marjoram	sweet cicely
cowslip	marshmallow	tagetes
curry plant	meadow clary	toadflax
dyer's chamomile	meadowsweet	vervain

The Astrology Garden

IN **Virgo,** August 21st - September 21st, we reach the end of the row of beds facing onto the lawn. The sign bears a particular relationship with the stomach and intestines. The dominant planet, Mercury, rules over a number of digestive herbs. Those I have chosen for this bed have generally shared a use against all manner of poisons, and tend to be hot and dry. It is a bed given almost entirely to foliage, and so I have also aimed to make the contrasts of leaves and heights as imaginative as possible.

The tallest is **Fennel,** attractive with its fern-like leaves, fennel provides autumn interest with umbelliferous seedheads. Culpeper makes the fascinating observation that because it is a herb of Mercury, and ruled by Virgo, it bears an antipathy to Pisces. He relates this as the reason it is cooked with fish, since it "consumes that phlegmatic humour, which fish ...... annoy the body with".

Fennel, as is well known, is good for wind and stomach ache from other causes, for hiccough and increasing a mother's milk. Culpeper also recommends it for treating those who have eaten poisonous herbs or mushrooms. Still grown in most herb gardens, it remains a herb regularly harvested for cookery and home remedies.

Winter and Summer savory are described by Culpeper as constant inhabitants in gardens, and both are so useful as culinary herbs, that they are returning to this level of appreciation. Mercury governs them, the summer being described as the best, "sharp and quick in taste, expelling wind in the stomach and bowels ..... provokes urine ....." and so on. Directing readers to dry the herb and make conserves and syrups of it, "if you love yourself and your ease." Culpeper gives savory high praise.

Savory jelly can be found in the recipes for July-August, and is one of my annual favourites. With culinary needs supplied, I also harvest it for stem baskets. The purple flowered savory is especially attractive when fresh or dried. Both perennial savory plants are suitable as edgings. Summer savory is a little taller and more delicate.

A larger herb, with strongly scented growth, **Southernwood** graces the bed. In truth, I chose it for the attractive bushy growth of fluffy foliage which it renews each year. It makes a perfect eye-catching bush beside the central path of the garden. Although Culpeper describes it as "a gallant mercurial plant, worthy of more esteem than it hath": he also reports that both ancient and modern writers regard it "to be more offensive to the stomach than wormwood."

To be fair, a herb given to kill worms in children's intestines probably has to be so. It does have several useful qualities which still interest garden visitors today. One of these is used in an ancient recipe when the ashes of the herb were mingled with old salad oil to apply as a cure for baldness. The bruised herb was also applied to draw out thorns and splinters. My own use is mainly in mixing the dried herb with others in moth sachets.

In the shade of the southernwood I grow **Parsley,** another mercurial herb which Culpeper writes "is very comfortable to the stomach." It has a similar nature to savory in expelling wind, provoking urine and opening the body. He also recommends it against the venom of poisonous creatures. No herb garden can be complete without parsley. In very early times being at the beginning of something, was referred to as 'being at the parsley and rue', for it was such a common habit to start a herb garden with edgings of these two herbs.

In my herb garden we now follow the path around the edge of the astrology to find Libra, which is planted 'back to back' with Virgo.

Libra, the sign of the scales and balance, is from September 21st - October 21st. In this sign as in Taurus, the dominant planet is Venus. Libra rules the kidneys, lumbar region and the skin. We find Culpeper giving the most interesting details of a herb under this sign for **Kidneywort,** *(Umbilicus Rupestris).* He writes, that this herb, also known as wall pennyroyal or wall pennywort, is challenged by Venus. He recommends the juice or distilled water applied outwardly, to treat pimples and St Anthony's fire. Taken internally, the juice or water "helps to heal sore kidneys, torn or fretted by the stone, . . . provokes urine, is available for the dropsy, and helps to break the stone."

He tells us this small herb with spikes of whitish green flowers in May, grows very plentifully in the West country on stone walls and rocks.

Pennyroyal is a herb under Venus and both the lesser, creeping plant and the taller pennyroyal come into this category. Culpeper tells us that "applied in a plaster, it takes away spots or marks in the face; applied with salt , it profits those that are splenetic, or livergrown." Since it was also for dropsy, we may presume an effect on the kidneys. Pennyroyal can be used as a minty deterrent against ants and fleas. Its pungent aroma is refreshing and welcome in the summer garden.

Yarrow is listed by Culpeper as a herb of Dame Venus. He tells us, it being so, "it stops the terms in women, being boiled in white wine." A herb then used to treat venereal disease, yarrow also "helps such as cannot hold their water." The virtues of the herb as a poultice or ointment for wounds and ulcers are still appreciated, as they have been for thousands of years. Yarrow may well be the best herb in this role. I have certainly had cause to be grateful for its extraordinary speed in removing sepsis and promoting healing. Yarrow tea remains in use and I include the herb in confetti and bridal posies. The wild herb which is often found in grassland will grow tall in a garden bed and may have a mass of tiny white or pink flowers.

Violets find a place here, as they do in Taurus. Culpeper writes they are effectual for pleurisy, "and the hoarseness of the throat, the heat also and sharpness of the urine and all the pains of the back or reins, and bladder." In Libra they add a third low growing herb, but are also a spring-time delight which makes them a very worthwhile addition.

Another spreading herb which seems determined to include itself in Libra whether I wish it or not, is the **Wild Strawberry**. Culpeper gives good reason for its presence, writing, "The leaves and roots boiled in wine and water, and drank, ... assuage all inflammations in the reins and bladder, provoke urine, and allay the heat and sharpness thereof."

These plants happily fill my herb bed for Libra as all have spreading natures. Kidneywort will be more at home amongst stones. I have used large flints from about the garden to mark the divisions between the beds, so making a better habitat for it. Should you wish to add taller herbs, mugwort and sea holly are both suitable. I have rejected mugwort as it can spread as rampantly as tansy.

Sea holly placed by Culpeper as Eringo, still grows wild on the Norfolk sands and the Welsh coast. It can be bought in some nurseries but can be difficult to raise from seed. Culpeper set it "under the celestial Balance", and recommended a decoction of the root for obstructions of the spleen and liver, as well as "dropsy, pains of the loins and wind cholic, provokes urine, and expels the stone, procures women's courses." A candied conserve of the root became a popular aphrodisiac at one time. The main modern use rests with arranging the spiky, but beautiful seedheads, which look brilliant sprayed gold at Christmas.

The cultivation details of fennel, savory, southernwood, parsley, pennyroyal, yarrow, violets and wild strawberry can all be found in Herbwise Naturally. Those of sea holly are included in Herbcraft Naturally. The details of kidneywort can be found in the Cultivation Section.

So ends our tour of Virgo and Libra and we move on to harvesting.

Main Harvests - Quick Reference

Angelica -	last leaves to dye wool or to make syrup. Harvest root for liqueur or to dry as a fixative for pot-pourri and fragrant beads.
Avens -	flowers for pressing.
Blackberry -	preserves and cordial, wine or dye from berries. Freeze. Bramble stems for basketry.
Borage -	last flowers freeze in ice cubes.
Calendula -	flowers for drying, more oil and ointment. Calendula sugar or marigold wine.
Comfrey -	last young leaves for ointment. Also dyeing. Mix chopped leaf with compost.
Dahlia -	red and bronze flowers for dyeing.
Dogwood -	prune for basketry.
Dyer's bistort -	cut back for dyeing.
Dyer's chamomile -	dry last flowers for dyeing.
Eau-de-cologne mint -	last harvest of new growth for drying. Use in rose based fragrant mixtures and bath sachets - see Herbwise Naturally.
Elderberries -	preserves and syrup. Wine and port. Dye for paper and fabrics. Ink. Can freeze or dry berries.
Elecampane -	seedheads for flowercrafts and Christmas decorations. Root to candy for cough sweets and preserves. Cough syrup. Dry as fixative for pot-pourri and fragrant beads. Possible dye as yet unsuccessful.
Fennel -	seeds for cookery, medicinal use and against fleas on dogs.
Geranium -	fresh leaves of rose and lemon-scented geraniums for jelly, syrup and leaf printing. Dried for pot-pourri and sachets.

Golden rod -	last flowers for wine, dye or to press. Seedheads and flowers dried for flowercrafts and Christmas decorations.
Greater Knapweed -	dry seedheads for flowercrafts.
Guelder rose -	berries for tart tasting jelly, or as an ingredient for ink.
Hawthorn -	berries in wine or medicinal tincture. Dry for pot-pourri decoration.
Hazel -	young growth for basketry.
Hollyhock -	dark flowers for dyeing wool or silk. Light pink single flowers for cough syrup. Set stems to ret for paper-making or spinning fibres.
Hop -	flowers in beer making, for hop pillows or with the leaves as a dye. Stems after the flowers have been gathered, for basketry. They have also been used in papermaking and for cloth but are laborious to prepare. Leaf print. Dry for harvest arrangements.
Horehound -	last chance to harvest fresh leaves for honey and rum cough liqueur. Dry leaves. Dry seedcases for flowercrafts.
Iris -	dry leaves for 'rushwork'.
Lavender -	late flowering stems for fans or to dry.
Lemon verbena -	fresh leaves for tea or furniture polish. Dry leaves for tea, fragrant sachets and pot-pourri.
Lovage -	dry root as fixative for pot-pourri, and fragrant beads.
Marshmallow -	candy root for confections or cough sweets. Dry leaves for use in cosmetic recipes or tea blends.
Meadowsweet -	root as dye.
Orris -	harvest root, cut in chunks and dry, keep for one year before grinding as a fixative for fragrant blends.
Peppermint -	dry or freeze new growth.
Pineapplemint -	last cut to dry.
Pineapple sage -	jelly from leaves. Dry leaves and flowers for pot-pourri.
Pokeweed -	harvest berries for dyeing.
Balsam poplar -	young branches for basketry.
Rose hip -	hips for preserves, syrup and wine. Dry for pot-pourri and tea. Freeze.
Rosemary -	jelly, vinegar or dry.
Sage -	dry green sage for cookery. Spanish sage for flowercrafts.
Sloe -	preserves and wine. Liqueur.
Snowberry -	berries for dyeing. Young growth for basketry.
Soapwort -	dry root for winter use.
Sunflower -	seeds dry for cookery. Ret stems for papermaking or spinning fibres.
Sweet cicely -	dry root as fixative for pot-pourri. Candy root and make syrup. Wine with damsons.
Tansy -	dry flowerheads for flowercrafts or dyeing. Use fresh as a dye. Dry leaves for moth sachets.
Teazle -	dry seedheads for flowercrafts or to deter pests.

Walnut -	as nuts are gathered, save husks for dyeing. Leaves and twigs also useful for lighter shades.
Wild strawberry -	runners for miniature baskets. Leaf prints.
Winter savory -	last cut for drying for cookery, or flowercrafts.
Wormwood -	dry to repel pests.

Preserves

THIS is a wonderfully rich harvest time with fruits, berries, hips, seeds and roots. Many autumn recipes are included in Herbcraft Naturally. The elderberry syrup is a personal favourite as it can be made up into a drink with hot water, thickened as a sauce, or taken by the spoonful to soothe a sore throat.

Another syrup, once a daily supplement for almost all babies and toddlers, is rose hip. This tastes delicious and is high in vitamin C. The following method seems to originate in instructions given by the Ministry of Food in wartime. It appears again and again in recipe books, with only slight variations.

Rose Hip Syrup

900g (2lb) ripe rose hips   water
550g (1¼lb) sugar

Gather the rose hips from your garden, or a hedgerow well away from traffic fumes. The hips from the wild rose, *Rosa canina* or those of the sweetbriar, *Rosa rubiginosa* - are the best. Their vitamin C content will be highest after a frost. If you wish to gather hips before the frost comes, put them in the freezer overnight before preparing them.

Put 1.7 litres (3 pints) of water in a large pan on the stove to heat. Bring to the boil. Wash the hips, discarding any imperfect ones. Chop by hand, or in a blender, and drop them straight into the pan of boiling water. Return the pan to the heat and bring back to the boil. Set it aside to cool for 10-15 minutes.

Pour through a fine straining bag into a jug. Hang the bag up to drip for a few minutes or squeeze gently if not too hot. Return the pulp to the pan and add 900ml (1½ pints) of water. Bring to the boil and remove from the heat. Leave to stand for 10 minutes. Strain, putting the first cupful back to drip through a second time.

Combine the two liquids in a pan and simmer until the quantity is reduced to 900ml (1½ pints). Add the sugar and dissolve this in over a gentle heat. Bring to the boil and boil for 5 minutes. Have ready 6 or 8 small, dark glass screwtop bottles. These should either have been pre-sterilised, or they will need to be simmered in a bath of water for 30 minutes after filling. In either case, the bottles should be warm as the syrup is poured in while still hot. Seal and label. Refrigerate once opened.

In addition to autumn fruit jellies, sweet herb flavours are also available. As the lemon-scented and rose geraniums and pineapple sages are potted up to put under protection, these are cut back. This harvest can make jellies to be used for cake fillings, desserts and to top scones, with cream. The recipe for lemon geranium jelly can be found in the January-February preserve section.

Pineapple Sage Jelly

3 cups sugar

½ cup herb infusion

1 cup pineapple juice

100ml (4fl oz) liquid pectin

Pour 1 cup of boiling water over 4 tablespoons of washed and chopped, pineapple sage leaves, in an enamel pan. Simmer till the liquid is reduced by half. While this is simmering, put the sugar and pineapple juice into a preserving pan and prepare 2 or 3 jars by sterilising with boiling water. Add the strained herb infusion to the sugar and fruit juice and heat gently, stirring to dissolve in the sugar. Turn up the heat bringing the jelly to the boil. Remove from the heat and add the liquid pectin and stir well. Boil for 2 minutes. Remove from the heat, skim if necessary. Stand to cool for a few minutes. Pour into the warmed jars. Seal and label. If liked, one leaf of pineapple sage can be added as the jelly is poured into each jar.

Chutneys

THE following recipe was first made when my friend Barbara was visiting and we invented it together. The tomato chutney is Barbara's own and a great favourite.

Barbara's Elderberry Chutney

900g (2lb) elderberries

900g (2lb) cooking apples, peeled, cores and chopped

225g (8oz) sultanas

100g (4oz) chopped dates

2 teaspoons salt

1 teaspoon mustard seeds

9 whole cloves

1 sprig tansy

1 sprig hyssop (optional)

225g (8oz) Barbados sugar

225g (8oz) onions, chopped

425ml (¾ pint) vinegar

12 peppercorns

2 sprigs rosemary

Stalk and wash the berries and place in a large mixing bowl. Add the apples, onions and dates. Pour over the vinegar and sprinkle with the salt. Mix in the dark sugar and sultanas. Leave all to steep for one hour.

Place the pounded rosemary, peppercorns, mustard seed and cloves in a small square of muslin, tie and add. Chop the tansy and hyssop finely and stir into the mixture. Pour into a large preserving pan and bring to the boil. Simmer gently over a low heat until the chutney thickens and there is no excess of liquid, approximately 2-2½ hours. Leave to cool for a few minutes. Remove the muslin bag of spices. Spoon into sterilised jars while still hot and seal with screwtop lids lined with greaseproof paper. Store one month before serving.

Makes 2-2.25 kg (4½ -5lb)

Copthorne Green Tomato Chutney
1.35kg (3lb) green tomatoes, skinned and roughly chopped
325g (¾lb) onions, peeled and chopped
275g (10oz) cooking apples, peeled, cored and chopped
170g (6oz) sultanas   1 teaspoon salt
325g (12oz) Demerara sugar   425ml (¾ pint) vinegar
½ teaspoon ground ginger   ½ teaspoon ground cinnamon
large pinch ground cloves
1 generous sprig of each herb. 6-8 leaves of sage, lemon balm and applemint. A
15cm (6ins) sprig of rosemary (finely chopped, discard rosemary stem)

Put all the ingredients together in a large preserving pan and bring to the boil.
Simmer until the liquid is reduced and the chutney takes on the consistency of jam.
Cook gently towards the end, turning the heat down and stirring frequently to
ensure it does not stick to the pan. Cool for a few minutes. Spoon into sterilised jars
while still hot. Seal with screwtop lids lined with greaseproof paper. Store for 3
weeks before serving.   **Makes 2-2.25 kg (4½ -5 lb)**

ROOTS are also harvested at this time and the recipe for candying sweet cicely
and elecampane roots is given in the January-February preserves section.
Sweet cicely and angelica syrups can be found in Herbcraft Naturally. Another
sweet root which can be harvested is the marshmallow. The first marshmallow
confections were made as cough syrup and sweets. The root was sometimes mixed
with fine sugar, gum tragacanth and orange flower water. It has its own individual
flavour which is fairly sweet and quite unlike anything else.

Dig 2nd or 3rd year roots and scrape the white pith from the very hard centre
which may be discarded. For herbal treatments, decoctions are always made from
the plant in cold water. Roots are also cooked as a food. Mallow roots are not the
same as marshmallow and should not be used. Rose water is now available from
some supermarkets.

Marshmallow treats
85g (3oz) cleaned, pared root   125ml (5fl oz) water
1 dessertspoon glucose   2 teaspoons gum arabic
25g (1oz) caster sugar   85g (3oz) icing sugar
5 dessertspoons dessicated coconut, 1 teaspoon rosewater **OR**
6 dessertspoons ground almond, 1 teaspoon clove pink conserve

Marshmallow root grows as many finger width roots from the main crown. Clean
the root, cutting away the thicker lengths for use. (If some fine root is left with the
crown it can be replanted.)

Take the best roots and peel very finely or scrape. This exposes the white pith
beneath the yellow skin. Pare this into the scalepan, discarding any very hard
centre. When you have sufficient, (a 2nd or 3rd year root should give enough for
this recipe) chop the root into a pan and cover with water. Stir in 25g (1oz) of sugar
over a low heat. Simmer until the root is soft and liquid has been reduced.

The gel which exudes from the root when it is in contact with water will have produced a thickening effect. When you have obtained a smooth soft paste remove the pan from the heat. Pass through a sieve. Pour into a blender with the gum arabic powder, glucose and icing sugar. Blend.

Return to a bowl and stir in 6 dessertspoons of ground almond with 1 teaspoon clove pink conserve. Alternatively flavour with 1 teaspoon of rosewater and add approximately 5 dessertspoons of dessicated coconut.

Line a tin either with ground almond or coconut and spoon in. Refrigerate. Cut into squares an hour or so later. Serve in petit-four paper cases.

Herb Teas

THIS is the time of year to be building up your health to resist coughs and colds. Thyme tea, drunk at breakfast is both antibacterial and refreshing. It is especially tasty if you make it from the lemon thyme which you dried earlier in the year, when flowering. Tea from fresh thyme is also pleasant, but dried thyme without flowers is not as good. One heaped teaspoon of dried thyme per cup will make an enjoyable tea.

Rose hip is another autumn tea which is both popular and health supportive. Rose hips can also be mixed (chopped) with an equal portion of elderberries and spiced with cloves or flakes of cinnamon or ginger. Dried hibiscus flowers can be added.

Put the mix into fine, double muslin bags or strain it through coffee filter paper to remove the irritant hairs of the rose hips. It may be sweetened with honey.

An effective hot drink can also be made by pouring boiling water on a tablespoon of elderberry syrup or elderberry jelly. This is especially soothing if you have a sore throat. (Recipes in Herbcraft Naturally.)

For a sore throat gargle with sage tea, make with one top of purple or green sage (6 leaves) to each 2 cups of boiling water. Do not take sage or rosemary when pregnant.

Wines and Liqueurs

MOST herb wines are white. Autumn fruits offer a special treat in providing rich red wines for the table, on cold winter evenings in the following year. The recipes for angelica liqueur and sloe gin are with my mother's rich and glorious 'Pump Cottage' elderberry port, and the lighter damson and sweet cicely wine in Herbcraft Naturally. The blackberry recipe below is different again as it contains some honey and spices and in a good year the haw wine can taste extraordinarily close to a sherry.

Haw Wine

1.35kg (3lb) haws	4.5 litres (8 pints) water
1.35kg (3lb) sugar	12g (½oz) fresh ginger root
rind of 1 lemon	25g (1oz) fresh yeast
rind of 1 orange	1 slice toast
2 Campden tablets	

Rinse the haws in a colander, removing any damaged or unripe fruits before putting them into a large preserving pan. Add 2.8 litres (5 pints) of water. Bring to the boil and simmer well for 20 minutes. Strain and discard the haws. Add the sugar, citrus rinds and chopped fresh ginger. Re-heat slowly to dissolve the sugar, stirring constantly. Bring to the boil, then cool a little before pouring into the fermenting bucket which should already contain 2 crushed Campden tablets. Although I usually regard these as an optional extra, previous experience without them has proved haw yeasts can become totally out of control when left to themselves. Wine which pushes its way out of the demijohn and overflows in all directions can be inconvenient to say the least.

Stir in the Campden tablet powder and leave the fermenting bucket covered for 24 hours. Then stir again and make the liquid up to 4.5 litres (8 pints) with boiling water. When at bloodheat, float the fresh yeast spread on toast on the surface for a further 24 hours. During this time the fermenting bucket should be kept at a warm temperature about 21°C (70°F). Carefully remove the slice of toast, squeezing the wine out of it and stir well. Stir night and morning for 7 days. Syphon into a sterilised demi-john, filling it to the point where the neck narrows and seal with a bored bung and fermentation lock. Bottle when the wine has stopped working.

Spiced Blackberry Wine

1.8kg (4lb) blackberries	1.15kg (2½lb) sugar
2 sticks cinnamon	325g (12oz) honey
25g (1oz) fresh yeast	1 slice toast
4.5 litres (8 pints) water	

Pick the blackberries on a sunny, dry day and leave them to stand overnight in a large bowl. Next morning put one tablespoon of water in the bottom of a large preserving pan. Add the fruit slowly, looking through the berries and discarding any which are imperfect. Heat gently in the pan until the juice runs from the fruit. Strain though a fine mesh straining bag. This should give about 1.2 litres (2 pints) of blackberry juice.

Put the sugar into a fermenting bucket and spoon on the honey. Pour the blackberry juice over. Flake in 2 sticks of cinnamon, breaking them into small pieces. Make the liquid up to 4.5 litres (8 pints) with boiling water. Stir well to dissolve the sugar while adding the water.

When it has cooled to bloodheat, add the fresh yeast spread on a slice of toast and leave covered, in a warm place at about 21°C (70°F) for 24 hours. Remove the toast, squeezing it against the side of the bucket. Stir night and morning for 6 days before straining and pouring into a sterilised demi-john and sealing with a bung and fermentation lock. Bottle when it has finished working. This has, perhaps the most beautiful colour of all the red wines and tastes delicious even before it goes into the demi-john.

In the Home

A S you bring out the winter woollies once again, this is a good point to use some of your dried herbs in refilling old moth sachets for the wardrobe. Here are two recipes, one with a sweet accent and the other with more of a masculine aroma. They each contain several herbs and essential oils which moths will find really unpleasant, while hopefully remaining acceptable to all who wear the protected clothes. Both blends will fill a couple of small sachets for drawers or a larger one to hang in a wardrobe. If something is especially valued you might like to hang a small sachet of the mix from the same hanger.

Sweet Moth-repellent

1 cup lavender	3 drops essential oil of rosemary
½ cup cotton lavender	2 drops essential oil of lavender
½ cup southernwood	or essential oil of patchouli
½ tablespoon ground orris root	1 teaspoon freshly ground clove

If you have a patchouli as a houseplant a few dried leaves can also be added to the mix.

Power Moth-repellent

1 cup tansy leaves	1 teaspoon freshly ground clove
½ cup wormwood	3 drops essential oil of eucalyptus
½ cup southernwood	2 drops essential oil of sandalwood
½ tablespoon ground orris root	

If you have had an ongoing battle with moths, either of these can be made even more potent by the addition of ½ cup of dried pyrethrum heads (*chrysanthemum cinerariifolium*) which contain insecticidal pyrethrums. This is not a highly dangerous sachet mixture but should be hung out of small childrens reach.

Sweet Lemon Furniture Polish

225g (8oz) beeswax	1 cup chopped lemon balm leaves
3 cups turpentine	1 cup chopped sweet cicely leaves
40g (1½oz) soapflakes	1 tablespoon sweet cicely seeds
1½ cups cold water	(can be used when green or brownish black)
4 drops essential oil of marjoram	4 x 15cm (6ins) sprigs lemon verbena
4 drops essential oil of melissa	2 tops sweet gale (optional)

With a sweet, lemon-fresh perfume, this polish will keep antique furniture in good heart. The marjoram oil helps to reduce the risk of woodworm, although furniture should still be treated against this. Use just a little and polish to a gleaming shine. It may take more effort to apply than a spray polish but will only need to be applied once in three weeks.

When making the polish, wear rubber gloves and ensure the stove area is well ventilated. The turpentine should be brought up to room temperature if you have been storing it in a shed. Do not place it on a heater to warm as it is highly inflammable.

To Begin

An ovenproof pyrex bowl may be used over a very gentle heat to melt the beeswax. If you find it difficult to control your hot plate at the lowest temperature, use a bowl set over a pan of boiling water. Beeswax can be bought in small blocks. If you have bought a larger block from a beekeeper, this may be cut into smaller chunks using a very hot knife.

Add the chopped sweet cicely, lemon balm, lemon verbena, (sweet gale or bog myrtle tops if used), and pounded or ground sweet cicely seeds to the cold water in a non-metal pan, (a glass pan is easier to clean). Bring slowly to simmer and simmer for 10 minutes. Strain out the herbs and add the soapflakes, stirring well until they are dissolved.

Remove the melted beeswax from the heat and stir in the warm turpentine. This should be dribbled carefully down, close to the side of the dish. Stir well with a glass rod or clean stick as you mix the two. If the turpentine is too cold, then the beeswax will set again.

Allow the beeswax and turpentine blend and the soap solution to cool to bloodheat, then slowly add the soap solution to the beeswax, stirring well. The consistency of the finished polish depends on the amount of soap added. To make a fairly hard block of polish you will not need all the soap solution. Add more or less for a polish or a cream. Practice will be your best guide, but remember you can always re-heat gently to add more - I have never tried adding more beeswax at the end but it may be possible. Lastly, stir in the essential oils and pour the polish into tins or shallow, wide-necked screwtop jars. Label.

Craft

Pokeberry Dye

AS September ends and October begins, the harvest of berries is well under way. I love the autumn with its glorious abundance of fruits, seeds and mellow roots. Sometimes so many are ready at one time that it is difficult to know which must be gathered on a particular day, and which can safely be left awhile.

It would certainly be difficult to overlook the pokeweed amongst other herbs, as the plants stand tall and majestic with long flame-red leaves in autumn. The berries look almost as if they are on small corn cobs as they are packed together along a central spine. When ripe, they resemble glistening, blackcurrant sweets. Attractive to children, they are a real danger, as a small child can only eat a few berries before showing symptoms of poisoning.

Serious cases of poisoning have generally come from using the root in a herbal home medicine for rheumatism, and taking too large a dose. The plant and dye liquor should be treated carefully however. The usual rules of wearing rubber gloves, keeping dye equipment separate from spoons and pans for cookery, and keeping the room well ventilated, should be applied with double caution.

To Prepare the Dye

Approx. 16 sprays berries, 1 cup white wine vinegar, 2 teaspoons citric acid to 50g (2oz) of wool.

Pick about 16 clusters of ripe berries and soak these in rainwater overnight. The next day make the quantity of water up to 2.8 litres (5 pints) and simmer them in a stainless steel dyepan for almost an hour. Allow the dye liquor to cool before straining the berries into a muslin straining bag.

Stir 1 cup of white wine vinegar and 2 teaspoons of citric acid into the dye liquor and add the sealed bag of berries before entering the wool which has been soaked and pre-mordanted with alum.

For instructions on preparing the wool and alum mordant see page 26. The wool and berries should be stirred and turned several times during the 50 minutes they are simmered in the dye liquor.

Leave to cool and steep overnight before rinsing and setting to dry.

Result: A vibrant pink/ginger.

On the first occasion I achieved this amazing shade, I dripped a little of the red dye liquor into a bowl as I rinsed the spoon. To remove the stain immediately, I squirted washing up liquid onto it and watched the liquor turn blue. In my excitement at the possibility of such an easy blue dye, I removed my brilliantly dyed wool from the dyepan and added 2 tablespoons of washing soda. Returning half of the wool, I set the pan back on the stove for a few minutes. Alas, I was left not with blue wool, but a rather wishy-washy yellow.

With Silk

Pokeberry dye liquor prepared as above gives a beautiful, deep, bronzed flesh-tone with silk pre-mordanted with alum (see page 26). It is a deeper colour than madder or henna and very attractive.

Walnut

The husks which are removed as walnuts are gathered, are a wonderful dye source. Anyone with a walnut tree will be glad of your help in removing the husks. They leave such a strong stain on unprotected hands. Do wear rubber gloves. 450g (1lb) of husks will dye 50g (2oz) of wool a deep, deep brown. Fresh husks are much stronger as a dye than dried. Soak them in 2.8 litres (5 pints) of rainwater for 24-36 hours, then pour the husks and water into your dyepan. Simmer them over a low heat for 2 hours. Cool the liquor and strain out the husks.

The wool need only be washed thoroughly and soaked in water for 2 hours before dyeing. No mordant is needed. Enter the wool at a hand-hot temperature and simmer for about 30 minutes. This has produced a really deep brown. A second batch of wool can be dyed on the next day; after the first wool has been removed, rinsed and set to drip dry. The second batch will be a shade or two paler.

With Silk

Deep browns are also obtained on alum mordanted silk. If you only have access to dried walnut husks from a dye supplier, 90g (3½oz) will dye sufficient silk for a scarf and a skein of silk thread. Soak the husks in 3.4 litres (5 pints) of water for

Virgo bed

(Top right) *Yarrow in Libra*

(Right) *Milk thistle brightens Sagittarius*

(Below) *Tarragon in Scorpio*

September - October

Pokeweed

(Above) *Ripe pokeberries*

(Below) *Dyer's bistort*

(Below) *Snowberries and guelder*

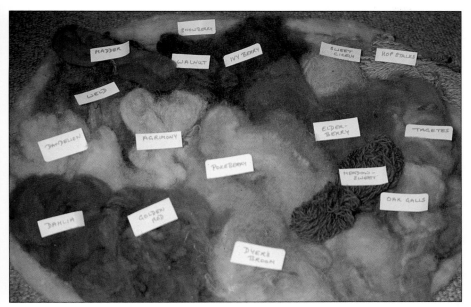

Dyed wood samples

(Below) *Dyed silks and leaf prints*

September - October

Rosehips over chamomile

(Below) *Basket in progress*

5 hours. Simmer for 1 hour and strain out the walnut. Enter the mordanted silk at just above hand hot temperature and leave steeping over a very low heat for 20 minutes. Turn off the heat and leave in the dye liquor for 2-4 days when the silk should have reached a very pleasant brown.

Other autumn dyes come mostly from fruits. Of these, the most useful is **Snowberry.** The berries are soaked overnight first, following the general rule with berries of 8 times the weight of wool. The recipe is found in Herbcraft Naturally and gives wonderfully vivid yellows through to khaki shades.

Elderberry
Also detailed in Herbcraft Naturally, elderberry gives exciting shades from pink to blue with afterbaths of vinegar or salt. The dye tends to fade on exposure to light with wool, however. Silk and paper both seem to hold the colour much better. Use 450g (1lb) of berries to dye a silk scarf. Soak for 3-4 days for a very regal purple.

Blackberry
Again a large quantity of berries is used. Both with blackberries and **sloes**, I have found the results rather pale and quick to fade.

Hop Stalks
Either the offcuts from basketry or longer lengths of stalks can be chopped up and boiled for 1 hour to give a deep, burgundy liquor. This needs no mordant to produce a pink dye. For full recipe see Herbcraft Naturally.

Meadowsweet Root
Also included in Herbcraft Naturally, the pre-soaked root with alum mordanted wool, gave grey-black. Since then a friend has obtained a good pink. To do this, she simmered the root in the original soaking water for 2 hours. The wool, which was unmordanted, was entered and simmered for 1 hour.

Hollyhock
The dark red flowers are best, but others may be tried. You will need about 20-30 flowers to dye 50g (2oz) of wool, or a silk scarf and some silk thread. Simmer the flowers in a stainless steel pan for about 30 minutes. By this time the liquor will have taken the red colouring from the flowers and may have a greenish tinge. Discard the rather sticky, soggy flowers when the liquor has cooled to hand-hot.

With Wool
Pre-mordant with alum as on page 26, enter and simmer for 30-40 minutes. After steeping the wool overnight in the cold dye, I was rewarded with a pretty, pale green. With wool pre-mordanted with chrome as on page 89 entered in the hand-hot dye liquor and simmered for 1 hour; a khaki shade was produced after soaking overnight. It should be noted that the flowers in this recipe had been quite severely frosted.

With Silk

The dye liquor was prepared as above. I then entered silk pre-mordanted with alum and cream of tartar as on page 26. It was steeped for 20 minutes over a very low heat and then soaked for 4 days. This gave a really strong mid-green. Another dyebath with alum mordant and a heavier silk, soaked for 2 days, gave a much paler shade.

Other greens can still be obtained from comfrey, angelica, and sages as you are harvesting.

Flowers and Foliage to press

THESE often seem to be the most precious flowers for pressing, since the very first to appear in spring. As September passes, there is a growing awareness that each day may be the last before a sudden frost takes them. With luck however, you are still able to gather many of these into October.

Flowers	**Foliage**
biennial clary sage	jasmine
borage	salad burnet
catmint	scented geraniums
golden rod	sweet cicely
heartsease	tansy
hyssop	wormwood
mullein	
pansies	
wild wallflower	
winter savory	

Autumn Harvest Ball

AN alternative to a larger dried flower and seedhead arrangement, this compact ball can be made to celebrate a safe harvest. The ball illustrated has been planned with 2 panels of seedheads pre-sprayed with gold. This is balanced at first by the 2 panels of natural materials. In December these are quickly removed to add red helichrysum and spices for a Christmas decoration.

You will need:

1½m (59ins) narrow ribbon, approx 0.25cm (⅛in) wide
a dry oasis ball, diameter 11.5-13cm (4½-5ins)
seedheads chosen from: betony, love-in-a-mist, elecampane, greater knapweed, poppies, *eryngium planum*
4 large seedheads chosen from: milk thistle, Jerusalem sage, safflower, hen and chickens poppy
pins

To Begin

Fold the ribbon in half to find the centre. Find the centre 'top' of the ball and lay the centre of the ribbon on this spot. Anchor it with a pin pushed straight into the ball. Take the 2 ends of the ribbon around the ball to the centre 'bottom'. Cross the ends of the ribbon and twist, as if wrapping a parcel. Anchor as before with a pin.

Take the ribbons back to your starting point, so dividing the ball into quarters. Remove your first pin while holding the ribbon taut, and lay the 2 ribbon ends across the first band of ribbon. Secure again with the pin through all 3. Put a couple of stitches in to be sure the pin won't work loose in time. You now have 2 free ends of ribbon to hang your ball and the rest neatly dividing it into quarters.

The Design

You may like to repeat one really attractive pattern on all sides, have 2 designs which are repeated on opposite sides, or make 4 entirely different patterns. Your decision must, of course, be based on how many of which seedheads are available.

If you have a lot of smaller seedheads and are restricted on variety, then you may choose to set these in rows of alternating forms. Triangles or diamond shapes can also be made within the segments. Trial designs can be set into the oasis and removed several times if necessary. With a few larger, dramatic seedheads, it can be effective to centre these, placing small seedheads around them.

It is helpful to draw a mid-line around the oasis ball before you start. This will be a valuable guide for all designs. Some may require another line drawn down the centre of each segment.

When planning your design, remember you will need to be able to hold the ball, pressing from both sides as you push the stems in. Make sure you have placed sturdy poppy heads, or open headed herbs such as elecampane, at the top and/or bottom of each segment. Pressing on love-in-a-mist and other delicate seedcases can have disastrous results.

The 4 segments on the ball illustrated are detailed below, with a rough guide to the numbers of each seedhead required.

Side 1 - Gold
Centre head - safflower
surrounded by -
love-in-a-mist - 9
betony - approx 33
elecampane - 6

Side 2 - Natural
Centre head - Jerusalem sage
surrounded by -
love-in-a-mist - 7
blue eryngium planum - approx 33
greater knapweed - 6

Side 3 - Gold
Centre head - hen and chickens poppy
surrounded by -
large single poppy heads - 8
smaller poppy heads - 7
small elecampane - 13

Side 4 - Natural
Centre head - milk thistle
surrounded by -
large seedheads of love-in-a-mist - 10
buff eryngium planum - approx 43
greater knapweed - 13

(a few evening primrose cases were used to fill tiny spaces)

Note: the smaller relative of sea holly, *eryngium planum* has seedheads which will dry blue if there are still some flowers left when picked. When fully ripe with seed, they will dry as a buff colour. I have used the blue heads on side 2 and buff on side 4.

Autumn Basket

HEDGEROW basketry is a seasonal craft. Most of the raw materials can only be gathered between the sap descending in autumn, and rising again in spring. The cool, damp mornings prepare the golden hop and honeysuckle beautifully. They can be cut and woven straight from the plants. Working on into sunny afternoons with the glorious autumn colours at your fingertips, is wonderfully satisfying.

The main instructions for basketry and several more projects, including the miniature baskets of strawberry runners, are given in Herbcraft Naturally. However, this basket sets out to explore new horizons in design. The finished basket might usefully hold balls of wool as you are knitting from them. It is well shaped to contain a bottle of wine, or would readily convert to a doll's cradle. Simpler yet, use it when gathering the last cut of herb flowers. The hood serves as an excellent handle.

When choosing materials, I have combined the best of the autumn colours with supple stems. Honeysuckle can be substituted for the golden hop, but will give a heavier basket without the wonderful shades of orange. Thornless bramble is a possible substitute for balsam poplar. When cutting the dogwood and balsam poplar stakes, take the longest supple branches with few side shoots. Avoid those more than 1.5cm (½in) in diameter with balsam poplar. Dogwood should have a steady tapering width. Cut away thick stem which is not supple.

Materials for the basket illustrated;
8 stakes of balsam poplar, approx. 1.37m (54ins) long
24 finer stakes of red dogwood, approx 76cm (30ins) long
stems from a mature hop or honeysuckle

To Begin
If the balsam poplar is worked immediately after cutting, it may not need to be pre-soaked. Should you decide to do so, please note resin in the branches can stain the container. Set the dogwood stakes to soak in cold water.

Find a shady spot in the garden and push the thickest ends of the balsam poplar branches firmly about 5cm (2ins) into the ground. Set them 2.5cm (1in) apart. (A patch of grass gives a firmer grip than newly dug flower bed.) Cut several lengths of golden hop, both close to the ground and as high up as you can reach.

Unwind them from their support as necessary, and remove their leaves. Lay all but one stem in the shade beside you. Kink the first stem a little way from one end, so that you can loop it around the edge stake. This will now be known as the weaver.

Take the short end of the weaver, behind one stake and in front of one, for the three stakes next to one edge. Bring the long end around the edge stake and weave it back across the row. Take it behind one, in front of one, turning at the edges. This is known as randing. (See diagram 1.)

Joining

Bring the old weaver out to the front, leaving a short end to overlay the next stake. Push the end of the new weaver down into the weaving on the left hand side of this stake, and bring it over the old end to continue weaving. (This cannot be done with firmer weavers). Join at the edges where you can, slotting both old and new weaver ends down into the side loops.

Continue weaving until the base of the basket is 28cm (11ins) long. Remove the thick stakes from the ground.

Begin shaping the end of the basket by bringing the long stakes of balsam poplar back over the base in a gentle curve. Pass a length of thick string around the base and stakes, holding them in place. See illustration. Continue weaving for another 8cm (3ins) to begin the end curve of the basket.

Foot-trac

Push half of the pre-soaked dogwood stakes, thicker ends downwards, into one side of the woven base. They should be set between the rows, just inside the first edge stake. Begin about 2.5cm (1in) in from the end of the weaving, and set them 2.5cm (1in) apart. Push each stake down until some 13cm (5¼ins) is showing below the base.

Work the foot-trac, beginning at the curved end of the basket base, with the basket held upside down. Take each stake behind 1, in front of 2, behind 1, and out towards you. (See diagram 2.) Press each one firmly against the base as you weave to give a firm base edge. When you reach the front edge continue the weave, taking the dogwood stakes behind and in front of the balsam poplar ends.

With one side completed, repeat the foot-trac for the other side with the remainder of the dogwood stakes. At the front edge, work across the balsam poplar as before. Trim ends beneath the basket with secateurs.

Sides

To give the basket strength, 2 rows of upsetting are worked. This is done using 3 weavers. Take the longest weaver and loop this around the first dogwood stake at the front of the basket. Set the 2nd weaver in to the right of stake 2. You now effectively have 3 weavers. Take the first weaver in front of 2 stakes and behind 1. (See diagram 3.) Repeat with each weaver in turn. Work around the basket, including the balsam poplar stakes at the curved end, pushing the weavers down tightly as you go.

Weave until the last 4 stakes at the front edge of the basket. Take the 1st weaver in front of 2, (the second of these is the 3rd stake from the end). Bring it round behind this stake and out. Take the second weaver in front of 2, turning behind the 2nd stake from the end, and out. Take the 3rd weaver in front of 2, turning around the edge stake and back out. You now have 3 weavers behind consecutive stakes. Continue the weave back along, turning at the other edge again. (See diagram 4.)

When you reach the last dogwood stake at the front of the basket, bring the first 2 weavers round this and back along, keeping the continuity of the weave. The third weaver passes behind the edge stake and out, so that you have 2 loops around it. (See diagram 5.)

At the end of the 2nd row, cut the ends of the 1st and 2nd weavers, pushing these down into the weaving. Continue randing with the 3rd weaver, (behind 1, in front 1) for 7 rows, looping around the edge stake at either front. On the 8th row, loop back around the 7th stake from the front. Work 7 rows, missing out the front 6 stakes at either side.

On the next row miss the front 7 stakes, looping the weaver around the 8th and returning. In this way two 'steps' are made in the weaving at either side. As you work, keep shaping the curved end of the basket. The balsam poplar stakes will need to be pushed into a curve and the weaving worked very firmly around the end. You could use a bag of stones or other material set inside the end of the basket to maintain the inner shape. Alternatively work standing, with the basket set on a bench or chair and position your knee inside the basket. This is the most effective way, but is not to be recommended for long periods. Pull the balsam poplar stakes firmly over and down as you work each row at that end. 14 more rows are worked. Where weavers are joined in, overlap the ends slightly behind a stake so that they are left inside the basket.

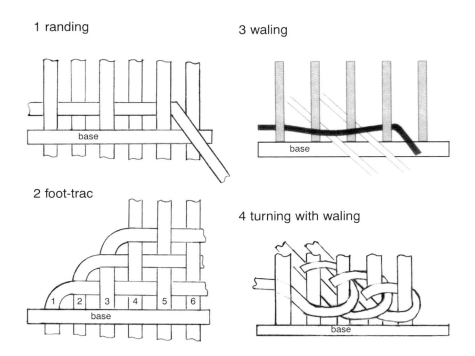

1 randing

3 waling

2 foot-trac

4 turning with waling

With the 'hood' formed, untie the string, and weave in the side stakes. Starting with the edge stake at the front, take the first 4 stakes at each side behind 1, in front of 2, behind 1, and out to the side. Push these down for a firm edge. The last of these will emerge from behind the first stake at the higher level.

Work next from the back of the basket. Take the end dogwood stake, (next to the balsam poplar), under 1, over 1, up over the curve of the hood and down. Leave the end on the inside of the basket. Now work the end dogwood stake on the other side of the basket back across in the same way. Pull the balsam poplar into position as you work. Keep weaving the stakes back and forth over the hood until you have woven 5 at either side.

You now have 3 dogwood stakes left standing at each side. Plait each set of 3 stakes until you reach the height of the first balsam poplar stake. At each side, include the balsam poplar in the plait by placing the left weaver behind it and continue plaiting. The next balsam stake is included by the next weaver, and so on. Take in 4 stakes with each plait, then secure the dogwood ends by threading them under and over into the opposite plait. Trim ends.

Finish by bringing the thin ends of balsam poplar in smooth rounded curves, 4 to either side of the basket. If long enough, the 2 at either side can be brought through the base of the plait, up and behind the first dogwood stake at the highest level of weaving. The centre stakes are threaded back through the plait and into the hood weaving. Leave generous curves in the shaping and do not force them. Wrap a wet cloth round them for a few hours if in difficulty. Then re-try. Trim ends.

November - December

The damp air hangs low
in the valley.
A sepia landscape, drained
of colour. No birdsong.
The robin sits hunched,
feathers fluffed, waiting for the sun.
Pale, it slowly lifts the veil,
life stirs and is comforted.
'Neath cold winter's icy blanket
nature slumbers, seeds and goodness
sealed, protected. Roots and berries
hold it fast.
Evergreens yet rich and glossy,
symbols of a new beginning;
near the solstice, hang in splendour.
Deck the houses, deck the churches.
Holly, ivy, round the fireplace.
Mistletoe and bay o'er doors.
Rosemary to line the manger,
welcome Christ in hearts re-born.

In the Garden

I always aim to have finished 'putting the garden to bed', by the second week in November. By this time all frost-shy plants should have been moved into shelter, or given a good covering of compost and dried stems. The compost heap will have been reduced as the beds are mulched, taking well rotted matter from the bottom. It will also have been raised again from the top, with the debris of autumn, dead annuals, leaves and some cut and chopped stems.

With all fencing, pergolas and other structures checked, painted with a preservative if necessary, and secured against high winds; I retreat to the fireside. There will still be brilliant sunny days to walk in the garden, appreciating the beauty of frost on the herb hedges and seedheads, or watching the birds. Harvesting will be restricted to gathering evergreens for Christmas decorations. Gardening, as such, is suspended, until spring draws me outside again.

This is not to say the garden is bare at this time. The evergreens-box, bay, sages, rosemary, holly, ivy, juniper, salad burnet and germander, retain their beauty alongside the giant green-grey leaved Jerusalem sage, silver santolina, curry plant and lavenders.

The winter pansies flower stoically on into the bad weather. The climbing rose on my covered way, *Rosa moschat*a has also flowered well into November in some years.

The Astrology Garden

AFTER the Balance of Libra before October 21st, we find the contrast of the scorpion sign. **Scorpio,** October 21st to November 21st, has, as you might expect from such a strong symbol, Mars as the dominant planet.The hot, spiky Martial herbs are here, as in Aries. This time they are mainly concerned with treating the sexual organs, pelvis and circulation.

Looking in Culpeper, we find **Basil** has a particular connection with scorpions. At least, he records the case of a friend of a French physician, who - "by common smelling to it, had a scorpion bred in his brain." Whether this story was entirely believed or not, basil was the subject of a storm of controversy at that time. Partly because it had been noticed that basil does not thrive if it is planted next to rue. Since rue was a well known antidote to poisons, this put the herb under suspicion.

Basil holds a place near the edge of the Scorpio bed as a medicinal herb. It was taken both to speed the birth and to give all-important aid in delivering the afterbirth easily. The plant makes a pretty edging, and is even more attractive when intermixed with a modern hybrid, such as opal basil. The purple leaves amongst green sweet basil, or green ruffles, are a lovely combination. There are many decorative basils to choose from.

Since basil graces the bed for such a short season, I grow another low edging herb in **Chives.** Culpeper includes them in his herbal as an afterthought, confessing he had been reminded of their existence by a reader. He seems to have considerable distrust for the hurtful vapours they might send to the brain, but recommends them for releasing stoppage of urine. He rates them as "hot and dry to the fourth degree", and so places the herb under Mars. Their green leaves, shooting up through the earth are one of the first, welcome signs of spring.

I decided to include one herb of Venus under this sign. It makes a cool oasis of green leaves amongst the hot herbs. With the female menopausal symptoms in mind, I chose **Lady's mantle**. Its soft, delicate nature is best known in *Alchemilla mollis,* grown for flower arrangements. The medicinal herb is a smaller version, the wild *Alchemilla vulgaris*, which has a black root. I have seen Alchemilla growing wild in upper Teesdale. *Alchemilla alpina* is also valued medicinally.

Culpeper writes that taking the distilled water of the herb helps conception and it was also used "to retain the birth". He makes a claim that it can reduce the size of large breasts. The herb remains in medicinal use with herbalists, helping women through the menopause. To the best of my knowledge there are no complaints of any unexpected side effects to the patient's figure.

Our last Martial herb in Scorpio is **Tarragon.** Such a dominant herb, it has little trouble in filling the remainder of the bed. The Russian tarragon, is of course, far worse in this respect than the French. As Culpeper remarks, "The plant is under the dominion of Mars, and therefore it would be a wonder if it should want some obnoxious quality or other,". With tarragon he recommends the herb for, "the flux, or any prenatural discharge". It was also given as it "gently promotes the menses".

In Scorpio, tarragon adds height and a contrast of foliage to the generally rounded leaves of lady's mantle, and the basils. This is one area where I am tempted to allow the chives to flower for a touch of colour. There are plentiful clove gillyflowers in the neighbouring sign however.

Sagittarius, November 21st to December 21st, completes our tour of the astrology garden. Here, Jupiter governs the sign of the archer, half man, half beast. The parts of the body of special concern are the hips, thighs and arteries. The lungs and throat may also be affected.

The **clove gillyflowers** may be planted in one of their old forms of sops-in-wine, or as bright red doubles, or, indeed any of the clove-perfumed pinks. For a time a mat of Mrs Sinkins pinks were deliciously fragrant in my astrology garden. This plant made such rampant progress however, that it overlaid the houseleeks in a very short time. It has now been replaced with more of the bright red *Dianthus caryophyllus* for use in cookery.

Culpeper clearly had a great affection for what he termed "gallant, fine temperate flowers". He administered them as strengtheners of the heart and brain in the form of syrups or conserves. Definitely a physic we may still enjoy.

The **houseleek,** now released from its covering, again edges the bed with rosettes of thick, succulent leaves. A wonderfully cooling herb, it was given to temper the blood, and restrain inflammations. Culpeper remarks that it is so well known that he does not need to write a description. He also writes of the belief, old even then, that growing houseleek on a roof might preserve it from being struck by lightning. A superstition which survives today and is much better appreciated than the herb's medicinal role.

Behind the houseleek and clove gillyflowers, I have set two plants of the most beautifully variegated thistle - **Milk thistle.** A favourite of mine, the milk thistle, surprisingly, is under Jupiter rather than Mars. Although few thistles can be sharper, the milk thistle, then known as Our Lady's thistle, was administered as a cooling herb. The seed and distilled water were applied outwardly for pains of the sides and gripings. Also to cool the liver and for passions of the heart. It was, and remains, a blood cleanser. It is in medicinal use today to protect and restore the liver.

Where the milk thistle was turned to in order to prevent infections, so the **Sage** growing behind it, was given to cure them. Initially, I planned to plant contrasting sages, such as the golden and purple, next to each other. My own Sagittarius bed really doesn't have enough space for the two bushes in one sign, however.

According to Culpeper, the purple, medicinal sage is good, "for all pains of the joints". This was in addition to cleansing wounds and ulcers, treating head pains, palsy, hoarseness, and much more. Strongly antiseptic, sage remains a useful and powerful medicinal herb.

The last herb in the Sagittarius bed adds tiny, yellow, star-like flowers, and spiky seedheads which remind me of the spokes of an umbrella. Anyone planting **Herb bennet** should not be fooled by the plant's innocent air. It spreads rapidly by seed and soon new seedlings will appear all around the garden. Even so, I remain fond of it, and set it here because of its old medicinal use, now almost forgotten.

Culpeper writes of its many applications. Amongst these we find, "It dissolves the inward congealed blood happening by falls or bruises, and the spitting of blood, if the roots, either green or dry, be boiled in wine and drank;". The root was steeped in wine and drunk fasting to comfort the heart.

For anyone shy of including herb bennet, ajuga reptans, or **Bugle** is a worthy alternative. An attractive herb with purplish leaves, it also spreads, but only by runners in the immediate vicinity. The vibrant blue flowers are particularly pretty. As Culpeper writes, "This herb belongs to Dame Venus", he goes on to say the virtues will make you fall in love with it, if you are wise. Once again the plant is effective for inward and outward wounds. It has the tell-tale local name of Carpenter's Herb, which always indicates especially healing plants. It was also given to those "that have broken any bone, or have any member out of joint".

Culpeper recommends it for curing some diseases of Saturn. I have taken this as a cue to set bugle in the next sign, **Capricorn,** where I had more space. It would be a shame to omit such a useful herb, one which Culpeper clearly loved, from a garden dedicated as much to his memory as medical astrology.

Whether readers are moved to plant herb beds on these lines or not, I hope this astrology garden will have encouraged closer reading of Culpeper's herbal. His knowledge and wit have given me many happy hours of study.

The cultivation details for basil, chives, tarragon, clove gilliflowers and herb bennet can be found in Herbwise Naturally. Those for lady's mantle are included in Herbcraft Naturally. Details on growing houseleek, milk thistle and bugle are in the Cultivation Section.

Preserves

WITH no fresh harvests from the garden, this is the time to appreciate the stocks of herb vinegars, jellies, sugars, wines and liqueurs on your shelves. As you prepare Christmas treats for entertaining, and have gifts to find; you will be glad of time spent earlier in making preserves. Many can be taken straight from your store and wrapped as original gifts. It is lovely to be able to make up a hamper of selected seasonings, sugars, jellies and perhaps a wine or liqueur, for a friend or relative.

You can also combine some preserves in making more.

Spiced Apricots

500g apricots, packed as ready to eat
175ml (6fl oz) elderflower vinegar
175ml (6fl oz) spiced primrose wine
425g (5oz) soft brown sugar

1 teaspoon coriander seeds
3 sprigs fresh rosemary
10 peppercorns
1 stick cinnamon

Heat the spices in the vinegar and wine, having washed and pounded the rosemary first. Stir in the sugar, dissolve it over a low heat. Add the apricots and simmer gently in a partially covered pan for 10-15 minutes. Remove the apricots with a slotted spoon and set these in a jar which you have pre-warmed and sterilised. Return the liquor to the heat and continue simmering until it starts to thicken, about 5 minutes. Remove the rosemary sprigs, cool slightly and pour the liquor over the apricots. This should cover them completely, filling the jar. Seal and label. Store for 2-3 weeks before serving.

Other vinegar and wine combinations can be made, giving varying flavours.

This is the easiest of preserves:
Pears in Clove Pink Conserve

1 tin pear halves in fruit juice
1 jar clove pink conserve

Jar with screwtop lid

Drain the pears completely. Pack them in a jar which you have already sterilised with boiling water. Pour sufficient clove pink conserve over the pears to cover them, filling the jar. Seal and label. The fringed edges of the clove pink petals look wonderful floating in the conserve against the pears. No extra spices are needed. Refrigerate once opened.

If fresh pears are used, prepare them as follows. Peel, core and simmer, covered in water with 2 teaspoons of lemon juice added, until tender. Drain, pack in the jar and cover with clove pink conserve.

Mincemeat

I have given one mincemeat recipe in Herbcraft Naturally in the section on Christmas cookery. However, this alternative recipe has a very different flavour, given by the tangy, elecampane root.

12g (½oz) flaked almonds

85g (3oz) sultanas

50g (2oz) currants

1 small cooking apple

3 teaspoons finely chopped, candied elecampane root

50ml (2 fl oz) sherry

50g (2oz) raisins

25g (1oz) dried apricot

Juice of ½ lemon

Put the dried fruits, including the finely chopped dried apricot, and flaked almonds, into a bowl. Stir in the finely chopped, candied elecampane root and pour over the sherry. Leave to stand for 2-3 hours. Peel, core and cook a small cooking apple with the juice of half a lemon added. Mash the apple. When cold stir into the dried fruits and nuts. Refrigerate until use. Use within 10 days.

The Elizabethan housewife produced decorative feasts from her store cupboard without the aid of a freezer. We too can delight in bringing out brightly coloured jellies to bake in tarts, contrasting red rose petals with green lemon geranium, and so on. Both jellies, together with the pineapple sage, are delicious spread on scones and lemon geranium jelly makes a superb filling for a plain sponge cake. It is even better when teamed with fresh cream. Rose petal tarts, rose biscuits, shortbread spiced with rosemary, gingerbread and other cake and dessert recipes using your preserves, can be found in my earlier books.

A selection of sweet recipes for a Christmas chocolate box has also been given, but such a selection can never have too many flavours. Here are more ideas.

Clove Pink Fondant

When making fondant with pot marigold or rose sugar an extra flavouring of 1 drop essential oil of rose geranium or peppermint is added to the mixture. With clove pink sugar the natural flavour from the petals is far stronger. This can then be intensified with just a teaspoon of either clove pink and rose liqueur, or clove pink conserve. The result is exceptional.

1½ cups icing sugar

1 teaspoon clove pink conserve or clove pink and rose liqueur

1 egg white

50g (2oz) clove pink sugar

Break up the egg white with a fork and add half the double sieved icing sugar, using a mixer. Stir in the clove pink sugar. This should be finely ground first, but need not be a powder, as occasional flecks of pink are attractive in the sweets. It does tend to react with the egg white in the same way as rose sugar however. After a short time the pink patches may turn green. Because of this you may like to add a drop of food colouring. Stir in the remainder of the double sieved icing sugar, together with the conserve or liqueur. When the mixture reaches a firm paste, roll this out and cut shapes of circles, square, oblongs or diamonds, approximately 1.25cm (½in) thick. Lay these on greaseproof paper to dry for about an hour, turn and dry again before coating with chocolate or carob if liked.

Alternatively, the fondant can be treated in the following ways before it dries:- roll shapes or balls of the fondant in ground almonds, perhaps with a flake of almond set into the top. Roll in ground hazelnut. Set a small piece of candied angelica into the shape. Or, just before the fondant is covered in melted chocolate, add a piece of candied angelica which has been steeped in sherry for 20 minutes.

If pot marigold sugar is used in the fondant in place of clove pink, add 1 drop essential oil of rose geranium to a whole mix. Round fondant sweets can be marked with a knife as they are made, to represent a marigold flower. Add a pinch of saffron or food colouring to a little of the mix to make a darker centre for each one. These can be seen in the illustration on page xxi.

Rose sugar in the fondant will give a green rather than pink colouring. Since this has flecks of pink in it, the mix makes perfect little Easter eggs, but is better coated in chocolate at Christmas.

To be at their best, all fondant sweets should be kept cool and eaten within 10 days if they are left uncoated. For anyone allergic to chocolate, a carob bar or carob drops can be melted to cover the fillings. This has a slightly bitter flavour which contrasts well with the sweeter centres.

Rose Petal Filling
Rose petal jelly is rich and delicious when cased in chocolate. Especially if it has a little clove pink and rose liqueur added.
1 tablespoon rose petal jelly
1 teaspoon clove pink and rose liqueur, clove pink conserve, or brandy
dessicated coconut (optional)

Melt some of the chocolate, use to coat the base and sides of petit-four cases. Leave to set. Stir the conserve, liqueur, or brandy into the rose petal jelly. Either spoon a little dessicated coconut into the chocolate cases beneath the rose petal jelly, or add as a top layer. Seal the case shut with more melted chocolate. When the chocolate is almost set, a candied clove pink petal can be set on top, or a squiggle of chocolate added. The petit-four case can be peeled away later.

Apricot and Lovage Filling
6 dried apricots   2 candied lovage stems
1 teaspoon peppermint liqueur or brandy

Grind the dried apricots to a paste. Stir in the finely chopped, candied lovage stems and peppermint liqueur or brandy. If you prefer a non-alcoholic sweet, a little peppermint syrup or peppermint flavouring can be added instead of the liqueur. Roll into balls or press into shapes.

Roll this filling in ground almond, or cover in chocolate - or both.

Fruit and Nut Filling
1½ dessertspoons ground hazelnuts   1 dessertspoon sultanas
¾ teaspoon rosemary liqueur   a pinch of ground rosemary

A substitute for the rosemary liqueur can be made by steeping a washed and pounded sprig of rosemary in brandy for 20 minutes. The resulting filling would be best wrapped in marzipan before covering in chocolate. Grind the hazelnuts again with the sultanas and rosemary. Make into a paste and cover in chocolate.

Sweet Cicely Filling

Candied sweet cicely root may be wrapped in marzipan and encased in chocolate. Alternatively, steep the candied root in sherry before setting in chocolate or adding the marzipan covering.

Many more fillings or separate sweets are possible with candied herb roots and stems. They can, for instance, be used to flavour a variety of toffee and fudge recipes. The possibilities are endless and require dedicated tasting.

Herb Teas

IN blending a herbal tea for mid-winter, I have thought about the seasonal ills and the seasonal festivities. The thyme will be helpful in combating infections, while I have always found nettle invaluable at treating and preventing chilblains. It is also rich in iron. Liquorice, fennel and parsley are all good for cleansing the body. Liquorice aids the liver and acts as a mild laxative. Fennel and parsley both have digestive and diuretic qualities. The flavour of the combined herbs is also very pleasant. All ingredients are dried.

1 part marigold petals
1 part nettle
½ part shredded liquorice stick
1 part parsley

½ part fennel seed - pounded
1 part flowering thyme

Mix and store. Take 1 cup per day, 2 if the effects are much needed. Change and alternate with other teas every few days.

Herb tea method

In general use one or two fresh tops of the herb, or one teaspoon of dried herb, per cup. Never make herb tea in a metal teapot. Try to keep a particular pot or jug just for herb teas. Warm the pot first and pour the boiling water over torn fresh herb or dried blend. Cover and leave to stand for about 5 minutes. Strain into a cup, adding honey if liked as a sweetener. All herb teas are potentially medicinal and should be restricted to one cup per day unless you require the medicinal effect.

Wines and Liqueurs

IN November and December all harvests are in. The time you might otherwise spend in making a new wine, can be given to bottling wines already made in the spring and summer. Of course, syphoning the wine out of the demi-john requires sucking the tube and tasting is inevitable. It can be a very enjoyable task, as long as you don't mix too many at the same session. This is unlikely however, as there are all the bottles to be prepared.

Wine bottles, whether your own or other peoples, can be recycled as long as they are in perfect condition. Simply wash them well as soon as they are emptied, and store in a clean place. Later, fill with warm, then hot, then boiling water, to sterilise in readiness for pouring in the wine. I should emphasise the bottles should be left to cool down first. Simply syphon the wine from the demi-john into the prepared bottles, carefully leaving any residue in the bottom. Fill the bottles to where the neck has narrowed but not completely to the top. Corks are readily bought, along with an instrument to push them in if you so wish. All wine must be labelled immediately. You may think you know exactly which one is which, but some can look remarkably similar.

The most popular wines at Christmas tend to be the agrimony and ginger which has such wonderful warming properties and the elderberry port for mulled wines. Redcurrant and pineapplemint or blackcurrant and curled mint can also be used in this role. Mulled wine recipes, both alcoholic and non-alcoholic can be found in Herbcraft Naturally.

Good mulled wine has some real body to it. When making mulled wine for guests at Christmas I often use half elderberry port and half redcurrant and pineapplemint wine. In this way the richness of the port comes through, without being too heavy.

For those occasions when elderberry port is not available, that same richness can be added with the syrup made a month or so earlier. The recipe below gives a light rosé a traditional mulled wine flavour.

Mulled Wine

1 bottle redcurrant and pineapplemint wine	½ nutmeg
3 tablespoons elderberry syrup	10 cloves
3 rounded tablespoons brown sugar	thin slice fresh ginger root
½ cinnamon stick	thinly peeled rind of ½ lemon
sprig of rosemary	

Pour the wine into a large pan, stir in the elderberry syrup and add the rind and spices, flaking the cinnamon stick. Wash and pound the rosemary before adding. Stir in the brown sugar over a low heat. Bring to the boil and simmer for a few minutes. Strain and serve.

Non-alcoholic Fruit Punch

8 lemon geranium leaves - medium size
150ml (¼ pint) peach and apple juice or peach juice
300ml (½ pint) grapefruit juice
2 dessertspoons clove pink syrup
6 cubes frozen elderflower cordial, or ½ cup bottled cordial
3 strips candied angelica
small knob fresh ginger root
small lemon geranium leaves to garnish

Wash the 8 lemon geranium leaves and tear them into an enamel pan. Pour over 600ml (1 pint) of cold water. Add the candied angelica and ginger root. Bring to the boil and simmer until the liquid is reduced by half. Strain into a bowl, return one piece of candied angelica and then leave to cool. Add the fruit juices, clove pink syrup and cubes of frozen elderflower cordial and serve. If bottled cordial is used, plain ice cubes could be avoided by freezing the cordial earlier.

To convert this to an alcoholic recipe, use clove pink conserve and elderflower wine rather than the syrups. If your clove pink syrup has petals left in it, or you have used clove pink conserve, the tiny pink petals will look lovely floating in the fruit juices.

Your punch can be garnished further by adding small pieces of candied angelica and the smallest lemon geranium leaves.

The combination of flavours brings out a Christmas richness with a hint of spice, while retaining the freshness of the fruits. Delicious.

In the Home

A house can be decked beautifully with coloured streamers and silver stars, and still not hold the magical feel of a traditional Christmas. Perfume is certainly part of the scene for me, from the low, heady notes of the spices, to the higher tones of mandarin orange.

In the recipes below, two ways of adding a special Christmas fragrance to the atmosphere are given. The pomander beads need to be made in the first week of November. They take 6 weeks to 'cure', before they can be hung as fragrant decorations. Some of the ingredients for these are a good deal cheaper when bought in bulk. These could be bought a month earlier to make beads for Christmas fairs. The spicy sacks are certainly extremely popular on fund-raising stalls. See list of suppliers on page 151 for ingredients in large or small quantities.

Pomander Beads

This paste is based on a recipe from the 17th century. I have omitted some of Culpeper's ingredients, adding a few extras not available then. The resulting perfume is strong and rich, both in the freshly made beads, and the cured ones, as they are gently heated.

You will need:

crochet thread	a large darning needle or bodkin
a little olive oil	small boxes
cotton wool	4 tbsp gum benzoin
4 tbsp frankincense	⅔ tbsp balsam poplar buds
⅔ tbsp of each of the following spices:	⅔ tbsp of each of the following herbs:
freshly ground or grated nutmeg	rose petals or buds
ground cloves	basil
ground coriander or aniseed	lavender
	marjoram
	rosemary

1 tbsp sandalwood or sanderswood, mixed with cypressus cones if available
¼ pint rosewater and 1 dessertspoon gum tragacanth for mucilage
4 drops essential oil of benzoin res.   3 drops essential oil of chamomile
4 drops essential oil of basil

Note: if you have sensitive skin or any cuts on your hands, rubber gloves should be worn when mixing the paste.

The mucilage of gum tragacanth is mixed 24 hours before using. The rosewater and powdered gum tragacanth can be mixed in a liquidiser. Always add the powder to the liquid. Alternatively, pour the rosewater into a large screwtop jar and add the powdered gum gradually, shaking well after each addition. The second method can take some time and effort to remove all lumps, and the mucilage will need to be stood in a fridge for 2 days before use. Add 1 drop essential oil of benzoin res. or a pinch of powdered gum benzoin as a preservative.

When the mucilage is ready, grind all the other ingredients into a fine powder. This can be done in a mortar with a pestle, or in an electric grinder. A grinder used for food will be fine with the spices and herbs, but do not use it for cypressus cones or the other gum resins. I have an old grinder which I keep separate for these.

Mix the powders together in a bowl and add as much of the mucilage as you need, to bring them to a workable paste. Add the essential oils, one drop at a time and work these into the whole mixture. It should be sufficiently stiff to pull small lumps away from the larger mass and roll or shape these into little beads. The beads can be formed as lozenges, rolls, globes, or even flat circles and oblongs. If you wish to decorate them later with star anise seeds, coloured beads or tiny gold balls, press these into the paste now, to leave 'settings' ready. Cloves can also be pushed into the larger beads for spicy decoration.

Set the beads on greaseproof paper at first, and allow them to dry out a little, for an hour or so. After this time thread the large needle with crochet thread and put a knot at the end. Dip both thread and needle into the olive oil to coat them, then pass the needle and thread through each bead you wish to hang. Make a knot between each of the beads, leaving a short length of thread to keep them from touching each other. You may like to make up several different strings. Lay the threaded beads between layers of paper kitchen towel, set in a warm, but not hot atmosphere. Turn them regularly, firming them into shape at the same time, for 3-4 days, until they are quite dry.

Pack the beads into small cardboard boxes with cotton wool keeping them apart from each other. Leave for 6 weeks to 'cure'. This will increase the perfume of the finished beads. Check every few days for the first 2 weeks in case they were not fully dried. If any mould should form, simply wipe the beads with a drop or two of the benzoin res. essential oil, (wear gloves to do this) and re-pack.

After 6 weeks take out the beads, wipe away the cotton wool and glue any decorations in place. Re-thread and hang where warm air will bring out the perfume. Do not place them over a naked flame.

If alterations are made to the recipe, remember half the total quantity should consist of gum resins such as gum benzoin, frankincense and myrrh.

Note: Balsam poplar buds and cypressus cones also contain resin. Care should be taken if children make up the mixture, or form the beads, as they contain poisonous ingredients. They should not be hung where small children might suck them, although they are unlikely to do so for long. The particularly strong perfumes involved may also be a problem to asthmatics and heart patients. The same applies to the recipe below.

Spicy Sacks

Making these little sacks of spices and herb, is a perfect way to put you in the mood for really going to town with your Christmas decorations. They may be added to the swags in the craft section, hung on the door wreath, or tree; or set amongst pine cones in a basket on the side. With so many wonderful Christmas theme fabrics available, they can look as attractive as they smell.

You will need;

3 tbsp dried rosemary	2 teaspoons ground clove
½ tbsp cloves	1 tbsp coriander seed
½ tbsp caraway seed	1 tbsp mixed star anise heads and seeds
5 small lumps dried root ginger	1 small cinnamon stick, flaked
½ teaspoon grated nutmeg	1 tbsp calamus or orris root
2 drops essential oil of cinnamon	2 drops essential oil of frankincense

Mix all the ingredients, pounding the rosemary and breaking the root ginger pieces open if you can, first. Add the essential oils last. The amount above will fill 2 sacks made simply by folding a piece of cotton fabric 10cm (4in) x 15cm (6in), stitching and hemming the opening, and 1 sack of half size; or 5 small sacks. The sacks are tied closed with a narrow ribbon. Keep sealed in a plastic bag for 24 hours before setting about the room or adding to decorations.

Craft

Dyes

AT this time of year, with a busy dyeing season just behind you, sometimes it feels right to take a break. However, if the autumn harvests have filled you with continued enthusiasm, it may be time to plunder the store cupboard. If you have not dried roots, flowers and leaves of dye plants earlier in the year, then a dye supplier can provide some exciting dyes. When using dried dye material it may be finely powdered. Anyone with respiratory problems should take extra care not to inhale this.

Brazilwood is not a dye you can grow at home. Even though I grow a large range of dye plants, the reds I obtain are generally not as deep as this. I enjoy using brazilwood chips in November and December, as it produces some perfect reds for Christmas projects. I particularly like to use it with silk, and last year dyed numerous skeins of silk thread and squares of silk fabric for projects.

I pounded the brazilwood first and soaked the chips in 1.2 litres (2 pints) of water overnight. 100g gave me a beautiful burgundy in 4 pints of water. An equal weight of dye to dry wool or silk is recommended. I tend to use more. After simmering the chips for one hour, I strained the dye liquor and entered the silks which had been pre-mordanted with alum. See page 26. I then kept the liquor over a very low heat for 20 minutes, leaving it to cool before pouring the silks carefully into a container with sufficient dye liquor to cover. The container was sealed and I returned to it, swirling the silks gently in the liquor at intervals, each day for 3 days.

At the end of this time the silks had become a rich burgundy colour. Rinsed three times and drip dried, they have remained fast. I experimented with more pre-mordanted silk, added to the cold liquor, but this was a much paler colour.

Madder can be grown in the garden but takes several years to mature, and so needs rather a large area for a continuous supply. Soak the dried, chopped root in water, after grinding or pounding it as above. This time, I soaked the dye material for just 5 hours in 1.2 litres (2 pints) of water. Following exactly the same recipe as with the brazilwood, the colour obtained was a brick red, dull by comparison.

On another occasion, I added silk to a madder dyebath in which I had already heated 50g (2oz) of wool. While mordanting the wool and silk, I had accidentally added twice the usual amount of alum. On seeing the rather lovely coral pink which resulted, I decided to repeat the mistake another time.

Alkanet root is another dye herb which you may find yourself buying, ready-dried. The garden-produced alkanet root, is more difficult to bring to a successful dyebath. Again, I pound the root, soak it overnight and follow the process above. This tends to be more of a purplish shade than the others.

Oak Galls may still be laying under oak trees, or you may have dried them earlier. Having tried, without success to find the black, shiny galls used in old recipes, I have taken to leaving them on a flower bed in autumn. By November they have turned black and can be pounded for dyeing or ink. Other galls left neatly on trays did not change colour in the same way.

When dyeing wool I use an equal quantity of galls to wool, obtaining a reddish dye liquor. Unfortunately this is considerably darker than the colour imparted to wool or fabric. So far I have obtained deep mustard yellows and greenish tan with a chrome mordant. Oak gall powder can be obtained from dye suppliers.

Oak Gall Ink

50g (2oz) dark coloured gall nuts   (¾ oz) gum arabic powder
275ml (½ pint beer)   1 teaspoon brown sugar
25g (1oz) copper sulphate

Gather the darkest, shiniest oak galls you can find. Pound them to powder, or grind if you have a grinder not used for food. Steep the pounded galls in the beer for 30 minutes. Add the gum arabic powder, brown sugar and copper sulphate and stir. Simmer in an old enamel pan or a dyepan for about one hour. Strain through a fine muslin and keep, bottled in a cool, dark place.

This ink is not as bright as the elderberry ink in Herbcraft Naturally, but is fun to use.

Sumach is an ornamental tree commonly found in gardens. Several varieties are grown in this country and the ***Rhus glabra*** and ***Rhus typhina,*** or stag's horn sumach are especially good. All parts of sumach trees contain large amounts of tannin. At this time of year there may be some berries left, or unwanted suckers to use. Either can give a range of shades with or without a mordant. Alum may be used.

A friend of mine experimented with eight times the weight of wool in berries, and soaked these for a day or so before preparing the dyebath. Using the same water, she simmered the berries over a moderate heat for 2-3 hours before straining the liquor. The wool was entered for only a short time, as we had read in several recipes that heating the wool in the dye liquor for more than 20 minutes, might spoil it. The resulting shade of tan was very pretty and rather delicate. It toned well with other autumn shades we had obtained from madder, walnut and dahlias.

Dyer's bistort leaves may have been preserved in a solution of sodium metabisulphate (available from winemaking counters), earlier in the autumn, in which case they can be used at this time to prepare a blue dye.

I have tried drying the leaves on harvesting for use at this time of year, but was not successful in producing blue with a simple recipe. I have come to the conclusion that fresh or preserved leaves are needed. Their preparation is given in Jill Goodwins book, **A Dyer's Manual.** Dyer's bistort can be treated either in a similar way to indigo, or as woad leaves. The second method would be better carried out earlier in the year.

Not all dye experiments work, as every dyer knows. In a way this is part of the beauty of the craft, for it keeps you experimenting with more ideas and combinations. As one year of dyeing closes, another opens with new opportunities.

Decorative Christmas Swag

IT has always been part of the traditional Christmas to bring in berry-bearing evergreens, such as holly, ivy and mistletoe. The ivy stems can be draped around pictures and set along the mantelpiece or windowsill, in the same way as holly. It offers another interesting possibility with the pliant nature of the long ground-covering stems, already explored in basketry. It will readily adapt to being plaited.

Search out the longest stems of reasonably consistent thickness. You will need at least 3 for each swag. With sufficient strength you can plait just 3 thickish stems together to make a swag base. You may find it easier to make 3 plaits of 3 thin stems, and then plait again to give a wide base for your decorations. Leave all foliage on the stems.

The best way to achieve a good tension is to tie one end of each of the 3 lengths together in a bundle. Hang them from a nail on the wall outside, or a shed door handle. Make a plait by bringing the stem on the left over the one in the centre, and then the one on the right over the central stem. Keep repeating the movement, pulling the lengths taut as you do so, for a neat plait. Every so often you will have to turn and unravel the trailing stems behind you, which will be making a second plait of their own, unless you have taken care to keep them apart. In general, the stems will provide a plait about ½ of their full lengths. When the plait is finished, tie tightly with string and trim the ends.

Tweak any trapped leaves clear of the plait and remove damaged ones. You are now ready to decorate the swag.

Choose from:

Lengths of red, green, gold or multi-coloured ribbon.

Bags of gold, silver or red net containing nuts or sweets.

Decorated circles of dried orange.

Cinnamon sticks, with or without star anise, and gold balls.

Light Christmas tree decorations.

Braids and Christmas trim.

Holly and rosemary.

Cypress or pine cones sprayed silver or gold.

Herb seedheads sprayed silver or gold.

Begin by making a ribbon bow at one end of the swag, leaving one very long end of ribbon free. Wind this diagonally along the ivy base, tying it off in the centre, by taking it in and out of the plaited stems. Take a second length of ribbon and make a bow at the opposite end of the swag in the same way, bringing the longer length back to the centre. Tie off.

Make spicy sacks as in 'In the home' section. Attach these to the swag, using lengths of silver or gold braid trim.

To make the dried orange slices. Slice an orange thinly and roll each slice in a mix of powdered orris root and ground cinnamon. Lay them on a rack in the oven on the lowest heat, 50°C for an hour or so. Turn at intervals. Test. The fruit should feel completely dry. Store in a box or tin until needed. Check each day for the first few days to make sure no moisture has been left, or mould will develop. These will then keep for use year after year.

Attach the orange slice by pushing wired imitation holly berries through the centre of the slice. Leave a loop at the back, with the berries at the front. Twist the loop of wire around a stem in the ivy swag.

Cinnamon sticks bound together with a little florists wire, with, or without a star anise seedhead laid on top of them, are good additions. A tiny gold ball or two can be threaded onto the centre of the wire first, to add sparkle.

Cones and herb seedheads, such as elecampane, sea holly, love-in-a-mist, evening primrose, and poppies can be tied on with narrow ribbon, tinsel or braid, or simply tucked into the main ribbon.

Simple gold, silver or red bags can be made by laying a few nuts or sweets onto a square of net. Pull up the four corners to the centre and tie round with narrow ribbon. Slip more ribbon or tinsel into the back of the tie to attach to the swag.

Finish with sprigs of holly and rosemary. Hang on the wall, or from a beam, by slotting the loops within the plait over panel pins or nails.

Many more decorations appear in Herbcraft Naturally. A pretty table decoration which is very quickly made:

Mini Christmas Trees

For each tree you will need:-

a few sprigs of juniper or rosemary	a liquorice stick
a piece of wet or dry oasis	a small flower pot
a little glue	dill weed
decorations of tinsel, gold or red balls	

When cutting juniper, choose sprigs with thick stems, rather than fresh, thin growth at the ends of the branches. If the branches have berries this is a bonus.

With the rosemary, again, thicker stems with close growth are best. With a 5cm (2ins) diameter pot, the spread of greenery should not be longer than 11.5cm (4½ins) at either side of the oasis. Most sprigs needed will be shorter than this.

Cut a piece of oasis to fit inside the flower pot up to the rim. Spread a thin layer of glue on the top of the oasis in the pot and sprinkle with dill weed to represent grass, or coriander seeds for stones. Alternatively you could cover the surface around the place for the tree trunk by pushing cloves into the oasis. Cut a second piece in a cone shape which is the same height or slightly more than the depth of the flowerpot. Push the liquorice stick up into the centre of the cone to form a trunk for the tree. With a larger tree a cinnamon stick could be used.

If you wish the greenery to last more than a few days, use wet oasis and soak this in water, before pushing in the sprigs of herb. Choose a bushy sprig to make the top of the tree and push this into the centre top of the cone shape. Next work from the base up each side of the tree to make a shape which is widest at the bottom and tapers upwards. With the general shape set, add more sprigs at the front and back of the tree. Finally, dip the tree trunk in glue and push it down into the centre of the oasis base.

Decorate the tree with narrow tinsel or braid trim, tiny gold balls on red or green thread, imitation holly berries or other miniature decorations.

A T this point in the year, with the busiest months of natural dyeing nearly over, you may have sufficient skeins of wool in various colours, to knit a jumper. If you have been dyeing unspun wool straight from a fleece, you may have more than you can readily spin.

A peg loom is the quick and easy answer to turning a mountain of dyed wool into garments, or colourful rugs. A source of peg looms is given in the list of suppliers. The simple loom consists of a long block of wood with 24 holes drilled into it at regular intervals. There are 24 pegs to fit the holes. Each has another hole bored through it, a short distance up from the base. The waistcoat illustrated could be worked on such a loom with just a few evenings work.

To Begin;
Take the measurements of the person for whom the waistcoat is intended. Measure length from the centre of their neck to their waist, or below. Measure across their back from shoulder to shoulder and again from the centre under-arm to centre under-arm. Repeat for one front, from centre to under-arm, and shoulder down to neckline.

The 24 pegs set the total length of the main waistcoat. As you work on the loom, you will be weaving up and down this length. The rows will build up a length of weaving to go across from under-arm to under-arm. The number of rows, therefore, sets the width of the waistcoat, across the back or front.

The length of the waistcoat can be increased by working a separate collar which is stitched on afterwards. To lengthen it further, a band can be worked to attach to the bottom. This will need to be made in 3 strips, one for the back and another for each front. With the collar, and any bands for the bottom of the waistcoat, the rows are worked the other way on. Note collar in illustration. With these, the number of pegs used, sets the length of the band, and the depth is set by the number of rows.

Pattern

With the measurements clearly set out, begin by looking at your choice of dyed wool. Strips of contrasting colours, or shades of the same colour, are easy to produce. Other patterns will soon come to mind. Ideas which involve a great many short strips of different colours, should be avoided. The illustration of the back of the waistcoat shows an easy tree pattern. Creativity is at the heart of each peg loom project, for the technique could not be simpler.

The Back

Cut 16 lengths of spun wool, approximately 2½ times the measurement from centre under-arm across the back to centre under-arm. Using the threader provided, thread each of these through the hole in one of the pegs. Set the pegs in position, leaving 8 holes free, (subject to measurement from top of shoulder to under-arm).

With a small ball of spun wool, start by taking the end, behind and in front of the 4 edge pegs, bringing it back around the end. Continue to weave, behind 1 in front of 1, until you reach the last threaded peg at the other end. Bring it around the last peg and back again. On the second row, you will pass the wool in front of those pegs which it passed behind, on the previous row, and vice versa. See illustration of wool on the loom. Keep the wool with a steady tension, but not taut. Work 3 rows. At the end peg, bring the wool around and back into the row for 3 pegs. Cut the thread. This is simply to give a firm edge and can be worked at the beginning and end of each piece of work.

Take your chosen colour of unspun wool and tease out a long length with your fingers. The wool can be carded first, preferably on a drum carder. Unless it is very tangled, teasing should be sufficient preparation. Remove any tight 'knots' of wool as you go. The width of your 'roll' of teased wool should be about 3-4cm (1-1½in). Begin by taking the end behind and in front of 3 or 4 pegs, close to the end of the row, overlaying the spun wool. Weave as before, pushing each row down slightly, as you move along.

Moving down

When your woven wool reaches about 2/3 of the height of the pegs, stop weaving a little way in from one edge. Pull away the main wool, tucking the end of your weaving roll behind a peg. Lift the peg at the left hand edge out of its hole and push the weaving off the peg, onto your warp threads. Set the peg back into the hole. Lift the next peg and repeat. When you have reached the other end of the row, you will have several rows of weaving hanging down in front of the loom, and be ready to weave more around the pegs. Each time you move weaving down, it can be pushed tightly against the previous rows. It will then appear as a continuous piece of work.

Joining Colours

In the waistcoat illustrated, I continued weaving with this number of pegs for 10 rows, in order to finish the under-arm section. To join in another colour, I pulled away the teased wool, leaving an end a little longer than I needed. I then overlapped the beginning of the new colour with this, and worked the 2 twisted together for several pegs before continuing.

Christmas conserves, wines, liqueurs, chocolates

(Below) *Pomander beads*

Autumn harvest ball

November - December

Christmas swag

(Left) *Sprayed seed heads*

(Below) *Spicy sack mixture*

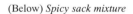

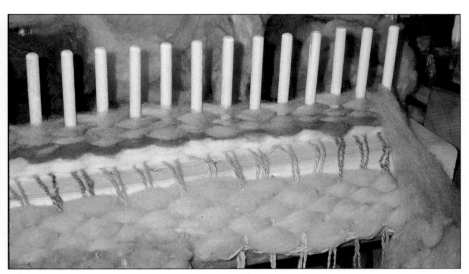

Weaving on the peg loam

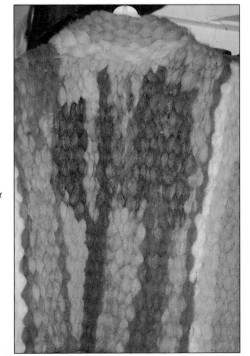

Back of waistcoat

Frosted teazle, motherwort, St. John's wort

To Increase

Add more pegs threaded with spun wool. I needed all 24 pegs for the full length from shoulder down. Work as before, including the extra pegs.

To Decrease

At the edge of the neck, I decreased the row by one peg, simply pulling it out of the frame and leaving it attached to the weaving I had already done. After 2 rows, I decreased by another peg and continued working with this number, until reaching the other side of the neck. I then reversed the process, increasing by 1 peg, then another, working the shoulder; and then decreasing by 8 pegs to work the under-arm.

Fronts

Work one front, beginning at the under-arm with 16 pegs - or as with the back. I increased the row to 24 pegs for the shoulder for approximately 16 rows. I then decreased by 5 pegs for the neck for approximately 13 rows. The last decrease of 3 pegs, left 16 pegs per row for the remainder of the front.

Note: Precise details of rows will vary according to the thickness of wool used and weaving tension. This is simply a guide to work by for a 92cm (36ins) chest measurement.

Collar

Clearly the length of the collar cannot be greater than the length of the peg loom. This was sufficient to reach exactly from the neck decrease on one front, round to the neck decrease on the other side on the waistcoat illustrated. It is 9 rows wide in two colours. If this is not long enough for your garment, a lapel could be worked to continue down along either front. This would need to be allowed for, when calculating the width of each front.

Ending Off

As you finish each piece, remove the pegs from the loom and adjust warp threads to leave an equal length at either end of the weaving. Knot the loose ends working from bottom to top. Knot the first two together and continue knotting each pair directly below the weaving. Then knot again taking the second and third threads together; fourth and fifth together, and so on. The ends may be left or cut.

Cut the loops at the other end, freeing the pegs, and knot in the same way. Adjust the tension of your weaving, pulling the knots tightly against it as you go.

Finishing

The under-arm seams can be stitched, or knotted together, using the free ends. The shoulder seams should be stitched, also the collar and any added bands of weaving. Fastenings can be made of toggles and loops of crocheted or plaited spun wool.

Washing

The garment can be hand washed in warm soapy water, rinsed and dried flat as for a pure wool jumper. With wearing and washing it will become a felt jacket in time, but will be tremendously warm, light and attractive.

Herb Cultivation

Common name	Latin name
alexanders -	smyrnium olisatrum
balsam poplar -	populus balsamifera
black hellebore -	helleborus niger
blessed thistle -	carduus benedictus
bugle -	ajuga reptans
dyer's bistort -	polygonatum tinctorium
fumitory -	fumaria officinalis
greater knapweed -	centaurea scabiosa
houseleek -	sempervivum tectorum
kidneywort -	umbilicus rupestris
lungwort -	sticta pulmonaria
milk thistle -	silybum marianum
pokeweed -	phytolacca americana
poppies -	papaver
self heal -	prunella vulgaris
Solomon's seal -	polygonatum multiflorum
wintergreen -	gaultheria procumbens
wormwood	artemisia absinthium

Some of the herbs in this section are toxic. When growing poisonous plants, care should be taken to keep these well identified and towards the back or centre of garden beds. Young children should be told about the danger of touching or eating the plants. In this way they will know not all flowers are harmless. If a child or pet does eat leaves from the garden and is unwell, always seek medical advice. Take a leaf of the plant with you for identification so that the poisons service can be contacted.

The two plants which have caused serious poisoning in recent years are laburnum and yew. Mezereon is also highly irritant and small children should be protected from the bushes. Most poisonous plants have a very unpleasant taste and many simply cause immediate vomiting.

Key to abbreviations

A	annual	S	shrub
B	biennial	T	tree
P	perennial		

Ajuga reptans   P   BUGLE

A popular garden plant, often grown as ground cover, ajuga may be a surprise in the herbal category. Also known as bugle, it belongs to the mint family, a fact which may help explain its land conquering habit. The herb can successfully be divided at almost any time of year. The runners, which are sent out from the main plant, grow leaves at intervals. By autumn when the runners die, roots have formed below these pairs of oval leaves to make new plants.

Personally, I am happy for the attractive purplish foliage to spread beneath the sloes in my Treasure garden, as well as on the north-facing bank of the Astrology. In Capricorn there is less shade, which means the plants make slower progress in their colonisation. They will cope without shade, so long as there is moist soil. I have always set new plants from division, but seed can also be sown in autumn or spring.

The stems are short, generally only about 15-23cm (6-9in). The intense blue colour of the flowers is striking, even though they are interspersed between bracts around the stem. In April-May they herald the change from spring to early summer. Their wide, 3-lobed lower lips appear almost to pout petulantly, defying anyone with a flower press to capture such beauty. The common name, bugle, comes from the likeness seen between the long, narrow corolla of the flower and similarly shaped glass beads. These are used in embroidery and called bugulus.

As a medicinal herb, ajuga provides healing leaves in the summer months for making ointment. This can be applied to wounds as a mild painkiller. The infusion was taken for internal bleeding and applied in the form of a lotion to treat sores.

A native of Europe, *Ajuga reptans* can be seen growing amongst grasses at the edges of woodland. Another pyramidal form, with longer bracts beneath the flowers is mentioned in the illustrated Flora. This grows from Cumbria northwards. An ajuga with an entirely different appearance, *Ajuga chamaepitys* with needle-like leaves and yellow flowers grows in southern counties. This herb also has medicinal qualities.

Artemisia absinthium   P   WORMWOOD

THE bitterness of wormwood is proverbial, we find it in Proverb 5 - "And her mouth is smoother than oil: But her end is bitter as wormwood." Absinthium has been translated as 'destitute of delight', which seems equally forbidding. If we needed any further warning of the nature of the herb, we find it in the legend that the plant first sprang from the track left by the serpent, as it wound its way out of the garden of Eden.

Therapeutically, wormwood has been valued over the centuries. With prolonged, or uncontrolled use, however, the thujone content will attack the central nervous system with disastrous results. A number of differing wormwoods, Roman, sweet, tree, and the Lambrook silver, are grown ornamentally. Several of these have some medicinal properties.

The common wormwood also has extremely attractive, soft grey leaves, on stems which grow to be just over 90cm (36in) high. The stems tend to lack strength and always need staking for support by summer, when the plants are flowering. The flowers are tiny and many, borne aloft like small yellow buttons. As the seeds are formed, the stems are cut for drying. This is traditionally the point in the year when they are thought to contain the most juice.

Germination of the seeds is supposed to be good, but I have never found any self-sown seedlings, I have always propagated the herb by division. In the wine and liqueur garden, wormwood enjoys semi-shade. Use of the essential oil in Absinthe and vermouth has been discontinued due to the danger of addiction. Its place here is strictly historical. The herb needs fairly poor ground to maintain the beauty of silvery foliage. Although the plants lose their leaves in winter, they are hardy, growing as far north as Siberia.

The perfume of the foliage is pungent and acts as a deterrent to many insects, including moths, midges and fleas. The herb has been used extensively in this role, dried and laid amongst clothes, strewn with rushes, and so on. Centuries ago, the bitter herb was added to ink in order to stop mice eating documents. As a fresh or dried herb, it also repels rats and mice, and generally has a reputation for keeping everything away - from animals to evil spirits.

Do not plant this herb next to delicate herbs, or those you intend to eat.

Carduus benedictus or
Cnicus benedictus   A   BLESSED THISTLE

SINCE first growing the blessed thistle, I have been fascinated by its appearance. It is a challenge to any photographer. The thick, downy hairs which cover the leaves and stems, make it appear out of focus. The leaves are typical of the thistle family in shape, but curl up around the stems, seeming to make the plant top heavy.

Perhaps this abundance of green growth is in response to garden soil. In the wild, the blessed thistle chooses to grow in stony, waste places. It originates in the Mediterranean area, having become naturalised in Europe and North America. The seeds are quite long and narrow, similar to those of the milk thistle, but lighter in colour. They may be sown in autumn or spring. The seedlings will need protective collars against cold winds and slugs. A further distraction for the slugs can be made by tearing up comfrey leaves, and setting these about, between the plants.

As the herb matures, it is best surrounded by others of a similar height, for support. When flowering, it may reach 45cm (18in) or more, and may well topple over. The yellow flowers are surrounded by heavy bracts which transform the 'bonnet' effect, to that of a 'lantern', as the seedhead hangs down. There may be two or three flowers from side-shoots of the same stem. The centres of the seedheads are filled with fluffy down, hiding the seeds ripening below. They are enclosed by a beautiful star-shape of now buff-coloured bracts. Outside these are another of four longer bracts, all of thin parchment-like quality.

I would happily grow blessed thistles for their decorative virtues alone, but their medicinal uses are also to be celebrated. The herb was commonly grown in physic gardens for centuries. An important stomach bitter, it found its way into liqueurs, such as Benedictine; which were medicinal at that time.

In the modern age the leaves and flowering tops are still harvested. The ancient role of increasing a nursing mother's milk remains, and the herb is combined with others to treat such problems as anorexia. Large doses of the herb will act as a strong emetic and it is not recommended for home remedies.

Centaurea scabiosa   P   GREATER KNAPWEED

MANY gardeners would only grow this herb as part of a wild flower area. Until the recent fashion of including wild flowers in gardens, it might even have been considered as a weed. Yet it is a lovely plant with attractive, almost evergreen leaves. Greater knapweed grows to a height of about 1-1.5m (3-5ft). It generally needs to be supported towards the end of the summer. By this time it has been flowering for weeks on end, and will have both more flowers and ripening seedheads.

The flowerheads, or buds, seem to have earned the herb many of its common names. These all refer to the knob-shaped buds which appear to be armoured, or covered in scales. Hardhead, Ironhead, Churls Head and Logger Head are just a few.

As the flowers open, throughout the summer, they attract bees and butterflies. The close relationship of this herb to the cornflower is evident in their form. Dense at the centre, they are purple with a coronet of tiny florets standing out around the base of the main flower. The seedheads are amazingly fragile, seeming paper thin. They have always reminded me of fairies' bonnets in children's book illustrations. Attractive in arrangements, I spray them gold at Christmas. Just the force of spray paint can blow them away if you don't hold tightly to the stems.

Greater knapweed likes a well-drained situation. It appears in the south along hedgebanks and in grasses, preferring dry, alkaline soils. The plant can be divided in autumn, or seeds sown in spring.

The roots and seed were once harvested for medicinal recipes, the most famous of these being an ointment called Save. Another common name, Felon herb, refers to the use of knapweed poultices to draw out sepsis from felons, or whitlows.

Fumaria officinalis   A   FUMITORY

A successful native of Europe, as far as Iran, fumitory has become naturalised in North America. It is a challenge to the photographer, for even a mass of the leafy stems, up to 30cm (12in) tall, have little substance. Often some trail out from the main plant in a rather untidy fashion. The **Illustrated Flora of Britain and Northern Europe,** lists nine forms of fumitory growing in the British Isles. Several of these are very localised, and all appear similar to the untrained eye.

Largely regarded by gardeners as a weed, fumitory is a peculiarly self-sufficient herb. Perhaps its self-fertilising ability, which seems to be extremely efficient, has helped to fuel the many legends about it. The delicate, ethereal grey-green foliage, rising like smoke from the ground; coupled with the lack of insect visitors, brought about imaginative interpretations.

Legend revealed that fumitory did not grow from seed as other plants, but simply emanated from the earth. Needless to say, this gave the plant power over evil spirits. The smoke effect was taken to its logical conclusion, and the herb burned to purify the area. The names fumaria and fumitory come from this same source.

Another common name, beggary, has two possible explanations. The first is that it may refer to the poor ground in which the plants often grow. Since fumitory thrives even better in well-fed earth; it seems more likely, to refer to the effect the rampant growth of fumitory in his cornfields, might have on the farmer.

For all this, the racemes of deep pink flowers in mid-summer give the herb an innocent air. Lotions of fumitory have been applied for removing unwanted freckles, cleansing the skin and to act as a depilatory. The last use we are led to believe, not only removed hairs, but ensured no more would grow. This together with a further use against scabies, suggests a powerful herb.

In fact, fumitory is related to the poppies and also contains alkaloids. The flowering plant is a bitter tonic. Its old use for aiding the liver function has survived, also the external application for eczema and dermatitis. The herb has found additional mention as a yellow dye. I have yet to experiment with this.

Gaultheria procumbens   S   WINTERGREEN

WINTERGREEN is unusual amongst the herbs, in needing an acid environment. If your soil is naturally alkaline as mine is, it can survive but will not flourish. A bed prepared with peat for azaleas or rhododendrons is the perfect habitat. The wintergreen will enjoy the shade from large shrubs.

I will always remember my first sight of a mass of wintergreen, growing as a 15cm (6in) ground cover in woodland near my Uncle's cabin in Ontario. I had followed the chipmunks in amongst the trees and suddenly became aware of the strong aroma of the herb, which was unmistakable. It was autumn, and by then the white flowers, touched with pink, had been replaced by attractive red berries, food of deer and birds. The berries are also cooked and stewed in tarts.

The common names of wintergreen - Mountain tea, Teaberry, Thé du Canada, all record the use of the leaves in herbal tea. Glossy and attractive, they were also added to tea as a flavouring which was much appreciated in the past. Taking wintergreen in such a way seems to have been tempting fate, remembering how poisonous the oil is. However, Mrs Grieve writes in her herbal that the oil only developed by fermentation as the leaves were steeped in water for 24 hours.

Wintergreen in analgesic liniments for all forms of rheumatism and muscular pain is now synthetic, being methyl salicylate. The chemical was also obtained from the bark of *Betula lenta.* Fatal poisoning accidents did happen with small children earlier this century who licked containers with traces of wintergreen oil in them.

Named after Dr Jean Francois Gaulthier, a botanist in the Quebec area in the mid 18th century, wintergreen is a native of Canada and the northern United States. It will flourish in Britain if given the right soil, some shade, and an occasional dressing of leaf mould.

Helleborus niger   P   BLACK HELLEBORE

A native of mountainous regions in Europe and Asia, the black hellebore shows its hardy nature in flowering close to Christmas. This has earned it the common names of Christ herb and Christmas rose. The white, star-like flowers, several inches across, light the dark January and February days in the herb garden. Gradually the brightness fades and they become pinkish, and finally green.

By March, 7 elegant greenish seedpods cluster at the centre of each of the 2 or 3 flowers on the plant. They are shaped quite beautifully, sitting, points outwards, like so many transfixed drops of green liquid. The mature seeds can be sown in a shady, sheltered situation, where the seedlings will need care for the first year. It will be three or four years before they reach their full potential.

The mature plants have large, leathery, deep green leaves on rather floppy stems. They have a tendency to lay on the ground rather than stand erect. The flowers rise from the root on a separate stem about 5-8cm (4-6in) above the earth. Good drainage and well fed soil, preferably of an alkaline nature, appear to be the most important requirements for the herb's success.

They can be divided in summer, giving the roots a chance to become established before winter. When handling and cutting the roots, it is wise to wear gloves, as the juice from them can be strongly irritant. Hellebore roots contain powerful poisons and must be treated with respect.

In earlier times the drug was used therapeutically. It found a place as a purgative, abortive, local anaesthetic and treatment for dropsy. Dioscorides lists the above, and adds a recipe for a poultice with vinegar to treat impetigo and leprosy. In the 18th century the roots were still being gathered and sent to London hospitals. Children were treated with hellebore to kill intestinal worms. Sadly when administered by the less experienced, this treatment could prove fatal to the young patient too.

All parts of the plant are poisonous and the only remaining medicinal use of the herb appears to be in homoeopathic medicine.

Papaver rhoeas   FIELD POPPY
Papaver somniferum   A   OPIUM POPPY

CULTIVATING poppies has to be one of the easiest tasks. In my experience, there is far more work in controlling their spread, than in encouraging them.

The red corn poppy with its black centre is a great pleasure to grow in a wild garden. In the past the red flowers have been harvested for medicinal use as a mild sedative, while the seeds were sprinkled on breads and pastries. Once you have sown the seeds in a freshly dug area, they should germinate and thrive, whether in chalky conditions or loam. If allowed, they will self-seed from that year onwards, being happiest amongst grasses. They may reach up to 90cm (36in) in height.

The opium poppy will be as tall or taller, growing anywhere up to 1.5m (5ft). It has lovely white or lilac tinted flowers, qualifying it as a plant of the moon for the Cancer bed in the Astrology. Even the grey leaves have an elegant, moon-lit quality. The herb is cultivated in Asia for the latex and alkaloid content of the seed capsules.

In this country the opium poppy is grown as an ornamental flower. A natural part of any physic bed, it has made a tremendous contribution as a painkiller in the forms of morphine and codeine. Ornamental cultivars of the opium poppy are varied and lovely, some having fringed and multi-coloured or layered petals.

As with the field poppy, once a place is prepared for the initial plant or seeds, the opium poppy may re-appear in any part of your garden if allowed to self-sow. Moving young plants is extremely difficult but can be done if they are still tiny. Water well with Bach Rescue Remedy and Walnut Remedy in the water and take the surrounding soil with the plant. Ideally, this should be done on a cool, overcast day. If not, give at least 24 hours of shade while the plant recovers.

Better 'spread control' can be made by harvesting the seedheads before the seeds are ripe and collecting them later, indoors. Poppy seeds keep their germination power for long periods.

Phytolacca americana   P   POKEWEED

POKEWEED, also known as pokeroot, is truly majestic. Once established, the sturdy red stems shoot up to some 1.5-2.4m (5-8ft), each summer. The sprays of pink flowers which hang down, arching out from the main plant on lesser stems, are truly ornamental. By the time the flowers have turned to berries, the long, pointed leaves are already streaked with their autumn red.

The berries almost glow with a rich, luscious purple colour when ripe. They are dangerously like blackcurrant sweets to look at. Dangerously, because they are actually poisonous, as is the root in large amounts. In North America, the home of this herb, the young leaves and stems are sometimes boiled and eaten. Far safer than other parts of the plant, even these have led to mild poisoning when not prepared with sufficient care.

The most common misuse leading to poisoning has come from taking too high a dose of the root. This has long been prepared as an anti-inflammatory and analgesic for rheumatism. Pokeweed does contain anti-inflammatory substances and anti-viral proteins. It is currently being researched for anti-AIDS drugs (see the **RHS Encyclopedia of Herbs and their uses).**

Although the seeds ripen very late in the year, and I harvest most of the berries for dyeing; there are still a few self-sown plants about the garden in spring. I move these to rich, moist ground in full sun. All plants die right back with the first frost, the tall stems collapsing dramatically to the ground. With the following spring however, the herb is rejuvenated. It sprouts again, steadily reaching a spread of 90cm-1.2m (3-4ft).

When clearing away collapsed stems, or cutting stems with berries, it is as well to note that sap from the plant can be an irritant to eyes and skin.

Polygonatum multiflorum   P   SOLOMON'S SEAL

THE name is thought to have come from a legend explaining the hieroglyphic markings within the root. They were said to have been stamped through it as a mark of approval from King Solomon. It was believed that he knew the virtues of all plants. Both the powdered rhizome and the leaves have been much used in poultices and ointments. These were applied for deep bruising, broken bones and freshly restored dislocations.

A decoction was taken for consumption in early times. Galen warned against drinking this. Gerard comments wryly in his herbal, centuries later, that those who had not read Galen's warning, drank the roots in ale with no after effects. Galen did, however, have a point. All parts of the herb can be harmful if eaten. Solomon's seal is a close relative of the poisonous lily of the valley. It is no longer thought to contain similar cardioactive glycosides, the effects being attributed to the saponins. (See **A Colour Atlas of Poisonous Plants.**)

Harmful, or not, the rows of white flowers, hanging as miniature bells from the long, curving stems in early summer, are a true delight. I grow them in the shade at the side of my knot garden, under trees in the craft garden and in Capricorn in the astrology. The last site, being open, is not ideal. In time the bugle may surround them sufficiently to keep their roots cool.

The natural home of Solomon's seal is at the edges of woodland. I have seen it growing wild in such a place, looking truly lovely. Both the multiflorum and odoratum can be used medicinally and are native to Europe.

The creeping rhizomes can be divided in autumn, or seeds sown from the bluish-black berries. Plant in shade or semi-shade in rich soil. A mulch of leaf-mould will be appreciated. The leaves which hang down from the 60cm (2ft) curved stems, should be watched carefully in early June for the eggs of sawfly larvae. If these are removed immediately the problem can be avoided. Left to feed, they will reduce the leaves to ribbons.

Polygonatum tinctorium   A   DYER'S BISTORT

THE seed should be sown in trays indoors, or in a heated propagator. The young seedlings need to be brought on with warmth, in sheltered conditions. Do not plant dyer's bistort in the garden until all danger of frosts is over. A plant of southeast Asia, they take sudden drops in temperature so badly, the leaves turn blue and shrivel up. The underside of the leaves is bluish throughout the year, in contrast to the dark green on their upper surfaces.

Related to Japanese knotweed, dyer's bistort might well spread beyond its usefulness in a warmer climate. In Britain, the temperature limits it to being an annual plant in the garden. When planting seedlings out, give them protection from cold winds and slugs. Plant in full sun with rich soil. Watering well will encourage lush growth, and a height of over 60cm (2ft). You will need 10-12 plants for a useful harvest of leaves, as they produce less pigment in our cooler weather.

The knotweed trait shows in the knobbly joints at intervals on the thick, reddish stems. Leaves can be harvested from late August onwards. It is often September before dyer's bistort produces the pretty and rather delicate, pink flowers, which resemble those of its relative, buckwheat. At this point, strip the leaves from most of your plants to prepare the dye.

While the remaining 2 or 3 plants are still healthy, pot them up and remove them to a sheltered position. As soon as the temperature drops below 10°C (mid 50°F), I take them indoors. They are easy houseplants, simply needing fairly good compost and cautious watering. They should not be encouraged to grow too fast, as you will not be able to cut them back until the seeds are safely harvested. So far, I have gathered them from the tight seedheads in December and January. It is difficult to tell when they are ready, as the flowerheads simply fade into seedcases, and take their time.

After gathering the seeds, cut the plants back. They may survive to be planted out for a second year. I am still experimenting with this.

Populus balsamifera   T   BALSAM POPLAR

MY balsam poplar is planted in the centre of the Treasure garden. In spring it perfumes this area for golden, silver and purple leaved herbs. It is a small, inspirational plot, where the spring leaves of the tree, gold tinted in the sunshine, open above silver herbal foliage. Left to grow unchecked, the hardy tree would reach anywhere up to 20-25m (70-85ft). For this reason, and just as importantly, for the regular harvest of young branches for basketry, the tree is pruned hard back once, if not twice a year.

In spring the sticky, resinous leaf buds are strongly aromatic, and many of these are harvested for making furniture polish, perfumed beads and pot-pourri, (see recipes). Several poplars, including the balsamifera, are known as Balm of Gilead, (mentioned in the Bible in Genesis, Jeremiah and Ezekiel). Collectively they provide leaf buds and bark for medicinal use.

The expectorant properties are used in Balm of Gilead cough mixture. The analgesic effect of the salicylates present is found in ointments for rheumatic and muscular pain. The bark of the main tree is grey. On the young branches it is a handsome, glistening, reddish brown.

The branches are strongly aromatic when cut and remain both aromatic and supple for some time. Beyond pruning, the tree needs little attention. It also produces suckers at distances of up to several feet away. These can be left to establish themselves for a few months and then potted up for friend's gardens. They do not take harm from the move, and are not considered to be particular about the soil conditions where they are planted. Cuttings can also be taken when the tree is pruned in spring or autumn.

Both ornamental and fragrant, this is, perhaps, one of the most delightful of the herb trees to grow.

Prunella vulgaris   P   SELF HEAL

THIS charming herb is an indispensable plant in any wild flower area. Having set a few plants in the edge of the Aries bed in my astrology garden, I watched their steady progress into other areas with delight. Bees love the flowers, and so I encouraged them to spread into the bed reserved for bee favourites. In front of that, in the lawn, the frequent grass cutting stimulates the self heal to flower at ground level. In more open circumstances, left alone, the plants grown to 15-23cm (6-9in) tall.

The stems are square, giving the herb something of the look of betony, but the leaves are quite different, being oblong and blunt. The plant is described as aromatic, unfortunately this is not noticeable when weeding next to it, or cutting the stems. Self heal flowers on and on. When the first flowers open, the flowerhead appears as a round ball, with tiers of tiny dark purple flower, divided by bracts. As more of these open, the shape is elongated.

The seeds can be sown in spring or autumn, or cuttings taken from the plants and rooted in a shady spot. They seem to thrive in moist soil. The established plants, meanwhile, fare better than the grass in the dry lawn, during a hot summer.

The herb is also a native in America, where it is know as 'blue curls' and grows in woodland clearings. The common names of the self heal in Britain direct us to its medicinal use. All-heal, Hook-heal and Slough heal all refer to application as a wound herb. It has been especially appreciated in this role, being anti-bacterial and acting as a styptic, stopping bleeding. Self heal is harvested when flowering to prepare the tincture and ointment. It is often compared to, and linked with bugle in its healing context.

Sempervivum tectorum   P   HOUSELEEK

THIS succulent plant is familiar to most gardeners, yet I would be surprised if many readers have thought of it as a herb. Nevertheless, the humble houseleek, known also as Jupiter's beard, Thor's beard, Bullock's eye and sengreen, has medicinal properties. The superstitious belief in the protection offered by the herb against fire, led to it being grown on thatch. A practice endorsed by the Emperor Charlemagne. The Latin tectorum refers to the plant's usual place on the roof.

Sempervivum emphasises houseleek's ability to survive almost any conditions, particularly long droughts. The juicy leaves store moisture and offer exceptional healing properties. It is certainly an excellent plant for a low maintenance garden. The rosettes of thick, pointed leaves grow out at ground level. They can become over 15cm (6in) across, and produce new plants around the edges. The only stem grows up, not from the centre, but at the side. Clothed in more small leaves, it bears clusters of deep pink, star-like flowers. Their profusion can make it appear unwieldy, sometimes bending over with the weight.

Introduced here from the Mediterranean, houseleek is also found on Greek islands. In addition to sites on many a roof across Europe, it will do well set into walls or in dry, stony places, in full sun. Evergreen, it has a reassuring air of permanence.

The juice of the leaves has been used for centuries to treat the inflamed skin conditions of eczema and psoriasis. It is included in herbal cosmetics for sensitive skin, and to combat wrinkles. Houseleek has also treated burns, sunburn, shingles, bites and stings. Internal use should be restricted to prescription only, as large doses are strongly emetic. Houseleek poultices, infusions and the tincture, remain in use.

Silybum marianum   A or B   MILK THISTLE

THE common name refers to the creamy splashes of variegation on the leaves. These were once identified with drops of the Virgin Mary's milk running down the foliage. Our Lady's thistle and Marian thistle also refer to this. The herb deserves a place of honour in the herb garden, for its beauty and medicinal usefulness.

Seeds may be sown in autumn to give flowers the following year, or sown in spring for an annual plant. Young seedlings grow quickly, needing protection from slugs, despite their already spiky leaves. Once established, they produce a wealth of large, shiny leaves with wavy, spiky edges. These are most attractive but hardly look edible. Despite this, the young shoots and roots were gathered in spring and boiled to be eaten. The flowerbuds were prepared as artichokes, which they resemble.

By mid-summer long stems have grown up amongst the striking foliage, bearing flowers which are deep pink and typical of thistles. These are followed by creamy down which floats out with the ripened seeds attached. At this point the herb may have reached a height of up to 1.2m (4ft), although mine are generally no more than 75-90cm (2½-3ft). The seedheads are dramatic, resembling crowns of thorns. They are quite vicious, but irresistible to flower arrangers.

Although the plants once grew almost as a weed on waste ground, the herb is now rarely seen, except in cultivation. It has only been a garden escape in this country, having been introduced from the Mediterranean and Western Europe. Since it is mentioned in Anglo-Saxon herbals, it may have been brought here by the Romans.

Medicinally the herb has been, and remains of great value. It both stimulates bile and protects and helps to regenerate liver cells. It is therefore indicated for herbal treatment of poisoning from alcohol or drugs and diseases such as hepatitis.

Smyrnium olisatrum   B   ALEXANDERS

ORIGINALLY a Mediterranean plant, alexanders was introduced to Britain by the Romans. It is hardy, but likes full sun. The herb has become naturalised along several coasts; in the South, East Anglia and Wales. I always associate it with happy days in North Wales. There it grows almost as a rampant weed, along the grass verges or narrow lanes, on the coastal strips of land. The alexanders are a mass of intense green tempting leaves, when I visit in spring. By summer, the flowers have opened in tight, creamy-yellow umbels and large black ridged seeds are formed.

The name olisatrum, is made up of olus - a pot herb, and atrum - black, referring to the seeds. In my herb garden, alexanders has plenty of foliage to offer as a spring vegetable, from early February. By mid-March the second year plants have overtaken many other herb's growth, being some 60cm (2ft) tall. The stems become thick and hollow as the plants mature, resembling angelica or lovage. Shorter than either of these giants, alexanders grows to about 1.5m (4-5ft) in height.

The herb self-seeds readily. I generally leave a few on the umbels to ensure an ongoing patch of the plants, and gather the remainder. These can be ground and used as a seasoning. Being a rather fascinating shape they are also useful for seed collage. See the Tree of Life design.

The flavour of alexanders has a hint of celery, rather like lovage. In addition to eating the leaves, cooks once pickled the flowerbuds for salads. The herb is no longer used medicinally, but the diuretic, cleansing effect may be felt if large quantities are eaten.

Sticta pulmonaria   P   LUNGWORT

THE most charming common name for this herb is surely, Jerusalem cowslip. The more usual, soldiers and sailors, refers to the two colours of the flowers - pink and blue. These were compared to the red and blue of our force's uniforms at the time. The flowers are very attractive, appearing as small, frilled trumpets to herald the spring. In some years the flowers on my plants seem to open with pink predominating at first, and then the blue takes over. Often there is a complete mix of colours. This spring the blue has shown first. Hardly a garden is without their cheery presence.

The name pulmonaria came from the perceived likeness of the spotted leaves to diseased lungs. By the doctrine of signatures, this meant the plant would prove to be a useful herb for treating such problems. Whether the doctrine is sound or not, this has turned out to be the case. Lungwort is effective in treating bronchitis and catarrh. The plants are cut in summer and dried for this use.

The shape of the leaves and presence of hairs on the stems, may betray a relationship between this plant, and borage and comfrey. Even without their sharper hairs on the leaves, the herb can be irritant to the skin. The herb remains low-growing, generally between 15-30cm (6-12in) tall.

I divide the plants in autumn or spring, so that they now dot several areas. They are equally in place in the physic beds, in Pisces in the astrology, in craft beds for the use of the pressed flowers, and in the wine and liqueur garden. This last site is justified by an early inclusion in vermouth. The plants thrive better in semi-shade or shade, with fairly rich soil. Lungwort is a native of European woodland, and has been introduced in North America.

Umbilicus rupestris   P   KIDNEYWORT

AS mentioned in the section on Libra in the Astrology garden, Culpeper's enthusiasm for this herb made me wish to grow it. The absence of a Latin name in Culpeper's herbal set me a problem which I first thought I had solved in **A Modern Herbal** by Mrs. Grieve. She quoted Culpeper and made an identification with *Cotyledon umbilicus* of the Crassulacae family. I was at a loss in searching for the plant under this name, except in Dioscorides. I searched for other common names, wall pennyroyal, and wall pennywort, without success.

Mrs. Grieve's description of the herb's habitat is clear. She writes it is, "mostly to be found on moist rocks and walls in the high-lying districts in the west of England". In the **Macdonald Encyclopedia of Medicinal Plants** I discovered *Umbilicus rupestris* was also identified as kidneywort, and grows in rocky places in southern and western Europe, including Britain.

Finally, I looked again in the **Illustrated Flora of Britain and Northern Europe,** and found the details of *Umbilicus rupestris* with the common name of navelwort. This name turned up again in Mrs. Grieve and the circle was complete. Having tracked down the elusive kidneywort, it is unmasked as a fairly common plant, preferring acid soil. It may be planted on a rockery or into a dry stone wall in a sunny position. A container of suitable soil could be provided for the plants, hidden amongst rocks in an alkaline area.

The leaves lie amongst the stones. They are thick, rounded and succulent. The central dip where the stem sits below, gives the appearance of a navel. The flower spikes remind me of lily of the valley, with many white or pinkish elongated bells hanging on all sides. The herb's healing uses in treating boils and haemorrhoids, have survived into this century. According to the Macdonald Encyclopedia, the juice is no longer taken for liver and kidney problems, being restricted to ear drops.

Bibliography and Further Reading

Valuable Secrets in Arts and Trades, London 1798

A Collection of Receipts in Cookery, Physick and Surgery,
By several hands, London 1746

Food for Free, Richard Mabey, Fontana 1972

Hedgerow Cookery, Rosamund Richardson, Penguin 1980

Dioscorides Greek Herbal, Edited by R. T. Gunther Hafner, 1968

Pliny the Elder, Natural History

Culpeper's Complete Herbal, London 1815

Paracelsus Essential Readings,
Selected and translated by Nicholas Goodrick-Clarke, Crucible 1990

A Modern Herbal, Mrs. M. Grieve, Savvas Publishing 1984

Herbwise Naturally, Christina Stapley, Heartsease Books 1993

Herbcraft Naturally, Christina Stapley, Heartsease Books 1994

The Gardener's Labyrinth,
Thomas Hill, Edited by Richard Mabey, Oxford University Press 1988

The Illustrated Flora of Britain and Northern Europe,
Marjorie Blamey and Christopher Grey-Wilson, Hodder A Stoughton 1989

The R.H.S. Encyclopedia of Herbs and their Uses,
Deni Bown, Dorling Kindersley 1995

The Encyclopedia of Herbs and Herbalism, Edited by Malcolm Stuart, Black Cat 1987

The MacDonald Encyclopedia of Medicinal Plants, MacDonald Orbis 1984

A Colour Atlas of Poisonous Plants, Frohne-Pfänder, Wolfe 1984

A Weaver's Garden, Rita Buchanan, Interweave Press 1987

A Dyer's Manual, Jill Goodwin, Pelham Books 1982

Delightes for Ladies, Sir Hugh Plat, Crosby Lockwood 1955

Perfumery With Herbs, Ivan Day, Darton, Longman and Todd 1979

The Bach Flower Remedies Step by Step, Judy Howard, C. W. Daniel Co Ltd 1990

List of Suppliers

Dye Suppliers

Fibrecrafts
Style Cottage
Lower Eashing
Godalming
SURREY
GU7 2QD

Fibrecrafts at Low Garth
Penruddock
Penrith
CUMBRIA
CA11 0QU

Gum Resins, dried herbs and spices - mail order

Hambleden Herbs
Court Farm
Milverton
SOMERSET
TA4 1NF

Bach Flower Remedies

The Dr Edward Bach Centre
Mount Vernon
Sotwell
Wallingford
OXON
OX10 0PZ

Peglooms

Spindlewood Turnery
23, Cedar Road
Sutton
SURREY
SM2 5DG

Index

A

acid soil 150
acorns 85
adders tongue .74, 80
agrimony 36, **37**, 39, 51, 52, 53, 60
. . . . .72, 74, **80**, 81, 88, 89, 100
agrimony and ginger wine 67, 128
ajuga - see bugle
alecost - see costmary
alehoof 52,72
alexanders 37, 39, 85, 138, **148-9**
seed 29, 31
alkaline soil 141, 143, 150
alkanet 9, 52, 74, 132
alum . . .25, **26**, 27, 50, 51, 71, 72, 89, 90, 112,
113, 114, 132
angelica . .16, 20, 42, 43, **46**, **62**, 71, **81**, 88, 89,
99, 103, 114, 148
root .103, 107, 108
seed .9, 29, 31, 98
anise seed 9, 22, 23
anise hyssop 100
antiseptic 59, 66
ants - see deter . . . .
aphids 34, 57
apothecary's rose - see rosa gallica officinalis
apricot and lovage filling 126
Aquarius **12**, 13, **14**, 37
aquilegia 72, 100
Aries 11, **12**, **38**, 39, 58, 59, 121, 146
arnica 9
ash 39
asthma 18, 59
astrology garden 11-14, 37-39, 58, 59, 74
80-81 ,100-103, 121-123, 139, 143, 145, 146, 149
avens 36, 52, 60, 72, 103

B

Bach flower remedies 10, 34, 79, 144
balsam poplar 42, 100, 104, 116, 129, 130, 138,
146

balsam furniture polish 42, 49, 146
basil . 9, 11, 36, 64, 65, 74, 77, 100, 121, 122,
123, 129
essential oil 129
basketry 35, 40, 41, 42, 100, 103, 104, 113,
116-119, 133, 146
bath sachets 60, 61, 103
bay 10, 33, 36, 81, 99, 121
basil and tarragon vinegar 64
bees 14, 34, 39, 141, 146
beeswax 49, 68, 69, 110, 111
Benedictine 140
berberis 54
bergamot 28, 36, 77, 81, 99
betony 36, 52, 60, 77, 81, 91, 100, 114, 115, 147
biennial clary sage - see clary sage
birds 8, 34, 35, 77, 99, 121, 142
bistort 28
blackberry .103 ,113
spiced blackberry wine 103, **109**
blackcurrant and curled mint wine . .84, 86, 128
black hellebore - see hellebore
blackthorn 33, 54, 104, 108, 113
blessed thistle . . .9, 11, **38**, 39, 74, 78, 138, **140**
borage . . .9, 29, 36, 62, 66, 77, 81, 85, 91, 100,
103, 114, 149
box 16, 34, 58, 98, 121
bramble tip 35, 50, 52
thornless 35, 50, 100, 103, 116
dye 42, **50**, 89
brazilwood 131-132
broken bones 13, 123, 145
buddleia 79
bugle 36, 72, 123, 138, **139**
burdock 88, 90
butcher's broom .74
butterflies 14, 34, 47, 50, 56, **79**, 141

C

calamint 74
calamus root 24, 29, 31, 131

calendula 9, 16, 25, 29, 31, 36, 65, 74, 77, 88-9, 100, 127
ointment 60, **68**, 81, 103
sugar 60, 81, **83**, 103, 125-6
calico 52
cancer 58
Cancer **12**, 13, **80**, 143
candied flowers 22, 38, 42, **44**, 62, 81
candied stems 60, 62, 125, 126, 128
Capricorn **12, 13**, 123, 139, 145
caraway 77, 83, 85, 98, 131
carnation 73
carpet sprinkle **24**
castor oil plant 9
catmint 25, 60, 72, 114
celandine .10, 27, 52
celery seed 15, 29, 31
chalky soil 21, 47, 143
chamomile 9, 36, 74, 77, 81, 100
double 66
essential oil 129
chervil 9, 34, 36, 65
chickweed 60
ointment 60, 68, **69**
chives 36, 65, 81, **121**, 123
Christmas decorations . .103, 104, 114, 131, 134
Christmas rose - see hellebore
chrome 25, 27, 51, **89-90**, 113, 132
chutney **106, 107**
citric acid 112
clary sage 74, **80**, 81, 91, 114
seed 9, 77, 98, 100
clove pinks . . .16, 28, 74, 77 ,85, 100, **122**, 123
conserve **84**, 107, 124, 125, 126, 129
petals - crystallised 60, 81, **84**
fondant 125
and rose liqueur . . . . .60 ,81, 125, 126
sugar . . . . .60 ,81, **83**, 125
syrup 60, 81, 128, 129
colds 66
coltsfoot 10, 21, 34, 42
coltsfoot lemon and ginger wine **21**
comfrey . .10, 13, 14, 33, 34, 36, 56, 60, 68, 74, 99, 103, 140, 149
dye 71, 88, 89, 114
ointment 60, **69**, 103
Compositae 11
compost 9, 34, 36, 56, 58, 99, 103, 121

confetti 60, 61, 83, 102
copper sulphate **71**, 90, 132
coreopsis tinctoria 9, 37, 39, 74, 100
coriander seed . . .15, 22 ,29, 31, 77, 81, 83, 85, 124, 129, 131
costmary 9, 36, **37**, 39, 74, 100
cotton 53
cotton lavender - see santolina
cough sweets 59, 103, 107
cowslip 9, 16, **38**, 39, 44, 46, 52, 77, 78, 85, 98, 100
sugar 42, **45**
syrup 42
wine 42, **47-48**
crab apple remedy .79
cream of tartar 26, 71, 114
Culpeper .11, 13, 14, 37, 38, 39, 58, 59, 80, 81, 101, 102, 103, 121, 122, 123, 149
cumin 85
curry plant 34, 98, 100, 121
cuttings 34, 98
cyclamen 10, 27
cypressus 35, 129, 130
cyprus 85, 134

D

daffodil 35, 42, **51**, 60, 95
dahlia 88, 89, 103, 133
dandelion 35, 42, 46, 48, 51
depression 13, 14, 45, 80
deterrent 38, 57, 104
ant 66, 102
aphid 57,60
flea 82, 102, 103, 140
insect 140
mice 56, 83, 140
rat 83, 140
dianthus - see clove pinks
dill 9, 15, 31, 65, 66, 74, 77, 81, 83, 85, 134, 135
Dioscorides 59, 149
diuretic 43, 46, 66, 149
dogwood 54, 74, 100, 103, 116
dropsy 37, 102, 103
drying herbs **65**
dyer's bistort 98, 103, 133, 138, **145**

dyer's broom 29, 31, 78, 88, **90**, 91
dyer's chamomile 9, 36, 77, 82, 88, 89, 100, 103
dyer's woodruff 72
dyes 25-27, 50-51, 71-72, 88-90, 111-113,
131-133

E

earache 13
Easter garland **54**
echinacea 100
eczema 13, 69, 87, 142, 147
elder 34, 60, 100
berries 57, 103, 108, 113, 132
leaves 71,91
stem 85
elderberry, chutney (Barbara's) **106**
port .103, 108, 128
syrup 105, 108, 128
elderflowers 57, 61, 65, 71, 72,85
elderflower, cordial 61, 64, 71, 128
and kiwi wine 67, 129
ointment . . . . .68, **69** ,71
vinegar 60, **64**, 124
elecampane 16, 59, 78, 79, 88, 90, 99, 100,
103, 114, 115, 134
marmalade 18
root 18, 19, 107, 124, 125
eringo - see sea holly
eryngium planum 114, 115, 116
essential oils 59, 61, 69, 130
eucalyptus oil 110
evening primrose .16, 36, 77, 99, 100, 115, 134

F

fennel 16, 27, 33, 36, 52, 53, 60, 64, 65, 66, 72,
74, 77, 78, 82, 83, 88, 90, 91,99, 100, 101,103,
127
vinegar **64,** 83
fennel, orange and lemon jelly 84
ferrous sulphate 26, 50, 51, 71, 89, 90
fibres - to spin 35, 99, 104
fixative 37, 59, 61, 69, 70, 103, 104
flax 9, 77
fleas - see deter
flowercrafts .38, 58, 60, 61, 80, 81, 82, 83, 104

forget-me-not 33, 52, 56, 72, 100
foxglove 36, 98
fragrant beads - see pomander beads
frankincense 70, 129, 130
essential oil 90, 131
freezing herbs 60, 61, **65**, 82, 83, 103, 104
French marigold 9
seed 29, 31
fruit and nut filling 126
fruit punch, non-alcoholic 61, 84, **128**
fudge 127
furniture polish 42
fumitory 14, 72, 138, **141-2**

G

Galen 145
galingale 29, 31
gall nuts - see oak galls
garlands - see also Easter 35, 61
garlic 34, **38**, 39, 57, 98
Gerard 145
geranium scented 20, 56, 99, 103, 114
see also lemon scented, rose scented
jelly 18, 19, 103
geranium essential oil 25, 49
germander 15, 16, 34, 58, 82, 98, 121
Gemini **12**, 58, **59**
gillyflowers - see clove pinks
ginger . .10, 15, 21, 67, 107, 108, 109, 128, 131
goat's rue 77
golden marjoram - see marjoram
golden rod 36, 77, 78, 82, 91, 99, 100, 114
dye **88,** 89, 90, 104
wine 82, **86**, 104
goldlace 52
gout 14, 37
greater burdock 36
greater celandine .72
greater knapweed 14, 77, 78, 100, 104, 114
115, 138, **141**
Greek oregano 9
Greek valerian . . .16, 35, 36, 55, 59, 72, 77, 99
gum arabic 44, 45, 107, 132
gum benzoin 70, 129, 130
essential oil 70, 129, 130

gum tragacanth 107, 129, 130
guelder rose 104
gypsywort 36, 88, 89, 100

H

harvesting seeds 77
hawthorn 60, 67, 99, 104
  liqueur 67
  wine 109
  red 74
hazel 100, 104
headache 66
heartsease 13, 14, 62, 72, 77, 83, 91, 114
helichrysum 9, 28, 114
hellebore 10
  black 4, 138, 143
henna 9
herb bennet 42, 72, 74, 77, 78, 123
herb Robert 72, 91
herbs to dry - see drying
herb, hedges 16, 58, 78, 98
  honey 42, 59, 61, 62, 64, 83
  jelly 42
  sachets 42, 60, 83, 104
  sugars 42, 45, 61, 62, 81
  swags 27, 28, 61, 133
  syrups 103, 107
  tea 20, 42, 46, 59, 66, 108, 127
hibiscus 108
holly 121, 133, 134
hollyhock 9, 53, 98, 104, 113
honesty 29, 31, 52, 72, 77, 78
honeysuckle 16, 34, 54, 79, 91, 100, 116
  see also winter honeysuckle
hop 104, 113
  golden 16, 52, 72, 91, 100, 116
horehound, white 15, 59, 61, 74, 77, 78, 83, 104
horseradish 11, 88, 90
horsetail 36
houseleek 122, 123, 138, 147
hypericum - see St John's wort
hypericum oil 88
hyssop 9, 28, 34, 35, 58, 74, 77, 80, 81, 82,
                91, 98, 100, 106, 114

I

indigo 9, 133
inhalations 60
ink 82, 103, 132
insomnia 59
iris 95, 104
iron - see ferrous sulphate
ivy 10, 25, 26, 27, 53, 121, 133, 134

J

jasmine 25, 52, 70, 72, 91, 114
  essential oil 25
  also see winter jasmine
jelly - see herb jelly
Jerusalem sage . . .28, 61, 73, 78, 114, 115, 121
juniper 33, 35, 56, 121, 134
Jupiter 37, 59, 74, 80, 122

K

kidneywort 102, 103, 138, 149-50
knot garden 8, 78
  miniature 8, 15, 16, 28, 58, 60, 61, 82, 83
knotweed, dyer's – see dyer's bistort
knotweed Japanese 145

L

laburnum 138
lacewing 57
ladybird 34, 57, 99
lady's bedstraw 36, 77, 91, 100
lady's mantle .15, 16, 52, 53, 72, 73, 74, 77, 82,
              91, 100, 122, 123
lavender . 15, 16, 20, 25, 28, 34, 56, 58, 59, 70,
    77, 78, 79, 82, 98, 99, 104, 110, 121, 129
  essential oil 59, 69, 110
  fan, favour, ...82
  fringe, star .91-93
lavandula dentata 10, 99
leaf mats .35, 95-96

leaf printing . .10, 35, 51, **52, 53**, 60, 61, 81, 82, 103, 104
lemon balm . .34, 37, 60, 65, 66, 73, 79, 80, 82, 99, 107, 110
 and lemon thyme wine 60, 67
lemon scented geranium . . 10, 18, 19, 29, 52, 53, 73, 99, 103, 105, 125, 128, 129
lemon thyme and grapefruit jelly 63
lemon verbena .10, 25, 56, 70, 82, 99, 104, 110
Leo **12, 80**
Libra **12, 102**, 121, 149
lilies 80
limeflower 25
liqueur **22**, 42, 60, 61, 104, 108, 125, 140
liquid feed 10, 13, 34, 42, 56, 58, 60
liquorice 127, 134, 135
lobelia 9
lovage 34, 35, 37, 42, **58**, 60, 65, 72, 77, 82, 83, 85, 99, 104, 148,149
 and grapefruit jelly **43**
 vinegar 60
 candied stems 42, **43, 44**, 62, 125, 126
love-in-a-mist 114, 115, 134
lungwort 37, 52, 138, **149**

M

madder .99, **132**, 133
mallow 35, 91, 98
marigold, pot - see calendula
French marigold see F
marjoram . . .9, 24, 36, **39**, 60, 65, 82, 100, 129
 dwarf 39
 essential oil 49, 110
 golden 16, 36, 39, 73
 winter 39
marmalade .17, 18
 grapefruit and elecampane 18
 grapefruit and sweet cicely 19
Mars 11, 38, 74, 121, 122
marshmallow 9, 16, 37, 91, 99, 100, 104
 treats **107**
marzipan 44, 126, 127
meadow clary 77, 100
meadowsweet 51, 52, 60, 72, 82, 88, 89, 91, 99, 100, 104, 113
melancholy thistle **13**

melissa - see lemon balm
melissa liqueur 67
 essential oil 110
Mercury 39, 59, 74, 101
mezereon 138
mildew 36
milk thistle .9, 29, 31, 54, 78, 100, 114, 115 122, 123, 138, 140, **148**
mincemeat **124**
miniature knot gardens – see knot gardens
mini Christmas trees 134
mint 5, 28, 34, 36, 37, 43, 44, 48, 56, 65, 79, 99
 apple 60, 107
 buddleia 82
 curled 63
 eau-de-cologne .16, 24, 59, 60, 70, 73, 82, 103
 ginger 59, 63, 91
 liqueur 67, 126
 pepper 16, 59, 60, 66, 73, 82, 104
 pineapple 73, 82, 104
 spear 43, 59, 60, 82
 syrup **63**
mistletoe 133
moon 9, 13, 36, 73, 74, 80, 143
moonwort 80
mordant, – see individual mordants
moth sachet 38, 58, 82, 101, 104, **110**
motherwort . .34, 36, 52, 77, 78, 81, 82, 91, 100
mugwort 37, 52, 91, 99, 103
mulled wine **128**
mullein .**13**, 14, 36, 57, 74, 77, 82, 98, 100, 114
 oil 60, 82, **87**
mullein moth caterpillar 57
muslin .53, 65, 95, 108
mustard seed 106
myrrh 130

N

nappy rash 68
nasturtium 9, 36, 82, 100
 vinegar 85
Neptune 37
nettle .10, 11, 34, 35, 36, 37, 42, 48, 51, 53, 56, 79, 98, 127
nettle and angelica syrup 43, **46**
nutmeg .38, 129, 131

O

oak gall 82, **132**
ointment   .14, 37, 38, **68, 69**, 71, 102, 139, 141, 145
olive flower remedy 10
orache 74
orange flower water 107
orange, dried .133, **134**
oregano 16, 28, 36, 82, 88, 89, 91, 100
   see also Greek
orris root 22, 24, 25, 29, 70, 104, 110, 131

P

pansy 114, 121
papermaking 35, 53, 60, 99, 104
Paracelsus 13
parsley 9, 46, 65, 101, 103, 127
   French 100
patchouli 10, 110
   essential oil 110
paths 33, 100
pears in clove pink conserve 124
peg loom **135-137**
pennyroyal .102, 103
peppercorns .106, 124
peppermint - see mint
periwinkle 36, 99
pests 33, 34, 57
pineapple sage - see sage
pine cones 134
   essential oil 33
pinks 60, 72, 73, 91, 99
   see also clove pinks
Pisces **37**, 38, 101, 149
Pliny 59
poisons . .14, 101, 111, 138, 142, 143, 144, 148
pokeweed 104, **111, 112**, 138, 144
pokeberry dye **111, 112**
pomander beads **129**, 146
Poplar, balsam - see balsam poplar
poppy 78, **80**, 81, 114, 115, 134, 138, 142
   corn **143-4**
   opium **143-4**

posy 61, **73**, 74, 82, 102
pot-pourri **24, 25**, 81, 146
   moist 60, 61, **69-70**, 82
predators 57
pressed flowers 27, 51-52, 72, 91, 114
primrose 16, 34, 43, 44, 47, 52
   candied 42
   sugar 42, **45**, 62
   syrup 42
   spiced primrose wine **47**, 124
pruning 42, 103, **106**, 146
pulmonaria - see lungwort
purslane 80
pyrethrum 110

R

ragwort 88, 90
redcurrant and pineapplemint wine 86, 128
Rescue remedy 10, 34, 56, 79, 144
rheumatism 13, 14, 59, 111, 142, 144, 146
rhubarb and sweet cicely jam **45**, 60
rhubarb and angelica wine 48
rock hyssop - see hyssop
rosa canina 105
rosa gallica officinalis 61, 62
rosa moschata 100, 121
rosa mundi 70
rosa rubiginosa 62, 105
rose . .16, 24, 25, 28, 36, 37, 39, 57, 60, 61, 65
         70, 72, 73, 74, 77, 83, 85, 99, 129
rose arbour pot-pourri 24
rose hip .99, 104, 108
   syrup 104, **105**
rose, petal jelly **62, 63**, 126
   sugar 37, **62**, 63, 125, 126
   syrup 37, **64**
   vinegar 60
   water 37, 45, 63, 107, 129, 130
   York and Lancaster 70
rose scented geranium .10, 19. 24, 99, 103, 105, 125
   essential oil 24, 70, 125, 126
rosemary .19, 33, 34, 35, **38**, 48, 52, 54, 56, 73,
         98, 99, 106, 107, 108
   silver 10
   essential oil 48, 49, 110

mint and nettle shampoo **48**
and mint jelly 42, **43**, 44
and orange jelly 18, **20**
spring liqueur 43, 48, 126
rue 102, 121
rum honey cough liqueur 86
rushes 95
rushwork 60, **95**, 104

S

sachets - see bath or herb
safflower .9, 114, 115
saffron 81, 126
sage 16, 34, **37**,39, 58, 61, 65, 82, 98, 104, 107,
                                        108, 114, 121
golden 61, 73, 123
pineapple 10, 56, 99, 104, 105
jelly **106**,125
purple 37, 61, 73, 82, 88, 89, 108, 123
Spanish 56, 60, 72, 104
tangerine 10, 56, 99
tricolor 61, 73, 99
Sagittarius **12, 122**-123
salads 35, 42, 58, 60, 81, 85
salad burnet . .36, 52, 72, 73, 91, 100, 114, 121
salad rocket 9, 36, 100
salix viminalis 40
sanicle 39
sandalwood 25, 70, 129
essential oil 25, 110
sanderswood 129
santolina 28, 34, 51, 60, 73, 74, 77, 98, 110, 121
rosmarinafolia 16
Saturn 12, **13, 14**, 58, 74, 81, 123
savory 9, 16
summer 101
winter16, 34, 35, 58, 74, 83, 91, 98, 101, 105, 114
purple flowered .101
savory and grapefruit jelly 85
scented geranium jelly . . . . .see G
Scorpio 11, **12**, 58, **121, 122**
Scotch thistle 34
sea holly 78, 100, 103, 116, 134
seeds **8, 9**, 13, 15, 29, **77, 78**
seed ball **114, 115**

seedheads 8, 15, 34, 38, 54, 59, 77, 78, 99, 103,
                                104, 114, 115, 134
self-heal . .36, **38**, 39, 74, 77, 91, 138, **146, 147**
shampoo 42, **48, 49**, 81
silk - to dye . .26, 27, 50, 51, 71, 112, 131, 132
silverweed 52
sloe - see blackthorn
slugs 33, 56, 60, 140, 148
snails 33, 34, 56, 60
sneezewort 16, 73, 82
snowberry 34, 104, **113**
snowdrop 10
soapwort 36, 48, 49, 82, 99, 100, 104
cleanser **86**, 87
Solomon's seal 13, **14**, 138, **144, 145**
Solstice 73
sorrel 79
southernwood 73, 74, 79, 82, 101, 103, 110
spiced apricots 124
spicy sacks 129, **131**, 134
star anise 24, 29, 31, 70, 130, 131, 134
St John's day 73
St John's wort 28, 36, 37, 57, 74, 77, 78, 82, 88,
                                        90, 91, 100
stem baskets **74-5**, 82, 83, 101
stonecrop 80
sugar - see herb sugar
Sun 11, **12**, 58, 74, 80, 81
sunflower 9, 36, 53, 56, 74, 77, 88, 98, 100, 104
sumach **132-133**
summer garden pot-pourri 25
swag, Christmas **133**
swag, herb - see herb swags
sweet almond oil 68, 69

sweet cicely9, 16, 35, 37, 43, 52, 61, 65, **71**, 72,
                                77, 82, 85, 91, 99, 100
root 18, **19**, 107, 127
seed 29, 31, 98, 104, **110, 111**, 114
syrup 19
and rhubarb jam 42, **45**
sweet cicely filling 127
sweet lemon furniture polish **110**
sweet gale 110
sweet moth repellent **110**
sweet rocket 77
sweet woodruff 52, 61, 72
syrup - see herb syrups

T

tagetes 77, 82, 88, 89, 100
tannin 132
tansy .15, 16, 27, 28, 33, 37, 52, **58**, 82, 88, 89,
                99, 104, 106, 110, 114
tarragon 37, 123
    French 64, 122
    Russian 99, 122
Taurus **12, 58**, 59, 102
tea - see herb tea
tea-tree, essential oil 48, 49
teazle 36, 77, 78, 99, 104
Thomas Hill 39
thrift 15, 16, 37, 61, 73, 77, 82
thyme 20, 28, 33, 34, 39, 46, 58, 61, 66, 72, 73,
                74, 83, 98, 108, 127
    mother of thyme 38
    essential oil 49
    lemon thyme 65, 108
toad 56
toadflax 100
tobacco 9
toffee 127
Treasure garden 139, 146
Tree of Life Seed Collage 8, **28, 29**, 149

U

Umbelliferae 11

V

Valerian 59
    Greek - see Greek valerian
vanilla 24
    pod 24, 70
Venus 11, **12**, 38, 58, 81, 102, 122
verbascum - see mullein
    oil **87, 88**
vermouth 149
vervain 100
vinegar 43, 60, 61, 62, **64**, 83, **85**
vines 39, 54
violet 10, 43, 44, 45, 52, **58, 59**, 85, **102**

liqueur **22, 23**, 42
    sugar 22, 42
viper's bugloss 72, 91
Virgo **12, 101**, 102

W

waistcoast **135-137**
walnut 105, **112**, 133
walnut flower remedy 34, 55, 144
wall pennyroyal 149
wall pennywort 149
washing soda 112
water lilies 80
weasel 57
weld 9, 77, 88, 89
wild basil 15, 78
wild pear 85
wild plum 54
wild strawberry . 33, 52, 56, 61, 72, 100, **102**,
                103, 105, 116
    basket 116
wild wallflower 114
willow 35, 39
    herbar 35, **39, 40, 41**
    flower remedy 79
wine .   **21**, 42, **47**, 60, 61, **67**, 81, 82, **86**, 104,
                109, 129
wintergreen 14, 138, **142**
winter honeysuckle 8, 27, 54
winter jasmine 8, 27
woad 29, 31, 36, 72, 74, 133
woodlice 33
woodsage 78
wounds 14, 38, 39, 102, 139, 147
wormwood . 74, **80**, 81, 83, 110, 114, 138, **139**,
                140
wrinkles 38

Y

yarrow . 16, 28, 37, 72, 73, 74, 83, 88, 90, 91,
                99, **102**, 103
yew 85, 138